From *Hitler* to *Heimat*

From *Hitler* to *Heimat*

The Return of History as Film

ANTON KAES

Harvard University Press
Cambridge, Massachusetts
London, England

First Harvard University Press paperback edition, 1992

Library of Congress Cataloging-in-Publication Data
Kaes, Anton.
  [Deutschlandbilder. English]
  From Hitler to Heimat : the return of history as film / Anton
Kaes.
    p.   cm.
  Rev. and enl. translation of: Deutschlandbilder.
  Bibliography: p.
  Includes index.
  ISBN 0-674-32455-2 (alk. paper) (cloth)
  ISBN 0-674-32456-0 (paper)
  1. Motion pictures—Germany (West)—History.   2. Motion picture
producers and directors—Germany (West).   3. Motion picture plays—
History and criticism.   4. Motion pictures and history.   I. Title.
PN1993.5.G3K2913   1989   89-2039
791.43′0943—dc19   CIP

To Bettina and Peter
who know little as yet about German history
but have often wondered
how someone can spend so much time on it

CONTENTS

PREFACE

The further the past recedes, the closer it becomes. Images, fixed on celluloid, stored in archives, and reproduced thousands of times, render the past ever-present. Gradually, but inexorably, these images have begun to supersede memory and experience. All of us, whether or not we have lived through the Hitler era, have partaken of its sights and sounds in a host of documentary and feature films. Cinematic representations have influenced—indeed shaped—our perspectives on the past; they function for us today as a technological memory bank. History, it would seem, has become widely accessible, but the power over memory has passed into the hands of those who create these images. It is not surprising that in recent years we have witnessed a virulent struggle over the production and administration of public memory.

The vehement reactions to Ronald Reagan's visit to the military cemetery of Bitburg in May 1985, expressly staged as a television spectacle; the heated debates about the function of two new museums of German history in Bonn and Berlin; the acrimonious dispute among West German historians about the place of the Holocaust and the Third Reich in German history—all these examples not only attest to the lack of a national consensus about German history but also demonstrate an increased sensitivity to matters of collective memory and national identity.

For more than a decade and with growing intensity, attempts have been made to rewrite German history, to fit the atrocities of the Hitler period into a tolerable master narrative. Since the mid-1970s countless books and articles, academic conferences, exhibitions, and television programs have focused on the discontinuities in German history and the lack of a national identity, trying to fill what is perceived as a vacuum. No other country has more politicians, journalists, academics, artists, and writers preoccupied with the history and identity of their homeland, their "Heimat."

Filmmakers play a special role in this undertaking. Their feature films—most of which have been shown, even repeatedly, on television—not only reach a much larger popular audience than, say, speeches, conference papers, or books; they also tend to move and manipulate spectators in a more direct emotional way. Moreover, films—as complex fictional constructs—offer ambivalent perspectives and contradictory attitudes that resist simple explanations and call for multiple readings. Fictional films are able to unlock the viewers' hidden wishes and fears, liberate fantasies, and give material shape to shared moods and dispositions. Films can thus be seen as interventions in cultural and political life. For example, Syberberg's 1977 filmic essay about Hitler or Edgar Reitz's sixteen-hour film chronicle *Heimat* of 1984 triggered debates that went far beyond the films that initiated them. The same holds true for the West German reception of the American television series *Holocaust* of 1979, which broke through thirty years of silence and left an indelible mark on German discussions of the Holocaust. But even films like Rainer Werner Fassbinder's *Die Ehe der Maria Braun* (*The Marriage of Maria Braun*, 1978), Alexander Kluge's *Die Patriotin* (*The Patriot*, 1979), and Helma Sanders-Brahms's *Deutschland, bleiche Mutter* (*Germany, Pale Mother*, 1980) became "discursive events" that emerged in response to specific concerns and took a position in the debates about German history and identity. It is this dynamic interplay between fiction, memory, and the present that will be explored here.

The title of my book alludes to Siegfried Kracauer's 1947 study, *From Caligari to Hitler: A Psychological History of the German Film,* which begins with the following sentence: "This book is not concerned with German films merely for their own sake." I have adopted this perspective for my own project as well. Yet I do not share Kracauer's intention to expose the "deep psychological dispositions" or some natural German propensity toward fascism, as he tried to demonstrate for the period 1918 to 1933 by using fictional films which, in his mind, foreshadowed Hitler's rise to power. Kracauer's trajectory from the fictional tyrant Caligari to the all-too-real Hitler is a bold and problematic construct, manifesting his strong belief in the social power of the cinema to influence perceptions and mold opinions. In contrast, *From "Hitler" to "Heimat"* traverses only a fictional space; Hitler has become today, literally, *Hitler, a Film from Germany,* and "Heimat" can exist only, some would argue, as memory evoked in a film. Still, Kracauer's resolve to study all art, especially film, as a fundamentally communal enterprise has undoubtedly influenced my work. I am therefore less concerned with reading the films as autonomous artifacts or as individual expressions of idiosyncratic artists than with situating them in the cultural, social, and political ambience from which they issue and within which they function. Seen in relation to the dominant discourses of their time and place, the films begin to resonate with various voices, with diverse political convictions and aesthetic traditions. Unlike Kracauer, who in his book pursued a single thesis, I will strive to focus on the complexity of the films so that they begin to tell not *one* story but *many*.

The films I selected deal with some of the most crucial and pressing debates in Germany over the last ten years: Hitler and the Holocaust, German identity and "Heimat." These debates are translated into filmic discourses that encode history in radically different ways, from the relatively traditional narratives of Fassbinder, Sanders-Brahms, and Reitz to the postmodernist films of Syberberg and Kluge. But despite their formal dissimilarities, all these films have one thing in common: they prefigure by several years, in one way or another, the ambiguities that surround current revisionist attempts by Germans to come to terms with their past—a past that will not go away precisely because its representations are everywhere.

This book is an adaptation, not a literal translation, of my German book, *Deutschlandbilder. Die Wiederkehr der Geschichte als Film,* which was published in 1987 by edition text + kritik, Munich. I have rearranged the chapters, changed emphasis, added sections, and updated the notes and bibliography. I am grateful to Ruth Crowley for the original version of the translation, and to Inter Nationes for a generous subsidy that made the translation possible.

My thanks go also to the Alexander von Humboldt Foundation for a research fellowship that enabled me to work on this project in

Berlin, where the consequences of the German past are more tangible than anywhere else. I also wish to thank the Institute of International Studies at Berkeley and the German Academic Exchange Service for short-term research grants. A list of all those colleagues, students, and friends, both at Berkeley and in Berlin, with whom I discussed the book would be too long; let me thank at least those who read one or more chapters and made suggestions for improvement: Edward Dimendberg, Miriam Hansen, Robert Holub, Martin Jay, Friedrich Knilli, Barbara Kosta, Roswitha Mueller, Hans Helmut Prinzler, Hinrich Seeba, and Siegfried Zielinski. I recall with pleasure the long and spirited discussions I had with Leo and Susanne Lowenthal about the films analyzed here. This book owes more than can be expressed to Eric Rentschler, colleague, friend, and collaborator, who was involved in every aspect of the project. His generosity in sharing his knowledge of German cinema is well known and has been instrumental in making the study of German film an exciting undertaking in the American university. I am also very grateful for the unfailing enthusiasm with which Patricia Williams of Harvard University Press supported this project from the beginning. Mary Ellen Geer did a splendid job of editing the manuscript.

Finally, I want to thank my students of the Interdisciplinary Summer Seminar in German Studies at Berkeley from 1982 to 1984 for their interest in discussing German films in cross-disciplinary and "new historicist" ways that took films seriously as multi-leveled texts that signify within larger discourses; many of the ideas presented here were first tested in the classroom.

Earlier (and much different) versions of three chapters have been published previously: Chapter 3 in *Persistence of Vision* 2 (Fall 1985) and in *German Film and Literature,* ed. Eric Rentschler (London/New York: Methuen, 1986); Chapter 4 in *Text + Kritik* 85 (1985); and Chapter 6 in *Augen-Blick: Marburger Hefte zur Medienwissenschaft* 1/2 (1985). Portions of the book were given as lectures at various American and European universities.

Excerpts from Hans Jürgen Syberberg, *Hitler, a Film from Germany,* translated by Joachim Neugroschel (translation copyright 1982) are reprinted by permission of Farrar, Straus and Giroux, Inc., and of Carcanet Press Limited; Bertolt Brecht's poem "Germany," in *Brecht Poems 1913–1956,* translated by John Willett and Ralph Manheim (London/New York, 1982), is cited by permission of Methuen, Inc.; Heine's poem "Night Thoughts," in *Complete Poems of Heinrich Heine: A Modern English Version by Hal Draper* (Boston, 1982), is reprinted by permission of Suhrkamp Publishers. The photographs on pp. 1, 73, 105, 137, and 161 are reproduced by courtesy of Stiftung Deutsche Kinemathek, Berlin; the photograph on p. 37 is reproduced by courtesy of TMS Film-Gesellschaft, Munich.

1
IMAGES OF HISTORY

Postwar German Films and the Third Reich

"We do not have the right to judge, but we have the duty to
accuse."
—Hildegard Knef and Ernst Wilhelm Borchert in
  The Murderers Are among Us

It is certain that the cloak of silence in which, for political reasons,
Nazism was enshrouded after 1945 has made it impossible to ask
what will come of it in the minds, the hearts, the bodies of the Germans. Something had to come of it, and one wondered with some
trepidation in what shape the repressed past would emerge at the
other side of the tunnel: as what myth, what history, what wound?

MICHEL FOUCAULT

The Politics of Representation

In the winter of 1944–45, while the Thousand-Year Reich was crum-
bling and life in Germany was moving underground to bunkers and
air-raid shelters, Veit Harlan, star director of the Third Reich, finished
shooting an epic war film in color about the famous battle of Kolberg.
Commissioned by Joseph Goebbels, the film was to evoke the memory of the citizens of Kolberg who stood firm in their hopeless fight
against the French in 1807; the example of their courage and bravery
was meant to inspire an increasingly desperate German population
to persevere. Despite shortages everywhere during the last year of
the war, no expense was spared to make Harlan's *Kolberg* the most
elaborate film production of the Hitler regime.[1] Some 187,000 soldiers were reportedly called back from the front in 1944 to serve as
extras in the battle scenes—more than actually fought in the battle
of Kolberg. Harlan's request for an additional 4,000 marines was at
first denied, but after a telephone call to Goebbels these men, too,
were made available. The shooting of the film turned out to be
cumbersome because the ongoing real war interfered repeatedly with
the simulated battles staged for the camera; the grim reality of the
foreseeable German defeat slowed down the production of a filmic
fiction showing a German victory.

The premiere of *Kolberg* took place in the besieged Atlantic fortress
of La Rochelle on January 30, 1945, on the twelfth and final anniversary of Hitler's rise to power and just a few months before Germany's surrender. When it was shown in one of the few movie houses
left standing in Berlin, in February 1945, its call to arms was lost in
a hail of bombs. Today, Harlan's *Kolberg* has become an emblem of

the Third Reich's unshakable belief in the demagogic power of images. In Paul Virilio's words, *Kolberg* is the most impressive illustration of the "osmosis between war and industrial cinema."[2]

On April 17, 1945, after a private screening of *Kolberg*, Propaganda Minister Goebbels spoke to his staff about the future, using the vocabulary of a film director: "Gentlemen," he said, "in a hundred years' time they will be showing a fine color film of the terrible days we are living through. Wouldn't you like to play a part in that film? Hold out now, so that a hundred years hence the audience will not hoot and whistle when you appear on the screen."[3] Goebbels's challenge to his officers not to disappoint the audience in the film version of their own history is a symptom of a political system that relied until its complete breakdown on appearances, histrionics, and simulation.

The "Third Reich" as film: Germany as the location, Hitler as the producer, Goebbels and his officers as directors and stars, Albert Speer as set designer, and the rest of the population as extras. Some of the lesser actors may have wondered what film they were really playing in, but most did not see the light until the film ripped. They had received too many promises and made too many sacrifices, had already paid too high a price, to sneak out before the end, even if they could have. The more questionable the staging of Germany's struggle and power became, the more dependent people grew on the deceitful images produced by Goebbels's propaganda machinery, which dangled the promise of German victories and triumphs before their eyes up to the very last day before the capitulation.

The production of images proceeded without interruption for twelve years, from the first days of Hitler's regime to the liberation by the Allies. Every commercial film, every documentary was examined for its ideological usefulness before being approved by the Reich's Film Bureau. Every movie house was required to show weekly newsreels; in the early, "successful" years of the war these would often last a full hour. Every week Goebbels himself, cynically aware of the newsreels' lies and distortions, appraised them with regard to their propaganda value; he even helped edit them.

No other film industry in the world has ever been so subservient to government propaganda; no other government has ever represented itself so obsessively on film. Yet the Propaganda Ministry made sure to conceal the political and pedagogic function of its films.

Speaking before the Reichsfilmkammer in 1941, Goebbels said: "This is the really great art—to educate without revealing the purpose of the education . . . The best propaganda is that which, as it were, works invisibly, penetrates the whole of life without the public having any knowledge at all of the propagandist initiative."[4] Goebbels knew what he was doing when he called for "apolitical" entertainment films that would cajole the public into (day)dreaming and implant in them indirectly, often only by insinuation and subtle allusion to autocratic rulers and authoritarian rules, the basic principles of National Socialist ideology. Mass culture and militarism went hand in hand. According to the film critic Karsten Witte, the spectacular revue films made by UFA, the famous 1920s film production company that became part of the Propaganda Ministry in 1933, and such opulent Nazi propaganda films as Leni Riefenstahl's *Triumph des Willens* (*Triumph of the Will*, 1935) complemented each other: "The enormous closing tableaux of revue films from *Premiere* to *Die grosse Liebe* are a continuation of *Triumph des Willens,* translating its ritualized expression into popular film genres. The overwhelming experience of the German masses, who had encountered themselves on the terrain of Nuremberg, had to acquire continuity in everyday production."[5]

The National Socialist propaganda film aimed to overwhelm the spectator by its monumentality, its dynamics and sheer massiveness. Sets, dramatic structure, and editing all follow this principle. In Triumph of the Will (generally regarded as the archetypal fascist film) cameras are constantly in motion, circling and moving, creating a compelling energy in the tightly composed spaces and around formations of masses of people, animating even buildings and monuments. The film uses symbolic lighting to produce a pseudoreligious, archaic, and mystical atmosphere and alternates between long shots and close-ups, between swaying masses and the static figure of the Führer in the center, shot from a low angle against the sky. Images such as these have become part of the public memory in Germany.[6]

"Never before and in no other country have images and language been abused so unscrupulously as here, never before and nowhere else have they been debased so deeply as vehicles to transmit lies."[7] These comments were made by the German director Wim Wenders in 1977 on the occasion of a documentary film that used these very images to illustrate Hitler's "career." The film, two and a half hours long, was *Hitler: Eine Karriere* (*Hitler: A Career*), directed by Joachim C. Fest, the influential editor of the *Frankfurter Allgemeine Zeitung,* and Christian Herrendoerfer. Based on Fest's highly regarded and widely read thousand-page biography, *Hitler* (1973), this documentary film intended to show the fascination that Hitler aroused in the German public.[8] A new image of Hitler, inspired by curiosity and nostalgia as well as commercial interest, had emerged with the publication of Albert Speer's diaries in 1968. No longer was Hitler the demonic criminal, the psychopathic monster, or the incarnation of evil, as he had usually been portrayed until then. Now he appeared as a complex, contradictory, and ultimately fascinating figure who radiated an attraction capable of captivating even intellectuals like Speer.[9] If we assume that, morally speaking, Hitler was a criminal, then, according to Fest, we must ask

> how Hitler was nonetheless able to win over so many people and exploit them for his purposes; how he convinced his contemporaries, broke down their resistance, corrupted them, and suspended their value systems; how he was able to overpower a state, to put a worldwide system of peace out of commission, and still make Germany one of the two great ideological centers of power in the thirties, the other being the Soviet Union . . . Yet most of Germany still holds on to an image of Hitler characterized by moral outrage without further inquiry. That is an image of Hitler for the politically naive.[10]

Film was the obvious medium for promulgating this new image of Hitler. Visual images, more immediate and intense than the printed word, became the most effective means of demonstrating the fascination and the demagogic power that Hitler exploited to hypnotize millions. To evoke this fascination and power, Fest and Herrendoerfer released a flood of images like those employed in the National Socialist propaganda films. They took clips from the propaganda films, synchronized them with sound effects (boot heels clicking, bombs exploding in stereo), enhanced the visual quality of the images, and edited them according to modern conventions. By using shot/countershot, they established the union between the Führer and the people as both pseudoreligious and erotic: masses of women listen raptly at the dictator's feet as he exhausts himself, fulfilling their libidinous, ecstatic desire to submit themselves. The carefully choreographed propaganda images of parades, public speeches, and party congresses radiate an opulence and a suggestive power that clearly overwhelm Fest's voice-over commentary, which is supposed to explain the pictures. In the cinema, visual pleasure always triumphs over critical resolve: what we see, not what we hear, is primary.[11] Fest's commentary is limited to the person and the myth of the Führer: "History on occasion loves to realize itself in a single person," a voice-over claims at the beginning of the film. The commentator sometimes even argues from Hitler's own perspective. We see little of the social, intellectual, and historical conditions that made Hitler's "career" possible. And with few exceptions, we are not shown the fears and suffering of the population, the suppression, torture, and murder in the concentration camps, or the persecution and resistance of dissidents. The documentary approach prides itself on using only historical film material, but that very approach undermines the critical intentions of the filmmakers. Since crime, suffering, and opposition were not documented by the Nazi propaganda films, they cannot be shown and are, according to the logic of this film, justifiably left out: whatever was not filmed does not exist. What *Hitler: A Career* in fact does is to pass off a reality produced by the Propaganda Ministry as an authentic documentation of the time. The film thus replicates, intentionally or not, fascist aesthetics and recycles, once again, an arsenal of deceptive and demagogic images.[12]

Fest's film on Hitler shows Hitler and the Third Reich as they wanted to be seen. "Scores of cameramen constantly surrounded him. Their pictures stylized him into a monument." Despite this critical voice-over commentary, Fest remains within the boundaries of the original images, as though Riefenstahl's manipulative and contrived shots imparted a true picture of National Socialist reality. "The 'career' that Fest and Herrendoerfer wanted to investigate," Wenders says in his polemic against the film, "was above all possible because there was a total control of all film material, because all of the images of this man and his ideas were made in a clever manner, were chosen skillfully and used tactically. As a result of this thoroughgoing demagogic treatment of images, all of those people in Germany involved with the conscientious and equally competent production of film images left this country."[13]

Wenders is thinking of Fritz Lang and more than fifteen hundred other directors, cameramen, technicians, actresses, and actors who were forced out of Germany or went voluntarily into exile because they did not want to conform to the Nazi line. He remains painfully aware of the disastrous long-term consequences of this mass exodus for German film culture:

> I speak for everyone who in recent years, after a long drought, has started once again to produce images and sounds in a country which has an unceasing distrust of images and sounds that tell its story, which for this reason has for thirty years greedily soaked up all foreign images, just as long as they have taken its mind off itself. I do not believe there is anywhere else where people have suffered such a loss of confidence in images of their own, their own stories and myths, as we have. We, the directors of the New Cinema, have felt this loss most keenly, in our own persons in the lack, the absence of a tradition of our own, as a fatherless generation, and in the spectators with their perplexed reaction and their initial hesitation. Only gradually has this defensive attitude, on the one hand, and this lack of self-confidence, on the other, broken down, and in a process that will perhaps take several years more, the feeling is arising here again that images and sounds do not have to be only something imported, but rather can be something concerned with this country that also comes out of this country.[14]

The legacy of the National Socialist film—an instinctive distrust of images and sounds that deal with Germany—has deeply preoccupied the younger generation of German filmmakers for the past quarter-century. How were they to find and create images of Germany and German history that deviated from those of the National Socialist film industry? The disjointed German film tradition caused Wenders to look to American directors like John Ford for his stylistic inspiration. Werner Herzog placed himself in the tradition of German Expressionism of the 1920s. Volker Schlöndorff went to France to learn filmmaking. An uncompromising rejection of the National Socialist film tradition has in fact become the secret unifying force of the New German Cinema since the 1960s.

The break with the film of the Nazi past became visible in 1962, at the Eighth West German Short Film Festival in Oberhausen. Twenty-six young filmmakers and journalists, among them Edgar Reitz and Alexander Kluge, published a manifesto declaring the death of the old German cinema and vowing to create "the new German feature film."[15] The authors of the "Oberhausen Manifesto" wanted to break with the film of their "fathers" in every respect: in matters of production, content, form, and style. The films of the New German

Cinema had artistic aspirations that were not seen in the commercial films of the 1950s. Taking their cue from Godard, Truffaut, Chabrol, and other *auteurs* of the French New Wave that began at the end of the 1950s, German directors also wanted their films to bear the unmistakable signature of an "author." The manifesto explicitly rejected the ideological and commercial exploitation of the film medium, seeking a new beginning both aesthetically and politically. The Oberhausen group wanted above all to serve as a critical voice in the life of the Federal Republic, as a filmic counterpart to the group of writers assembled in the influential "Gruppe 47."[16] This desire corresponded to a new interest by the young filmmakers in questions rarely even broached in the cinema of the Adenauer era, questions about the most recent German past and its persistence in the present of the Federal Republic. Not surprisingly, the first two productions of the "Young German Film," as the New German Cinema was called in the 1960s, emphasize this troubled relationship of Germans to their past.

Alexander Kluge's 1966 debut film became the first feature-length film of the New German Cinema to win an international prize. Its title reads like a slogan: *Abschied von gestern* (*Farewell to Yesterday*; in the English release, *Yesterday Girl*). Set in the mid-1950s, the film depicts a young Jewish woman from the German Democratic Republic who, after fleeing to the West, is unable to find a home in the Federal Republic. Her past catches up with her again and again. The film demonstrates that there can be no escape from the past: "No abyss separates us from yesterday, only the changed situation," proclaims the opening title. Like many later films of the New German Cinema, this film stresses continuities in German history where it seems most disjointed. Volker Schlöndorff's *Der junge Törless* (*Young Törless*, 1965–66), based on Robert Musil's 1906 novella of boarding school life, looks to the prehistory of the Third Reich. The film tells the story of a student who watches, half fascinated and half repelled, as two other students torment a fellow student of Jewish descent. The story is used to reflect the history of the many intellectual conformists during National Socialism who stood by silently as atrocities were committed.[17]

The films of Kluge and Schlöndorff are quite different in the formal treatment of their subject matter. Nonetheless, they share an interest in the causes and consequences of National Socialism—an interest that distinguishes the New German Cinema from the old. The new directors no longer considered German history taboo; they subjected contemporary West German society to critical scrutiny; and they gradually overcame their lack of ease around images depicting their own country. In the early 1960s, the Eichmann trial in Jerusalem and the Auschwitz trial in Frankfurt publicized the atrocities committed in concentration camps around the world. The German intelligentsia's collusion, whether passive or active, with the reign of terror finally became the subject of public discussion.[18] The time seemed ripe for films with a critical attitude toward Germany's most recent past. There were few models.

The Flight from Memory

How does memory function? Our knowledge—incomplete and contradictory in itself—insists that a basic mechanism is at work according to the system of gathering-storing-recalling. Furthermore, the first, easily erasable track is said to be recorded by the cells' bioelectrical action; whereas storing, the changeover to long-term memory, is probably a matter of chemistry: memory molecules, fixed in permanent storage . . . By the way, according to the latest research, this process supposedly takes place at night. In our dreams.

CHRISTA WOLF

When the Allied Forces took over the German film industry in 1945, the National Socialist production of images came to an abrupt halt. The few German films made in the first years after the war were subjected to a complicated licensing system that differed in each of the four occupation zones. The Western allies considered films above all a form of commercial entertainment. Their main concern was to regain and secure West Germany as a market for their own films; they were not particularly interested in reconstructing a native German film industry.[19] They also had a healthy distrust of the German film industry, which had served as an effective arm of the Ministry of Propaganda for twelve years.

The Soviets, on the other hand, soon began systematically to use film in their zone as a weapon in the fight against fascism and as an effective tool for reaching the masses in the "struggle for the education of the German people, especially the youth."[20] DEFA (Deutsche Film-AG) was founded under Russian license in 1946. Early on it produced a large number of films dealing with the psychological and social roots of National Socialism, excoriating those characteristics—subservience, obedience, political apathy—that allowed fascism to develop in Germany. From Erich Engel's *Affäre Blum* (*The Blum Affair*, 1947), Kurt Maetzig's *Ehe im Schatten* (*Marriage in the Shadow*, 1949), Falk Harnack's *Beil von Wandsbeck* (*The Axe of Wandsbeck*, 1949), and Slatan Dudow's *Stärker als die Nacht* (*Stronger Than the Night*, 1954) through Wolfgang Staudte's films *Rotation* (1949) and *Der Untertan* (*The Subject*, 1951) to historical works by Konrad Wolf including *Lissy* (1957), *Professor Mamlock* (1961), *Ich war 19* (*I was 19*, 1968), and *Mama, ich lebe* (*Mama, I Am Alive*, 1977), the films of the German Democratic Republic were profoundly concerned with the causes and effects of National Socialism, specifically with war, fascism, the persecution of Jews, and the resistance movement. These historical films, most of which follow the doctrine of Socialist Realism, served as a warning aimed at preventing a renewed alliance of fascism, capitalism, and war.

Wolfgang Staudte's film *Die Mörder sind unter uns* (*The Murderers Are among Us*, 1946) was the first DEFA film (the French and the Americans had refused to license the script) and the first German postwar film that dealt with the most recent past. It was nonpartisan. The film did not analyze the economic and political roots of fascism, but instead raised the questions of guilt and atonement. Dr. Mertens, an embittered war veteran, returns home and is unable to find a foothold in the ravaged present. When he learns that his former batallion commander, Brückner, lives in Berlin, he dreams of revenge. Mertens believes that Brückner must atone for his war crimes, for he is a "murderer among us." In a flashback to Christmas Eve, 1942, we see Brückner ordering hostages shot in Poland. The film, which is based on the belief that the crimes committed during the war must not go unpunished, presents one man's fantasies of revenge and seems to suggest they are justified until, at the last moment, they are converted into a demand for legitimate state justice. At the end of the film Mertens's friend, who has herself just been released from a concentration camp,[21] says, "We do not have the right to judge, but we have the duty to accuse, to demand atonement on behalf of millions of innocent people who were murdered in cold blood."

This appeal to the legal system of the state makes little impression primarily because it does not inevitably follow from the film's dramatic structure; it seems tacked on. Staudte uses a film vocabulary that consciously rejects the intoxicating style of National Socialist propaganda and instead adopts the expressionistic style of the Weimar Republic, decried as degenerate by the Nazis, as well as elements that recall Italian neorealism. Distorted camera angles, strongly outlined silhouettes, diagonal lines, and heavy shadows—familiar from such films as *Das Cabinet des Dr. Caligari* (*The Cabinet of Dr. Caligari*, 1920)—symbolize the inner distress and turmoil of the protagonists.

Staudte's *The Murderers Are among Us* is the best known of the so-called *Trümmerfilme* ("rubble films") made between 1946 and 1948. These films tried to come to grips with the recent past against the still contemporary background of ruined cities.[22] The films made in the Western occupation zones also exhibited the humanistic and existentialist mood of the immediate postwar years. The first feature film made in the American zone, Josef von Baky's *Und über uns der Himmel* (*And the Sky above Us*, 1947), describes the stages of a soldier's transformation from a life of hunger, poverty, and black marketeering to a moral and ethical existence. The story is strongly emotional and forward-looking: "For the heaven above us will not let us perish." Images of the devastated landscape and the black market document the loss of old values and serve as a foil for a depoliticized appeal to a new humanity.

Helmut Käutner's film, *In jenen Tagen* (*In Those Days*, 1947), licensed by the British, offers a sympathetic reading of German history from 1933 to 1945. In seven episodes, noble but powerless individuals are destroyed by fascism, seen as fate, because their very humanity makes them vulnerable. The film aims to show that even under the reign of terror, humanitarian behavior existed. The film is motivated by an ideology of self-purification—a retrospective attempt to lend meaning to senseless events, which explains its sentimental visual symbolism (the last shot is a close-up of a spring flower amidst the ruins of a building). Against the background of authentic ruins, fascism is mirrored in private conflicts; political implications are glossed over. The metaphysical question "What is a human being?" seems more important than an investigation into what human beings were actually capable of just a few years before.

The trauma of defeat and the resulting "political quarantine"[23] under which the occupation powers placed the Germans in 1945 inhibited an open political analysis of the conditions, mechanisms, and consequences of National Socialism. Questions about right and wrong, guilt and atonement were evaded by the adoption of a pre-dominantly existentialist-humanist approach, obscured by the psychology of love stories, or diverted into appeals to Christian forgiveness. The German people appear as the passive and suffering victims of Nazism, while Hitler and his entourage stand as the guilty ones— a view inadvertently strengthened in the public's mind by the Nuremberg trials, where the guilty supposedly found their just punishment. After the war the Germans were in fact more passive observers of their own fate than active participants. The reality of "denazification" was such that most Germans once again assumed a submissive role; they followed orders while others were making policy for them.[24] Pent-up energies surfaced with all the more force in the politically unthreatening free zone of culture, the sole arena in which German identity could express itself. Goethe was revived to represent the "other," humanistic and spiritual Germany, which became all the more vital with the destruction of the political Germany. Friedrich Meinecke, in his 1946 book *Die deutsche Katastrophe* (*The German Catastrophe*), suggested that German identity be renewed by the spirit of German Classicism and that the moral rebirth of the nation be promoted by hours set aside each Sunday to celebrate Goethe.[25]

As the debris was cleared away, the visible signs of the past were removed as well. Soon grass grew over the ruins and people began to build the foundations of new houses in bomb craters. In order to avoid another false commitment, people shied away from politics in general: once burned, twice shy. The Germans seemed particularly demoralized and stricken with apathy in matters of national identity. In Leni Riefenstahl's *Triumph of the Will*, which documented the Nuremberg Party Congress in 1934, Rudolf Hess shouted out into a crowded arena, "Germany is Hitler and Hitler is Germany!" But Hitler was dead; was Germany too? German identity, as it was defined by the Führer, was destroyed; the rhetoric of German supremacy proved absurd by the pitiful end in 1945. With surprisingly little resistance the Germans accepted their division into two states in 1949, just as they had earlier accepted denazification, their "reeducation" by the Western Allies, and the outrages committed, primarily against women, by American and Russian occupation soldiers. In 1945 Germany was a nation without state sovereignty or political power, a burnt-out crater of world politics.

Paradoxically, in the early postwar years the Nuremberg war trials, the denazification program (satirized as early as 1951 in Ernst von Salomon's *Der Fragebogen* [*The Questionnaire*]) and Allied control of all public media and institutions did more to impede than to promote free discussion among Germans about their own past. It seemed as if even the German past were now under the jurisdiction of the Allies; it was *their* business. Since the Germans had not liberated themselves from Hitler, they were held to be incapable of acknowledging their crimes. Moreover, the Allies seemed to believe that the Germans possessed an incorrigibly fascistic national character. The sociologist Sven Papcke argues that this blanket suspicion corresponded to an equally universal hardening of conscience on the part of the German populace.[26] The mounting resentment against the conquering powers could not, however, be articulated in the immediate postwar years. Just like the Hitler era itself, this resentment had to be repressed. It did not surface until thirty or forty years later, in debates about the crimes committed by the occupation troops and in obliquely political films of the late seventies. The negative view of the American occupation in some of the films discussed here must be seen in this light.

During the 1950s repressed political and psychological energies were rechanneled into the physical reconstruction of Germany. With initial help from the Marshall Plan and the currency reform of 1948 (which irrevocably separated the Soviet occupation zone from the rest of Germany), the West German economy flourished and soon outdid most of the nations that had won the war. With such a promising future ahead, it was easy to forget the past. Looking back would have numbed the Germans—so thought the majority—and slowed down their progress. Nor could the twelve million refugees from the former German territories in Eastern Europe afford to think much about the past if they wanted to survive and succeed in the new achievement-oriented society. It was the role of mass culture to make up for the resulting emotional deficits and spiritual deformations.

The cinema of the Adenauer and Erhard era functioned as a dream world fulfilling the desires for a healthy Germany, for beautiful German landscapes and naive but noble German people.[27] Countless stories of star-crossed couples, reunited in the inevitable happy ending against a background of the Black Forest, replete with music and color, present an illusory image of German reality and history that indirectly points up the repressions, self-deceptions, and collective wishes that were at work. The characters move about as if they were in an Arcadia of trivial myth where evil obtrudes only in the form of an outsider, typically someone from the city. More than 300 of these so-called *Heimatfilme* ("homeland films") were made in the 1950s, with more or less uniform narrative structures and similar images. Products of a typical German tradition, they can be traced back to the mountain films of Arnold Fanck, Luis Trenker, and Leni Riefenstahl in the late 1920s and 1930s, with their idealization of nature. They also derive from the Nazi "blood and soil" productions, which glorified the rural life as the mystical embodiment of German blood and German soil. The Heimatfilm of the 1950s became a genre that (like the American western) shows imaginary spaces, pure movie lives, and a strong moral undercurrent. As a refuge from dirt, debris, and poverty and as a compensation for the many deprivations of the postwar era, these movies fulfilled real collective needs: in 1951, no fewer than 20 million viewers saw Hans Deppe's *Grün ist die Heide* (*Green is the Heather*), one of the classics of this genre. It was no secret that these Heimatfilme of the 1950s also tried to impart a new feeling of home, of "Heimat," to the millions of refugees and exiles who had lost their homelands. These films, which painted an unabashedly idealized, nostalgic picture of Germany, may indeed have helped all those who were made homeless (*heimatlos*) by the war to identify with West Germany and accept it as their new Heimat. The German homeland: at once movie dream and trauma.

Among the popular film genres attacked by the Oberhausen filmmakers in 1962, the Heimatfilm of the 1950s received particularly harsh criticism. Its cliché-ridden, Agfa-colored images of German forests, landscapes, and customs, of happiness and security, appeared to the young directors to be deceitful movie kitsch. They also took offense at the continuity of themes and forms from the thirties to the fifties. Many of the successful Heimatfilme were indeed remakes of films from the Hitler era. Most of the well-known Heimatfilm directors, such as Hans Deppe, Paul May, and Rolf Hansen, were seasoned professionals who had learned their craft—the commercial entertainment film—at the UFA studios in the 1930s and 1940s.[28] Under Hitler the Heimatfilm was an arch-German film genre, with all its negative connotations: national chauvinism, "blood and soil" ideology, and overwrought emotionalism. Nevertheless, despite their contempt for the genre, young German filmmakers considered it a challenge to tackle the Heimatfilm, which was, after all, one of the few indigenous film genres. From the "critical homeland films" of Peter Fleischmann (*Jagdszenen aus Niederbayern* [*Hunting Scenes from Lower Bavaria*], 1968), of Volker Schlöndorff (*Der plötzliche Reichtum der armen Leute von Kombach* [*The Sudden Wealth of the Poor People of Kombach*], 1971), and of Reinhard Hauff (*Mathias Kneissl*, 1971) to Edgar Reitz's highly ambivalent adoption of the genre in *Heimat* (1984)—all these films work with, and rework, images and narratives that focus on Germany as homeland, as Heimat, both hated and loved.[29]

The war films of the fifties were just as popular—and just as burdened with a negative tradition—as the homeland films. In the wake of the rearmament debate these films generated particular interest in the Federal Republic because they showed a direct relation to the propaganda films of the Nazi past. Here, too, we find directors who had made films under Goebbels. Alfred Weidenmann, for instance, who directed the Luftwaffe film *Junge Adler* (*Young Eagles*) for the Hitler Youth in 1942, won prizes for his (anti)war film *Canaris* in 1954. Continuities can be seen particularly in the choice of images and the narrative presentation of war. Although these films differ from Nazi films in their professed antiwar attitude, they undermine such a resolve in their naturalistic evocations of battle scenes: the images overpower any critical intentions; moral messages evaporate when up against visual pleasure and spectacle. Even films as different as Paul May's three-part version of Hans Hellmut Kirst's bestseller, *08/15* (1954–55), and Helmut Käutner's *Des Teufels General* (*The Devil's General,* 1954), based on Carl Zuckmayer's play, show the upright, duty-conscious soldier as the powerless victim of a mad Führer and a merciless general staff. The soldier as the hero pitted against criminal and crazy authority: this tried-and-true narrative war-film formula still works in Wolfgang Petersen's film *Das Boot* (*The Boat,* 1982) and may account for its international success.[30]

The power structures and relations of dependency shown in these films remain irrational and inexorable. They thus succeed, indirectly and perhaps unconsciously, in valorizing and rehabilitating the old military virtues like "manly" courage and heroism, obedience and honor, martyrdom and unquestioned love of the fatherland.[31] Even such a widely respected antiwar film as Bernhard Wicki's *Die Brücke* (*The Bridge,* 1959) retains a political ambivalence. The film shows the senseless death of a group of young boys charged with defending a strategically useless bridge against advancing American tanks. The ambivalence derives from Wicki's concentration on the fate of the German child-soldiers as victims, who are as innocent as they are apolitical.

The arsenal of images from World War II was taken up and used again only five years after the end of the war, not only in the Federal Republic but also in the United States. Indeed, more than half of the 224 war films shown in the Federal Republic between 1948 and 1959 came from the United States. The best-known titles, Henry Hathaway's *The Desert Fox* (1951), Fred Zinnemann's *From Here to Eternity* (1953), and David Lean's *The Bridge on the River Kwai* (1957), all shown in dubbed versions in West Germany, deal with the "great themes"—life and death, tortured conscience, pitched battle, and the test of manhood—against a background of exotic landscapes. These themes had much in common with the National Socialist image production during World War II; in the petit-bourgeois social welfare state under Adenauer, they served to vent frustrations and compensate for deprivations. These films fueled nostalgic fantasies about adventures in exotic lands and the heroic life on the front. They also distinguished between the honest soldier and the unreasonable, despicable regime, and thus succeeded in intensifying already prevalent apologist tendencies.

The Cold War brought a premature end to the denazification program, and this fostered the growing view, strongly held in the 1950s, that the past should be laid to rest. Even Konrad Adenauer felt moved to launch a categorical protest against this tendency as early as in 1952:

A dynamic person forgets the past too easily and perhaps with relief, especially when the past is not as he would have liked it. That presents a great danger, because the past is a reality. It does not disappear, and it continues to have an effect even when we shut our eyes to it . . . When I think of the nameless misery that was visited on our fatherland and the whole world largely through the fault of Germany, I am outraged at the glorifying descriptions of the truly guilty and truly responsible parties of that time which appear time and again in certain of our newspapers. The fact that it was possible to lead a considerable portion of the German people down such a fateful path must open serious, very serious questions for every thinking person, especially the question as to how it was possible in the first place. We must ask these questions in order to devote all our strength to preventing the return of such a deep and disastrous fall.[32]

This is the official, unmistakable discourse of West German politicians with respect to the past, a discourse of admonishment that has not changed much between the early fifties and the present.[33] Most of the population, however, considered Adenauer's questions about the "fateful path" and "how it was possible" less urgent. They went to the movies, more popular in those pretelevision days than they ever were, to be entertained. In addition to the escapist homeland films and the nostalgic war films, there were costume epics (the Sissi series, based on the life of the Bavarian princess Elizabeth who later, as the wife of Franz Josef, became the Austrian Empress), comedies (many starring the popular Heinz Erhardt and Heinz Rühmann), melodramas, and thrillers. Films that took a critical view of the past (particularly in its relationship to the present) were the exception in the 1950s.[34] The German cinema of the fifties had no one like Heinrich Böll, who in all of his writings made it his mission to confront Germany with its own past.[35]

In 1962 Jean-Marie Straub and Danièle Huillet based their first film on a short story by Heinrich Böll. A decade after Adenauer's speech, they tried to provide a serious response to his query about the "fateful path" and its causes. They provoked enraged attacks, not least because they introduced a new way of treating history in film. Straub was born in Alsace and had lived in the Federal Republic since 1958; he and his co-director were pioneers who greatly influenced the new German *Autorenfilm* because they rigorously separated the medium from the sphere of commercial entertainment and re-positioned it in the realm of avant-garde literary art. Politically, too, Straub and Huillet were ahead of their time.

In *Machorka-Muff* (1962), a short film following Böll's satiric *Hauptstädtisches Journal* (*Bonn Diary*), Erich von Machorka-Muff, a former general under Hitler, fulfills a dream of his youth by founding an "academy for military memories." Here soldiers from the rank of major up can write their memoirs in peace. The title of his first lecture, "Memory as a Historical Task," points not only to the nostalgic tendencies of the old military men who were speaking openly once more but also to the collective amnesia in the era of the economic miracle. The film, says Straub, dealt with the "rape of a land that had the chance to be free of the military. *Machorka-Muff* was a kind of didactic piece. Germany missed out on its revolution and did not free itself from fascism. For me it is a country that moves in a circle and cannot free itself from its past."[36] The film begins with a title, "An abstract dream of images, not a story," but it is as if an awakening occurs at the end, in the last sentence, when the general asks, "Opposition? What's that?"

Straub and Huillet's radical film adaptation of Böll's novel *Billiard um halbzehn (Billiards at Half Past Nine)*, with the revealing title *Nicht versöhnt oder Es hilft nur Gewalt, wo Gewalt herrscht (Not Reconciled; or, 'Only Violence Helps Where Violence Rules,'* 1965) is even more overtly political. Through sudden unmarked flashbacks, the film conjoins the fascist past with the West German present. The film focuses on a Catholic architect's family over three generations as it builds and destroys a monastery, only to rebuild it again. The youngest son is "not reconciled" with his present, which exists without a sense of its guilty past.

Böll's literary texts provided only a point of departure for both films: in *Machorka-Muff* Straub and Huillet added excerpts from newspaper articles about rearmament; in *Not Reconciled,* they incorporated a short documentary segment as part of the fiction. In keeping with Brecht's theory of the epic theater, Straub and Huillet are concerned with the relative independence and separation of the various filmic elements: images, sound, acting, dialogue, and written text on title cards, which in the tradition of silent films interrupt the flow of images. Instead of blending these diverse enunciations into a coherent narrative that effaces all traces of its making, they want the spectator to have access at all times to the process of constructing meaning in filmed fiction. For only if the viewer is always aware of fiction *as* fiction, that is, as something staged and constructed, can enlightenment and learning ensue, rather than further obfuscation. In strict opposition to the opulent images of the Nazi cinema, Straub and Huillet maintain an almost ascetic relation to images, which seem bled dry in their early films: the camera usually remains static, the dramatic structure limited to bare essentials; gaps, leaps, and ellipses abound. Straub and Huillet prefer nonprofessionals as actors, who follow Brecht's method and do not "become" the fictional characters but instead "quote" them. In order to document the act of filming in the film itself, Straub and Huillet leave the originally recorded soundtrack unchanged. In short, their films violate nearly every Hollywood convention. The spectator is activated, forced to see differently, and—in the tradition of modernism—invited to reflect critically on the very construction of filmic images; identification with onscreen characters is often interrupted and visual pleasure frustrated.

According to Straub and Huillet, the truly political film must not treat political subject matter in a conventional narrative; rather what is needed is a revolution in the filmic representation itself. They insist that the representation of history in film poses special problems that cannot be solved with traditional strategies of narration. As their film *Geschichtsunterricht* (*History Lessons*, 1972) makes clear, it is not so much the story as the very act of representing the story as history (and history as story) that is at stake. *History Lessons* is based on Brecht's fragmentary novel *Die Geschäfte des Herrn Julius Cäsar* (*The Business Affairs of Mr. Julius Caesar*), which Brecht wrote during his exile in Denmark in the late 1930s. Like the novel, Straub and Huillet's film challenges historical representation by eliminating both narrative continuity and naive referentiality; it calls attention to the impossibility of recapturing the past in the present by way of simplistic reconstruction. Brecht's own film of 1932, *Kuhle Wampe oder wem gehört die Welt?* (*Kuhle Wampe or Who Owns the World?*), with its calculated mixture of cinematic enunciations (images, titles, music, sound, documentary as well as staged parts), served as a model. Straub and Huillet's translation of Brechtian principles into film exerted a strong influence not only on the aesthetics of Alexander Kluge and Rainer Werner Fassbinder but also on the judgment of such authoritative film critics as Enno Patalas and Frieda Grafe. Straub and Huillet's avant-garde renderings of Böll's texts won numerous prizes in foreign film festivals. In the Federal Republic, however, audiences reacted to their films either with hostility or, more often, with indifference.

Straub and Huillet were part of a small group of West German film directors in the early 1960s who were dissatisfied with the state of the film industry as it turned out film after film, uninspired and provincial beyond belief. But the "Young German Film" was not a movement, nor was it a school. The individual temperaments and stylistic interests of its members were too varied. Like the New

German Cinema that succeeded it in the mid-1970s, Young German Film became distinctive in the international scene primarily because of the conditions of production under which it arose (and still operates to this day). These conditions to a large degree reflect the willingness of the state to fund selected films through an elaborate system of subsidies, loans, advances, prizes, and awards. From the 1970s on, German television increasingly functioned as a co-producer. This economic independence from the marketplace allowed the directors of the Young German Film as well as the New German Cinema to see themselves from the beginning as "counter-cinema," as avant-garde. Predictably, and almost on purpose, these filmmakers never gained a mass following. And they never really needed to gain one, because from the beginning they could rely on government support. In his critical survey, "New German Cinema: Economics without Miracle," Kraft Wetzel writes: "Since the films made in the Federal Republic of Germany usually don't even gross enough to cover distribution costs—not to mention production expenditures— there is no possibility of establishing a fund for financing other films. Therefore, West German filmmakers can only produce as many films as the government can afford to subsidize. Consequently, the history of West German film is the history of a struggle to convince the government to create subsidies, to gain access to these funds, and then to persuade the State to increase the amount of money available."[37]

In 1981 the German states and the federal government spent a total of 80 million marks on its patronage of film production. Although the government subsidies for opera, concerts, and theater are significantly higher, a sum of this magnitude carries obligations. The state-subsidized German film has, more than in any other country, accepted a secret cultural mission: for twenty-five years the "artistically ambitious" New German Cinema has represented the Federal Republic with astonishing success at foreign film festivals. Goethe Institutes all over the world show films of the New German Cinema in retrospectives or in theme-oriented series;[38] teachers at foreign schools and universities can borrow films of the New German Cinema for a nominal fee from the embassies and consulates of the Federal Republic. Thus the New German Cinema plays an important part in the promotion of West German culture abroad. Considering how little known and appreciated some of the films of the New German

Cinema are inside West Germany—foreigners are always amazed to learn this—one is tempted to conclude that the publicly subsidized film functions mainly as an export article for distribution abroad.

The Federal Republic presents itself to the rest of the world in the mirror of these films. It is not surprising, therefore, that films dealing with the recent German past arouse particular attention. Occasionally the federal government launches a protest against the often self-critical image of Germany that these films display, fearing damage to the reputation of the Federal Republic.[39] Nonetheless, particularly in the last ten years, an astoundingly large proportion of government-sponsored films have dealt with the period 1933 to 1945, possibly as sort of a compensatory mechanism that leaves the painful task of coming to terms with the past to the simulated reality of the media. Between 1975 and 1985 alone, more than fifty new feature films dealing with National Socialism were made in West Germany, nearly as many as in all the thirty years before.[40] The numbers are impressive, but from an aesthetic point of view most of these films mean very little: they recycle images of images.

Starting in the 1970s, an iconography of the Nazi era has evolved that is now routinely reproduced over and over in these films. The great international art films of the early 1970s—Luchino Visconti's *The Damned,* Louis Malle's *Lacombe, Lucien,* François Truffaut's *The Last Metro,* and Liliana Cavani's *The Night Porter*—presented the fascist past through imagery so powerful that most subsequent films about the Third Reich were invariably influenced by these films.[41] Their visual style became a convention for historical films dealing with Nazism. The Third Reich itself was often reduced in these representations to a semiotic phenomenon: SS uniforms, swastikas, shaved napes, black leather belts and boots, intimidating corridors and marble stairs have become mere signs unmistakably signaling "fascism"; they serve as a suggestive backdrop that lends the private events in the foreground historical weight and consequence. Already in 1977, Karsten Witte attacked the clichéd use of fascist images:

> Haven't we speculated enough on the past under the pretext of coming to terms with it? Haven't we been exposed to the Nazi past enough under the pretext of "immunization"? What is left for the visual analysis of fascism to discover except the tautological reproduction of the material

with which we started? This supply of images is exhausted. We have already seen them all, but seldom from a new perspective. Public opinion should protect itself from the blight of these fascist products that are nonchalantly televised on holidays, and force speculators who exploit collective fascinations in the name of enlightenment to publicly admit their true intentions.[42]

Many of these films and television productions figured in the so-called "Hitler wave" of the 1970s.[43] We do not know whether any of these representations caused Germans to begin remembering. Their straightforward, realistic narrative form made it easy to take them as entertainment—gripping but harmless. Television, ever hungry for stories, swallowed the historical films about the Nazi era without difficulty. These were films in the past tense, narratively closed to the viewer's present. Their "authentic" reconstructions showed the past as finished and done with; no one needed to be affected by it.

The Return of the Repressed

The dead, too, write on the paper of the future, with flames already threatening to destroy it.

HEINER MÜLLER

On September 5, 1977, Hanns Martin Schleyer, chairman of the Daimler-Benz company and one of the most prominent West German industrialists, was kidnapped by members of the Red Army Faction (RAF). Four of his companions were shot to death. On October 13, a Lufthansa airliner carrying eighty-six passengers was hijacked and compelled to land in Mogadischu, Somalia, to force the release of captured RAF members. On October 18, an antiterrorist team of the West German border police liberated the hostages. On the same day, in the maximum-security prison of Stammheim, Andreas Baader, Gudrun Ensslin, and Jan-Carl Raspe, members of the Baader-Meinhof group of terrorists, were found dead, apparent suicide victims in circumstances so mysterious that an international commission convened to investigate the matter. On October 19, Schleyer's corpse was found in an abandoned car in Mulhouse, Alsace. These were the events of the autumn of 1977, the "German Autumn," as it was later called. In April of the same year members of the RAF had murdered the attorney general, Siegfried Buback, and in June the banker Jürgen

Ponto. In a climate of suspicion, anxiety, and hysteria, the government countered not only with intensified security measures but also with an active and undifferentiated persecution of anyone suspected of sympathy with the RAF terrorists, including all those who, like Heinrich Böll, had dared to criticize the government policy of repression. It became dangerous to express one's opinions; a general fear of surveillance and censure lay heavy over the country. The senseless accumulation of terrorist crimes exposed an underlying political madness that had, if not method, at least a history. Norbert Elias, then eighty years old, referred to this in his comments about the Autumn of 1977: "The violent acts of small, hermetic groups of terrorists in the Federal Republic and the reaction of declaring open season on sympathizers have only the function of a trigger: they suddenly brought to light the latent fissures that exist in West German society and made them visible to the whole world. The reasons for these fissures go further back."[44]

The postwar generation in Germany, from which most of the terrorists came—in the mid-1960s they were about twenty years old, on their way to the university—had broken more radically than elsewhere with the political values and attitudes of their parents' generation. Margarethe von Trotta's fiction film *Die bleierne Zeit* (*Marianne and Juliane,* 1981) explores the only thinly disguised life history of one such terrorist, Gudrun Ensslin. In von Trotta's view, Ensslin, a minister's daughter, was radicalized by her awareness of the monstrous guilt passed on to her by her parents. The filmmaker shows the Ensslin character as a child watching documentary footage of the concentration camps in Alain Resnais's *Night and Fog*; she is so shaken by the images of horror that she vomits. For those born at the end of the war, the atrocities of the Nazi regime were an ineradicable mark of Cain, a stigma that did not allow them to identify with a country capable of such barbarity. Since members of this generation saw the Federal Republic as the successor of the old fascist state, they violently opposed it—almost as if they wanted to show their parents how they should have battled the fascist state thirty years earlier. Thus they offered belatedly the resistance that their parents had failed to offer. In their futile struggle against the alleged contemporary "fascist system" of West Germany, they symbolically wrestled with the demons of their own past.

According to Norbert Elias, German crimes under Hitler were

distinguished from the crimes of other nations by their disregard of the reality principle and by their excessive senselessness.[45] These features, he says, also characterize the terrorist acts of Autumn 1977. They ultimately stem from the collective trauma of learning the truth about the horrifying German past, usually not from one's parents but from books or in school. It was only a matter of time before this repressed trauma would coalesce with the frustration about the "petrified conditions" in the Federal Republic. The memory of the Nazi reign of terror had been excluded from public discussion during the entire reconstruction phase of German postwar history; Germans had thus been denied the chance to work through the past and come to terms with it. This omission now seemed to be taking its revenge in the terrorism of the younger generation. The title of the English book *Hitler's Children* mistakes the true motive of the terrorists, who had "Antifascism" inscribed on their red flags.[46] Nevertheless, in the memory of older Germans, terrorism, restricted freedom of expression, and the Hitler regime were all too closely related. Writing about the German Autumn, Alexander Kluge stated: "The fatal catastrophe succeeded in cutting through the amnesia of many. The events did not have much to do with war directly, but '1945' and 'war' were associated with them. It is no coincidence that we have an emotional movement that *is posing questions about Germany and about the history that takes the form it has.* The repressed shock breaks out in terrorism, a point that is actually not suited to genuinely coming to terms with the previously repressed material; it may even produce new distortions."[47]

In October of 1977, nine directors of the New German Cinema decided to produce a collective film about Germany in 1977 that would be both a chronicle and a commentary. The suggestion came from the Filmverlag der Autoren, a distribution organization founded in 1971 by a group of filmmakers and, from February 1977, partly owned by the magazine *Der Spiegel*. The film, entitled *Deutschland im Herbst* (*Germany in Autumn*, 1978), was intended to document the immediate reactions to the events of fall 1977 and also to reflect the anxieties of that time in short fictional scenes. The communal project was also meant to be a means of countering the government's news blackout and an attempt to answer the "official" version of events with an unofficial one. Like the 1967 French film *Loin du Vietnam* (*Far from Vietnam*) by Alain Resnais, Chris Marker, Jean-

Luc Godard, and others, *Germany in Autumn* is a collective production. The 15- to 30-minute contributions by the nine filmmakers are not individually identified. Nonetheless, the film unmistakably shows Alexander Kluge's overall guidance, since he and his editor, Beate Mainka-Jellinghaus, were in charge of cutting the two-hour film (from nine hours of material). On the surface the film imitates the structure of a television program, with its mixture of documentary shots, interviews, and fictional scenes. But it presents images, tells stories, and offers perspectives not to be found on German television.

The film is framed by two public ceremonies of mourning: the state funeral of Hanns Martin Schleyer and the burial of the dead terrorists, with the police out in force. In between there are funerals and images of violence in German history: documentary shots of Rosa Luxemburg before she was murdered and old footage of the state funeral of Field Marshall Erwin Rommel, who was forced by Hitler to commit suicide in 1944. The nexus of the present and the past is strikingly evident when we see (in an interview) Manfred Rommel, son of the war hero and mayor of Stuttgart, personally demanding a burial with dignity for the terrorists.

The contribution of Heinrich Böll and Volker Schlöndorff centers around the (fictional) cancellation of a television broadcast of Sophocles' *Antigone*. Denied burial, rebellion, and suicide: these themes, seen from the perspective of myth in the play, are associatively related to the efforts of Gudrun Ensslin's sister to care for the common grave of the three RAF members who died in Stammheim. The bitter satire makes clear that a television broadcast of *Antigone* would be too inflammatory in the political situation of Autumn 1977; a classical play about the themes of violence and resistance has become unpresentable.

The mix of forms in *Germany in Autumn* corresponds to the ambiguity of its political agendas. In discussing the goals of their undertaking, the filmmakers emphasized that they had not tried to present a theory to explain terrorism because that would be a "film without images":

> It is something seemingly simple which roused us: the lack of memory. First the news blockade, then the imageless verbal usages of the news media. After the fall of '77—Kappler, Schleyer, Mogadischu, the Stammheim deaths—followed, like every year, Christmas '77 and the New Year.

As if nothing had happened. In this traveling express train of history we are pulling the emergency brake. For two hours of film we are trying to hold onto memory in the form of a subjective momentary impression. As best we can. No one can do more than he can. In this regard our film is a document—this too is another weakness that we do not want to hide . . . *Autumn 1977 is the history of confusion. Exactly this must be held onto. Whoever knows the truth lies. Whoever does not know it seeks. This is our own bias, even if we have different political views.*[48]

At a press conference held to publicize *Germany in Autumn,* the first film of the New German Cinema made without public assistance and without the support of governmental committees or commissions, and, above all, the first cooperative work, the nine filmmakers stated their future program as succinctly as possible: "We want to concern ourselves with the images of our country."[49]

It is no accident that *Germany in Autumn* inspired several projects concerned with "the images of our country." Alexander Kluge continued his short episode showing Gabi Teichert, the Hessian history teacher who digs with her spade for the roots of German history, in his film *Die Patriotin* (*The Patriot,* 1979). Fassbinder's contribution included a staged conversation with his mother about the formation of political opinion and about public behavior today and under National Socialism. He used this revealing conversation as an impetus to reflect on the beginnings of the Federal Republic in his "FRG Trilogy," consisting of *Die Ehe der Maria Braun* (*The Marriage of Maria Braun,* 1979), *Lola* (1981), and *Die Sehnsucht der Veronika Voss* (*Veronika Voss,* 1982). Edgar Reitz, in his segment of *Germany in Autumn,* had shown a border guard speaking in dialect, dreaming of becoming an aviator. He took those dreams up again in his filmic chronicle *Heimat,* begun in 1979. Volker Schlöndorff made a film based on Günter Grass's novel *Die Blechtrommel* (*The Tin Drum*) in 1979, intrigued by the unruly "terrorist" dwarf Oskar who refuses to grow up in the Nazi period. Bernhard Sinkel, another director involved in *Germany in Autumn,* also tried to work through a chapter of recent German history—the unholy alliance of the German chemical industry and National Socialism—in his eight-hour family epic, *Väter und Söhne* (*Sins of the Fathers*), begun in 1979 and shown in four parts on West German television in 1986.

Germany in Autumn consciously sought to counter the collective amnesia by relating images from the present to the past. It could have served as a model of how filmic "images of our country" could be exhibited in a critical and detached manner. But the public resonance of *Germany in Autumn* was limited because its thematic interest in questions of memory and mourning as well as its experimental montage form contradicted most viewers' expectations for a feature film. There were no characters to identify with, no elaborate historical sets, and no engrossing story to follow. Only a year after *Germany in Autumn,* these expectations found fulfillment in the American television series *Holocaust.*

Holocaust was the first major commercial film to deal with the persecution and systematic slaughter of millions of European Jews in a fictional form. As such, it was destined to evoke an especially strong response in the Federal Republic. The German discussion began already in mid-April 1978, when NBC broadcast the four-part, eight-hour-long television series to an audience of approximately 120 million viewers.[50] Initial reports from America castigated the commercial motives of the film, its consistently kitschy style, and the tasteless blend of concentration camp scenes and commercials. When the series began on April 16, 1978, Elie Wiesel, himself a survivor of Auschwitz, described his revulsion at the series in a *New York Times* article called "Trivializing the Holocaust: Semi-Fact and Semi-Fiction." To most German critics, his objections served as a substitute for an argument of their own:

> Untrue, offensive, cheap: as a TV production, the film is an insult to those who perished and to those who survived. In spite of its name, this "docu-drama" is not about what some of us remember as the Holocaust.
> Am I too harsh? Too sensitive, perhaps? But then, the film is not sensitive enough. It tries to show what cannot even be imagined. It transforms an ontological event into soap-opera. Whatever the intentions, the result is shocking. Contrived situations, sentimental episodes, implausible coincidences: If they make you cry, you will cry for the wrong reasons . . .
> Holocaust, a TV drama. Holocaust, a work of semi-fact and semi-fiction. Isn't this what so many morally deranged "scholars" have been claiming recently all over the world? That the Holocaust was nothing else but an "invention"? . . . The Holocaust *must* be remembered. But not as a show.[51]

Following the classical narrative pattern of historical fiction, *Holocaust* tells the story of a fictive family to reflect a larger general history. The scripted lives of fictional characters are woven into the historical "text" of verifiable data and occurrences; private events intersect with political and public ones. The series uses a doctor's family to show the stages of the systematic persecution and annihilation of German Jews in the Third Reich between 1933 and 1945. The viewer learns about the Nuremberg Laws, the "Kristallnacht," the euthanasia program, and about the concentration camps of Warsaw, Buchenwald, Theresienstadt, Babi-Yar, Sobibor, and Auschwitz, through the personal lives of these imaginary characters. In terms of dramatic structure, the Weiss family is paired against the family of the unemployed Eric Dorf, who hopes that joining the Nazi Party will enable him to find work. Pushed by his ambitious wife, he makes a career as the assistant to SS leaders Heydrich and Kaltenbrunner. After the collapse of the Third Reich, Dorf commits suicide. The characters and their love stories, their coincidental meetings and forced partings, are obvious fictions, staged and artificial, but the history that intervenes in their lives is real.

This commingling of historical events with invented characters, of political *Geschichte* (history) with private *Geschichten* (stories), characterizes the genre of the classical historical novel in the tradition of Walter Scott.[52] Televised history tends to follow this formula, but, as a result of television's habitual claim to authenticity, the distinctions between imagined and factual history, between fictional and real spaces, are blurred even further. Presented as a television mini-series, the historical Holocaust shares in this medium-specific dilemma of ambiguous factuality. "Is fact watched as fiction? And fiction fact?" This question, posed by Gerald Green, author of the *Holocaust* screenplay, remains unanswered.[53]

In the case of *Holocaust,* an answer is not necessary, since it exploits this very indeterminacy. The realistic style, the carefully reconstructed historical mise-en-scène, and the occasional intercutting of documentary photographs and authentic film footage from the concentration camps, always motivated by the dramatic action, impart to the film a strong "reality effect." This effect gains intensity in its appeal to the visual memory of the spectator. The pictures of concentration camps are well-known ones; no one would fail to recognize them. Seeing these images again as part of a television series produces a déjà-vu effect that implicitly validates the historical "correctness" of the film.

Holocaust is a *mixtum compositum* in view of its narrative structure and visual style, offering something for everyone, much like a consumer commodity.[54] The series includes domestic happiness and its dissolution, love, war, humiliation, incarceration, survival, rebellion, and ultimate liberation—all universally valid dramatic set pieces whose combination guarantees the broadest possible public appeal. Not surprisingly, in the year of its first broadcast *Holocaust* was sold to fifty countries—including the Federal Republic of Germany, where it played on four evenings in the last week of January 1979.

After its popular success in the United States, the broadcast of this series in the "land of the guilty" promised to draw strong reactions, yet the extent of the collective preoccupation with this film exceeded all predictions. *Holocaust*—the word became a German neologism in 1979[55]—encountered a sensitive political situation. It coincided with the ongoing Majdanek trial, which lasted from 1975 to 1981, the most extensive trial for concentration camp crimes in the history of the Federal Republic. It also coincided with the Filbinger affair, in which the governing president of Baden-Württemberg was accused of having sentenced a deserter to death in the last days of the war. And it coincided with heated debates in Parliament about extending the statute of limitations for Nazi crimes. Even so, the statistics are startling: over 20 million West Germans—which means every other adult—watched *Holocaust*.

The television station WDR, responsible for the broadcast, received more than 30,000 telephone calls and thousands of letters.[56] Radio stations, newspapers, and magazines addressed the issue of German war crimes in the wake of *Holocaust*. The publishers of the two largest weekly magazines in the Federal Republic, *Spiegel* and *Stern*, wrote editorials confessing that they too had taken part in discriminating against German Jews because they had looked the other way. During each of the four episodes telephone numbers were superimposed over the film, inviting viewers who wanted to share their experiences to call in and talk—before the whole nation—with experts from the press and academia. These open-ended discussions followed each segment of *Holocaust* and ran for hours. Heinz Höhne, writing for *Spiegel*, described the public climate of opinion:

> An American television series, made in a trivial style, produced more for commercial than for moral reasons, more for entertainment than for

enlightenment, accomplished what hundreds of books, plays, films, and television programs, thousands of documents, and all the concentration camp trials have failed to do in the more than three decades since the end of the war: to inform Germans about crimes against Jews committed in their name so that millions were emotionally touched and moved . . . Only since, and thanks to, *Holocaust* does a large majority of the nation know what was hidden behind the seemingly innocuous bureaucratic phrase, "the final solution." They know it because U.S. filmmakers had the courage to free themselves from the crippling precept that it is impossible to portray mass murder.[57]

Günter Rohrbach, director of the entertainment division of the television station WDR, stated: "*Holocaust* not only changed our consciousness of history, it also taught us what mass communication can be. After *Holocaust* television can no longer be what it was before."[58] The American series provided a marked break with previous attempts to address the past on German television, which had never attracted a large audience. "A society of educated citizens communicates with each other," Rohrbach said, "in hopes that the news will someday, somehow, filter down."[59] This "arrogance of the educational elite" could not develop in the United States, he continued, where "lines of communication run from below to above." This populist view of American television does not mention that unlike West German television, which is largely state-controlled with a strong educational mandate, American television is part and parcel of the advertising industry and very much dependent on mass audiences and high ratings.

The intellectual elite in particular was disturbed by the runaway success of the American television series. The conventional German distinction between "high culture" and the "soulless" products of commercial American "mass culture"—a distinction that goes back to debates in the Weimar Republic—seemed suddenly rather questionable.[60] The long-cherished German dream of cultural superiority over the "shallow entertainment culture" of America found a rude awakening. German pride in high culture—an essential part of its national identity since the eighteenth century—had to face the question of its actual effect and social function. Those who felt responsible for the state of German culture chastised themselves publicly. Even someone as enmeshed in tradition as the literary critic Marcel Reich-Ranicki asked testily why the Germans had not managed to produce a work like *Holocaust*. And Marion von Dönhoff, publisher of the influential weekly *Die Zeit,* questioned her own aesthetic objections: "The league of film critics, led last year by the *New York Times,* raised many critical objections in this country as well: it is a melodramatic tear-jerker, a trivial entertainment cliché, an impermissible mixture of love story and horror story—as if these aesthetic categories had even the slightest significance in the face of the moral dimension and the message of this series. Some critics overvalue the aesthetic at the expense of the moral in a truly horrifying way."[61] She went on to say that placing value on the purely aesthetic was a typical feature of fascism. "Even during the Hitler business the aesthetic perfection of the flag parades or the grandiose choreography of the Nuremberg Party Congresses infected many and made them 'fellow travelers.'" The rigid, undialectical opposition between aesthetics and morality, between quality and mass effect, as well as the demonization of the aesthetic as tainted by fascism, demonstrate the journalistic excesses that the media event *Holocaust* called forth in Germany.

The shifts in the press's response before and after the showing of *Holocaust* are especially telling. Sabina Lietzmann, journalist for the *Frankfurter Allgemeine Zeitung,* wrote one of the first articles about the American mini-series on April 20, 1978, using the pejorative headline, "The Annihilation of the Jews as Soap Opera." She described her discomfort with the trivialization of suffering and the watering down of history as story. She revised her opinion on September 28, 1978, several months before the German showing, convinced now that the theme was so central to national self-awareness that it "promotes constant thought, which sometimes, as in this case, can lead to a total rethinking":

Why? The response of the American public to *Holocaust,* many of them delayed reactions, taught us that intellectual and critical reaction is one thing, whereas the spontaneous effect on the naive emotions is something altogether different. For millions of viewers throughout the country, *Holocaust* was the first and only access to that otherwise unimaginable phenomenon of the destruction of the Jews. We still consider a good, objective documentary to be a superior instrument of information, but we know that "in terms of people," the television series compelled the mass audience to watch and to empathize. This is a power that no documentary has, however well made. If we are faced with the choice whether to allow no information to be presented or to permit information tailored for easy access as a "story" and produced for people who want entertainment, today, resigning ourselves to the realities, we choose the story. In this sense *Holocaust* has a function, however much our taste and our critical purism rebel against it.[62]

When the series was finally broadcast on West German television in January 1979, it seemed as if for the first time an entire nation dared to remember and to look at its own past. Collective mourning in the Federal Republic itself became a public spectacle, played out, consciously or unconsciously, before the eyes of the world. The Germans knew the rest of the world would be waiting with bated breath for their reception of this film. The influential American columnist Mary McGrory, for instance, intimated this in her commentary on *Holocaust*: "What would be most encouraging, perhaps, to those who are drained from watching this harrowing and often inept re-creation of recent history would be the news that Germany had ordered a print of the film."[63] And Günter Rohrbach, the person mainly responsible for showing the film in Germany, wrote in the same vein: "It would be remarkable if the Germans, whose protagonists proceeded so purposefully in the annihilation of the Jews, were to raise special objections to the treatment of this theme by others."[64] Similarly, Heinz Werner Hübner, the television director of WDR, admitted candidly: "The film is a political event, and if it is shown in the land of those who were affected by the Holocaust, in Israel, then we should expect the people in Germany who participated in those events and their successors to view it as well."[65] Günther Rühle described the international horizon of expectations even more explicitly before the series was shown in Germany:

> During the past thirty years the rest of the world has constantly reminded us of what happened in Germany between 1933 and 1945. The four-part television series *Holocaust* . . . comes to us as a new reminder . . . It is a film that has provoked the most contradictory reactions in America, in England, in Israel. But people in these very countries have also been asking how Germany will deal with the presentation of those events in which almost six of the eleven million European Jews were annihilated in a campaign that included virtually the whole of Europe.[66]

From this perspective, the *Holocaust* series seemed to be a challenge to the Germans to recognize themselves in the mirror held up by Hollywood. One advantage of the "right" reaction would be the chance to show the rest of the world that the Germans had learned from history, that they had changed.

It is not surprising that this confrontation with a long-repressed history met with resistance and criticism. Peter Schulz-Rohr, director of the station SWR, spoke about the "almost exhibitionistic German inclination to engage in self-abnegation," which "combines in a fatal way with the performance of public acts of atonement and exemplifies the kind of moral gesture made to impress others that, for anyone with a sensitive conscience, calls into question the very morality it is meant to demonstrate."[67] For Edgar Reitz, even worse than the dreaded spectacle of guilt and atonement was the fact that the "commercial aesthetic of America" had taken charge of German history, had even "ripped" German history "out of the hands" of the Germans.[68] This insistence on retaining one's own history, even in its most inhuman form, introduces a new, highly ambivalent note in the chronicle of Germany's coming to terms with its own past—a note that became unmistakable a few years later, during Reagan's controversial visit to the military cemetery at Bitburg in May 1985[69] and in the so-called "historians' debate" in 1986.[70] Both events highlight the new revisionist struggle over German history, memory, and national identity.

Even with several empirical studies at our disposal, it is still difficult to assess the actual effect of the *Holocaust* series on the German public. Its aesthetic structure, deliberately organized to meet a large variety of expectations (and thus to be commercially successful), allows, not surprisingly, a large variety of reactions. Letters from German viewers ranged from aggressive rejection to demonstrative, self-chastising confessions of guilt. Whatever the individual strategies of dealing with *Holocaust*, however short-lived the tears it provoked, one thing is certain: the film ignited a new, broad-based interest in the images and stories of the German past.

The *Holocaust* series also inspired renewed vigorous discussion about the various ways in which history should be presented on film. The innovations in narrative technique and film aesthetics that characterize several of the films in the wake of *Holocaust* can be seen as indirect reactions to the aesthetic and dramatic structure of the American television series. The German Autumn of 1977 had evoked an "excess motivation" (Kluge) among intellectuals and filmmakers to deal with German history, but only the broad reception of *Holocaust* allowed the numerous films about the recent German past to find an audience. *Germany in Autumn* presented impressions of a country on which the past weighs heavily; the German reaction to *Holocaust* showed how much still had to be done to master that past.

It seemed in 1979 as though the Germans had finally become able to look their history in the eye. *Holocaust* allowed the Germans to work through their most recent past, this time from the perspective of the victims, by proxy, in the innocuous form of a television show that viewers could switch off at any time. Because the collective catharsis felt by many viewers came about through a *film* (that is, through a fiction, a simulation), one might well suspect that the catharsis, if there indeed was one, rested on a self-deception.[71] Still, no matter how skeptical one may be about the long-term effect of a media event like *Holocaust,* it cannot be denied that in its wake a new historical consciousness emerged in the Federal Republic. The past suddenly seemed very present. German filmmakers felt challenged to come to terms with German history and its images.

2

GERMANY AS MYTH

**Hans Jürgen Syberberg's *Hitler,*
a *Film from Germany***

*"I was and am the end of your most secret wishes, the legend and
reality of your dreams."*
—Heinz Schubert in *Hitler, a Film from Germany*

Masses of people accept as myth what they would reject if it were suggested by reason. Since we ourselves are personified insignificances, accidental products of a nature that has no particular plan for us, we need metaphysical crutches to carry on at all. That accounts for our strained craving for some sense to our lives, for myth, which gives transcendence to meaningless existence. We want a destiny, even if we have to win it with fire and sword, concentration camps and gas chambers. Before we admit our own nothingness, we will serve the myth with the many names.

GÜNTER KUNERT

If you believe in the unity of aesthetics and politics, you are already living in the period of *post-histoire.*

WOLF LEPENIES

History at a Standstill

Ladies and gentlemen, now that we're rid of the Kaiser and God—off we go.

The Song of Songs, the greatest story ever told. Let's give him his chance, let's give ourselves our chance. Taboos, this show's about taboos. The greatest show of the century, big business, the show of shows . . . No human story, but a history of mankind, no disaster film, but disaster as a film. The end of the world, Deluge, the cosmos biting the dust.

Hence, no scenes of the private life, of the fear and misery of the Third Reich, and nothing of the "cabbage trust," the political racketeering of thirty years ago. Rather, something of the faith that moves mountains. Of a popular tribune without parallel. So gather all your strength, your gladness, and your sorrow.

Anyone who wants to see Stalingrad again or the Twentieth of July plot or the lone wolf's last days in the bunker or Riefenstahls' Nuremberg will be disappointed. We are not showing the unrepeatable reality, nor the feelings of the victims with their stories, nor the non-fiction of the authors, nor the big business of trading on morality and horror, on fear and death and atonement and arrogance and righteous wrath. (41–43)[1]

We have adequate warning. At the beginning of Syberberg's six-hour-45-minute film, the circus barker in whiteface promises us a show without equal. He announces not a historical film, not a reconstruction of the Third Reich, but a circus spectacle; not a story, either invented or authentic, but a tribunal; not education, not nostalgia or sentiment, but history as theater, history as a horror picture show. From the very start, the film distances itself from the conventions of its own genre and the attendant expectations of the viewer. The barker enumerates everything the film will *not* show; his long list reveals at once the film's polemical and self-reflexive dimension. The film constructs itself from the beginning by setting itself apart from all other approaches to history. Like a video recorder, it erases what has already been recorded in order to record over it.

The film claims in numerous ways to be something absolutely original. This claim is legitimated through the choice of Hitler as a subject. Hitler, according to Syberberg, was a singular phenomenon; an extraordinary film aesthetics is necessary to do justice to this person, who was loved by millions and hated by millions. No 90-minute feature film could give a sense of Hitler's significance for his followers, for his victims, for German history, for the world. Syberberg's film is also the result of an obsessive search for an adequate filmic expression of the phenomenon Hitler. One symptom of this search is the often abrupt shift in tone: from pathos to travesty, from the sublime to the ridiculous, from the elevated to the everyday. Another is the series of exasperatingly long monologues, alternating between sarcasm and bombast, most of which are spoken off-camera. Since there are no characters to propel the action forward and no mimetic relationship to any kind of present reality, the film constantly refers only to itself; it keeps inventing itself anew.

Against the background of traditional narrative cinema, these monologues, which constantly call into question the very possibility of historical representation, must have appeared to be manically narcissistic on Syberberg's part. Viewers took the many provocative voice-over comments and the often monstrous arguments, conclusions, and prognoses as direct expressions of Syberberg's own opinions. Critics began to suspect that the whole film was simply a platform to express the resentments of a megalomaniac's misunderstood genius, a genius so fascinated by fascism that he himself had become a "fascist." The dispute soon came to center less on the film than on Syberberg himself, who, it must be said, seemed to thrive on the abuse heaped upon him; he returned the sharp attacks with equally acidic commentaries that showed the extent to which he despised the whole phalanx of West German film critics.

But Syberberg's notorious battling with his critics (and vice versa) was not necessary to make his Hitler film a scandal. The controversies were already triply inscribed in the film itself. First, it was provocation enough to treat Hitler not in a didactic, documentary fashion but poetically and with a sense of awe. Second, the theatrical, "unfilmic" form, which replaced story and dialogue with static tableaux and long, reflective monologues, disoriented and frustrated viewers (particularly those not familiar with the meditative, stationary cinema of, for example, Marguerite Duras or Alain Robbe-Grillet). Finally, Syberberg's provocative assertion in his film that irrationalism lies at the core of German identity met with instinctive rejection in the Federal Republic. The condemnation of the film by West German film critics was so vehement that Syberberg initially refused to show *Hitler* at all; he did not submit it to the Berlin Festival in 1978. After premieres in Cannes in 1977 (in a preliminary one-hour-long version), London (November 1977), Paris (June 1978), and Vienna (October 1978), a single copy of his film was made available for public showing in West Germany. It ran mostly in museums or theaters, rarely in movie houses.[2] It was not until December 1979 that the film was shown on German television. In 1979 and 1980, distributed by Francis Ford Coppola, Syberberg's film appeared under the title *Our Hitler* at all the major film festivals in the United States, with great success; in February 1980, Susan Sontag published a review of the film in the *New York Review of Books,* placing Syberberg in a class with Wagner, Artaud, Céline, and Joyce.[3] This review undoubtedly marked the breakthrough for Syberberg's film in the United States.

An amply illustrated filmscript was published in German as a paperback in 1978, allowing the public to "read" the film. Although the tension between sound and visuals, the opulence of the images, and, of course, the experience of watching a film in a public setting are lost on the printed page, the publication of the script was important for Syberberg because he was no longer completely at the mercy of the institution of cinema, which is ruled, as far as he is concerned, by commercial interests and nothing else.

The title, *Hitler, a Film from Germany,* emphasizes that we are dealing with a film. Still, nothing occupies Syberberg more than to challenge radically all assumptions about this medium as we have come to know it. He began his systematic (and self-consciously quixotic) vendetta against Hollywood film conventions in 1972 with

Ludwig: Requiem für einen jungfräulichen König (*Ludwig: Requiem for a Virgin King*), calling it "a declaration of war against the dominant forms of the cinema of dialogue and the entertainment film in the tradition of Hollywood and its colonies."[4] He continues: "It was also a declaration of war against psychological dribble, plots based on gags and action, the philosophy of continuity editing and its shot/countershot technique, its metaphysics of the automobile and the gun, its excitement of opening and closing doors, and its melodramas based on sex and crime, in short, against the domination of narrative cinema in principle."[5]

Syberberg believes, and Alexander Kluge would emphatically agree, that the realistic narrative cinema, which dominates filmmaking in Hollywood today, has closed off and buried the revolutionary beginnings of the film medium. The magician George Méliès and the German Expressionist filmmakers had created autonomous worlds in the studio; their theatrical and painterly films do not rely as much on story line as on mise-en-scène and atmosphere. What seems "unfilmic" today was in fact the prevalent form of filmic expression until the end of the 1920s, that is, until sound made the film more "realistic." Especially Méliès's trick and fantasy films seem to Syberberg to inaugurate "the birth of a new myth, at least the instrument of its realization, with the opportunity to work with magic and spectacle."[6]

Syberberg's debt to this original, nonmimetic tradition of filmmaking is clear not only from his various visual quotations of Méliès's surreal, fantastic films (like *Le voyage dans la lune,* 1902) but also from his return to the studio as the place where cinematic fantasies arise. He reconstructs in miniature the first film studio, Thomas Edison's "Black Maria," in a glass ball and has the camera zoom in on it in the film's prelude. After a lap dissolve, we are inside the studio, where the film proper begins. This camera voyage through the archetypal film studio of 1900 expresses Syberberg's wish to return to the origins of the cinema, to locate his historical film where it was actually produced: in a truly fictional space where, for the time of the filming, the laws of logic are suspended, where tricks and magic reign and we are mesmerized by an artificial, illusory world of magic.

A circus barker with top hat, tuxedo, and walking stick, standing in front of the sketched backdrop of a circus crowd and beside a stuffed imperial eagle, opens the film proper. The barker is also a master of ceremonies in Méliès's sense, inviting us to watch carefully, to enjoy the show, without getting emotionally involved. Presenting (not representing) events is a theatrical tradition, which goes back to the late Middle Ages. It was resuscitated by the theater director in the prelude to Goethe's *Faust* and then developed in the antipsychological theater of Wedekind and Brecht. Max Ophüls also used this device in his film *Lola Montès* (1955)—and just as the circus director introduces Lola Montès as the "extraordinary and absolutely unique case from which we all can learn," the barker in Syberberg's film introduces his Hitler as a singular, unprecedented specimen of mankind. The presentational mode distances the film—and the viewer—from its material. Here the viewer does not become a contemporary of the past but always remains aware of his position as a viewer. Direct address, a theatrical and "deictic" manner of acting, stylistic ruptures and swings of mood that disrupt continuity and destroy illusion keep the viewers emotionally detached from the events and force them into the role of constantly surprised observers. At the same time, as in Brecht's theater, spectators are intellectually challenged; they are both subject and object of the film: "There will be no heroes, except ourselves. And there will be no story, except the one about ourselves" (42).

Syberberg became interested in translating theater into film with his first 8-millimeter films in 1952–1953, when Brecht gave the seventeen-year-old student permission to document the rehearsals of his Berlin Ensemble's productions of *Puntila und sein Knecht Matti* (*Puntila*) and *Die Mutter* (*The Mother*) as well as a complete production of Goethe's *Urfaust*.[7] In 1965, at about the same time when Syberberg was writing his doctoral dissertation on Friedrich Dürrenmatt's theater plays, he made an almost two-hour documentary called *Fünfter Akt, siebente Szene: Fritz Kortner probt Kabale und Liebe* (*Fifth Act, Seventh Scene: Fritz Kortner Rehearses Kabale und Liebe*).[8] Unlike Kracauer and Bazin, Syberberg sees the basis of the film medium less in photography, that is, in the tradition of Lumière, than in the theater, in the tradition of Méliès, a tradition that has also shaped the cinema of German Expressionism.[9] The Expressionist film sought to counter the strong penchant of the filmic medium for a "realistic," direct rendering of the world. According to Expressionist theory, film could become art only to the degree that it turned away from the "mere" technical recording of "unformed" nature and instead borrowed from the already established, very much flourishing theater tradition of the educated elite. It was no accident that artistically ambitious films after 1910 increasingly employed stage actors and adopted the expressive vocabulary of the theater. The stylistic domination of the silent film by the theater was specific to the German cinema of the 1920s. According to the film historian Ulrich Kurowski, the nonrealistic film in the Expressionist tradition, which does not aim at portraying the world "as it is" but wants to create it anew in the studio (artificially, under controlled conditions, with subjective distortion), is typical of German cinema in general; the conscious theatricality makes a film, says Kurowski, a typical "German" film.[10] In this light, Syberberg's histrionic film style revives and carries on a film tradition that is specifically *German*.

In addition to the theater, music was another medium that had a strong influence on Syberberg's aesthetics. The new magic worlds that film creates can be structured according to musical principles, which remove Syberberg's film even further from linear storytelling.[11] Music allows his film—beyond Méliès and the German Expressionist film, both of which were still dependent on the purely visual—to come close to the *Gesamtkunstwerk,* the total work of art, which Richard Wagner had envisioned in the late nineteenth century.[12] Wagner's music drama, with its demand for total darkness in the audience and its trancelike musical images, had to a certain extent already prefigured cinema; if Wagner were living today, his grandson once said, he would probably be making films in Hollywood. Syberberg acknowledges his debt to Wagner not only through numerous musical quotations, in particular from *Rienzi,* Hitler's favorite opera, and from *Götterdämmerung* but also through the overall structure of his film: like the *Ring* cycle, *Hitler* consists of four parts. Given also Syberberg's fascination with German mythology, it is not far-fetched to regard his film as a continuation of Wagner's project in the age of technical reproducibility.

Thus, in his battle against Hollywood, Syberberg has brought about an irreconcilable alliance: Brecht and Wagner. And Syberberg knows that these antipodes cannot really be joined: "I made the aesthetically scandalous attempt of combining Brecht's doctrine of the epic theater with Richard Wagner's musical aesthetics, of linking the epic system as anti-aristotelian cinema with the laws of the new myth."[13] This hybrid origin leads to sudden breaks, to unmotivated shifts of mood and perspective, and results in ambivalences that challenge any attempt at interpretation.

The rebirth of Syberberg's film from the spirit of music and theater also has far-reaching consequences for his treatment of historical material. Past events and characters, removed from their original contexts, become quotable set pieces in an aesthetic structure that follows its own laws. History is "produced" (in both meanings of the word) and exhibited in the form of a "show," appearing as a revue that consists of a number of self-contained sketches. Syberberg is less interested in constructs of history that deal with cause and effect than in evoking moods in which interconnections are recognized. His radically contrived mode of presentation also attacks all those allegedly authentic (in actual fact clichéd) reconstructions of the past in which, as in Joachim Fest's film on Hitler, all the deceptive images of the old propaganda films are naively reproduced or reconstructed. Syberberg's film destroys all referential illusion. What reality, after all, should the film mirror? Past reality is absent and not repeatable; a deep chasm lies between history and its re-presentation. What is presented is never identical with the presentation itself.

Syberberg favors a self-reflexive play with images and linguistic signs that *refer* to history in associations that are not bound by time and place. It is not a matter of documentary reality when Himmler, in dream images, is confronted with the victims he never met. It is not "real" when Hitler arises from Wagner's grave (the motif is borrowed from Gustave Doré's illustrations for Dante's *Divine Comedy*) or when he sarcastically praises all those leaders in the world who continue his work. Various temporal layers are interlocked through blatant anachronisms, radically undermining the illusion of continuity in narrated history. Historical time is stopped and recombined according to principles that derive not from chronology but from the power of association. Visual and aural leitmotifs recur throughout the film, often as only one layer of several on the soundtrack or in the image construction. Syberberg's complex sound-image collages neutralize the linear progress of time and bring history to a standstill. Instead of the "horizontal" development of a story, we have a *vertical* structure in which various levels of meaning and association coexist and resonate polyphonically.

Everything the camera registers takes place on a studio stage, which is hermetically sealed off from the outer world. Time becomes spatial, a dense web of quotations and intertextual references from literature, music, and film. Unlike Alexander Kluge, however, who also uses montage as his principal method, Syberberg aims at a totality which he believes can be achieved through the very medium of film. His confession about the Hitler film, "Everything is in it. The viewer has to decide. Anyone who wants things to be more direct starts to lie, preparing for the next errors" (27), demonstrates this will to totality. Kluge's approach is different; in editing a film, he seeks to bring about a "change of perspective" through ironic juxtapositions and collisions of preexisting, found images and sounds. Syberberg, in contrast, builds his multilevel mise-en-scènes from scratch, assembling and "layering" images, sounds, speeches, music, and stage effects precisely in order to produce a contradictory whole, a totality—a notion that Alexander Kluge is extremely suspicious of. Nor is there an equivalent in Kluge's work for Syberberg's surrealistic tableaux, which transform history into a gigantic sign system.

For instance, at one point in the first part of the Hitler film we hear a sound montage, consisting of a reading of the *Muspilli*, an apocalyptic poem from the ninth century—"The mountains burn, the trees vanish from the earth, the rivers run dry, the moon falls, and finally the entire earth burns"—and simultaneously, in original sound, a Hitler speech of 1932: "We have a goal and we will advocate it fanatically and relentlessly until the grave" (40). The mythical prophecy of the end of the world is associatively related to Hitler's expression of a collective death wish. At the same time, we see on stage a girl place a stuffed dog with Hitler's face in a cradle. She is surrounded by life-size cardboard cutouts which loom through the artificial ground fog that lends a Wagnerian touch to the visuals. The cutouts represent figures from German Expressionist films of the 1920s, including the hypnotist and charlatan Dr. Caligari, his somnambulist murderer Cesare, and the vampire Nosferatu. Here the spectator may remember Siegfried Kracauer's argument in his 1947 study *From Caligari to Hitler,* namely that the power-hungry villains of German Expressionist cinema have anticipated Hitler. These fictional film figures may function also as reminders that Hitler—like Caligari or Nosferatu—is available to us today only as a celluloid image, one signifier among others.[14]

This proliferation of aural and visual signs cannot be interpreted in a conventional sense. As multilayered collages they contain no transparent, simple messages, but rather impressions and polyvalent possibilities; no representative images of an independent reality, but articulations of autonomous artificial worlds; no straightforward stories, but intricate constellations and meandering paths of associations that do not converge at a single point. History cut loose from time and space seems like a dream. Syberberg himself once called his Hitler film an attempt "to dream history."[15]

As though embodying this dream, a young girl dressed in black wanders like a somnambulist across the stage, cradling a Hitler doll. She is Syberberg's own daughter. Her image functions as a positive countermyth of childlike innocence and naiveté; she is the angel of history, fleeing from the past that seems to tower like a monstrous mountain of rubble. "His face is turned toward the past," writes Walter Benjamin about Klee's Angelus Novus. "Where we perceive a chain of events, he sees one single catastrophe which keeps piling wreckage upon wreckage and hurls it in front of his feet."[16] The girl returns like a leitmotif at the beginning and end of all four parts of the film, accompanied by Mozart's Piano Concerto in D Minor. The static nature of these scenes, intensified through several repetitions, de-emphasizes history as an experience of passing time.

History appears in this film as a bazaar in which old and new myths are offered *en masse,* coming from the most diverse realms: from Germanic mythology to American mass culture, from Hölderlin to Hitler and Himmler. Syberberg's film is like a carnival in which, as in the preclassical age, the differences between high and popular culture do not matter, and all styles mix promiscuously. Western cultural history of the last 2,000 years provides the building blocks which the author, as *bricoleur,* constantly rearranges and regroups. *Hitler, a Film from Germany* consists of a seemingly endless string of quotations picked eclectically from literary, biographical, and historical sources and woven into the film's spoken text that accompanies the images, most of which are also quotations from paintings, theater productions, and other films. Syberberg's stylistic strategies of proliferation, juxtaposition, contradiction, and intertextuality betray his affinity to a poetics of postmodernism, while his apocalyptic world view, his cultural pessimism, and his denial of history as progress place him in the tradition of *post-histoire.*[17] The easiness with which a postmodernist artist like Syberberg uses the past as "material" that can be quoted at will is based on the belief that history and progress have reached their limit and have come to a standstill; the present is itself no more than an assemblage of quotations from the past. In the epoch of the *post-histoire* originality and innovation mean recycling and pastiche. In this sense postmodernism and *post-histoire* are related concepts. But while postmodernism has engendered a critical debate that is still growing by leaps and bounds,[18] the term *post-histoire* has almost gone unnoticed. Looking at its origins, we find surprising interconnections with Syberberg's project. As early as 1952 the German sociologist Arnold Gehlen adopted the term from Hendrik de Man and used it to designate an epoch characterized by a state of stability and rigidity, when neither change nor development is to be expected.[19] (It is no accident that Gehlen introduced this term in the restoration era of Adenauer, and that he stands in the tradition of cultural pessimism that began with Oswald Spengler.) In 1961, in an article appropriately entitled "Über kulturelle Kristallisation" ("On Cultural Crystallization"), Gehlen wrote: "I am predicting that the history of ideas has come to an end and that we have arrived at the *post-histoire,* so that now the advice Gottfried Benn gave the individual, 'make do with what you have,' is valid for humanity as a whole. In the age in which the earth has become optically and informationally surveyable, when no event of importance can happen unnoticed, there are no more surprises."[20]

Syberberg takes up this motif of crystallization, of glacial rigidity, in the second part of *Hitler,* in the scene in which the Nazi myth of ice cosmology is explained; Kluge, too, is fascinated with images of crystallization, ice, and ossification in his film *The Patriot.* In Syberberg's *Hitler* the stage itself on which history is simulated stands as an emblem of the frozen world. Since, according to Syberberg, the future has no further prospects and history seems to have come to a halt, there is no longer any existing force that could function like a magnet to pull the fragments of the past into a meaningful (narrative) order. The fragments remain fragments; they lie scattered around on Syberberg's stage, dead and without context. The "spatialization" of time to a confined area in which disconnected fragments from many historical eras are strewn about—the bits and pieces after the catastrophe, as it were—corresponds exactly to the idea of an eternal present expressed by the adherents of *post-histoire.* Syberberg's *Hitler* has no forward movement; it evokes instead elegiac memories of past glories, nostalgia, and a sense of the apocalypse.[21] Where no development or change is considered possible, the future vanishes. At the end of history, the artist works in an eternal process of recycling what is at hand. The entirety of Western culture is now available, a quarry to which one goes to pick out quotations. This is how Syberberg expressed it in 1981:

> Now the world is divided up, relinquished to history and the traditions of culture, the source of our works. Huge mines of the old cultures for quotations, which build up by layers to new cultures. Everything we show or speak has been used before, been touched, and only a rearrangement of the systems and fragments produces, if it functions, something new. What is new to us has been built from the old, that is our fate, our luck, and the new joy that desires its own eternity, just as before. Today's mythologies of the wandering Odysseus are constructed of quotations from the discipline of our history, and the fear of today's Penelope threatens to create chaos on the horizon of our inner landscapes as a foreboding about the future—the end of all history.[22]

Postmodernist Staging

> A tormenting thought: as of a certain point, history was no longer real. Without noticing it, all mankind suddenly left reality: everything happening since then was supposedly not true; but we supposedly didn't notice. Our task would now be to find that point, and as long as we didn't have it, we would be forced to abide in our present destruction.
>
> ELIAS CANETTI

Syberberg's translation of historical reality into a self-sufficient cosmos of signs, intertexts, quotations, allusions, personal memories, and visual associations gave him the freedom to encode German history in a variety of presentational forms: as a circus and amusement park, as a horror cabinet, a puppet theater, a cabaret and side show, as tribunal, Grand Guignol, commedia dell'arte, and as an allegorical, baroque Theatrum Mundi. The central project of the film is not the representation of Hitler himself but the presentation of the various ways in which Hitler has been represented. Syberberg's interest lies in the *possibilities* of presenting a figure which, he feels, "essentially cannot be represented realistically,"[23] because today the historical subject Hitler has dissolved into a plurality of images. Instead of reducing the phenomenon Hitler to *one* image, Syberberg

proliferates images. Thus we are confronted, at the very beginning
of the film, with the different roles Hitler played: Hitler as house
painter, as raving maniac, as Nero who pulls the limbs off dolls and
eats them, as Charlie Chaplin in a scene from *The Great Dictator,*
and finally as the compulsive sex killer from Fritz Lang's *M,* who
recites his famous defense before invisible judges: "But who will
believe me, who, who knows what compels me! I have to, I don't
want to, I, I have to, I don't want, I have to, I can't help myself, I
can't help myself. I have to, I have to do it, but nobody will believe
me. I can't help it, I, I . . ." (61). The monologue is spoken with self-
lacerating theatricality by the Austrian actor Peter Kern, wearing an
SA uniform. It is superimposed over a recording from Berlin of 1939,
in which masses break out into "Sieg Heil, Sieg Heil" at Hitler's
appearance. As the murderer is still whimpering "I can't help it, I,
I . . . ," we hear the original soundtrack of an SA song:

> The banner high! Our ranks are serried tight.
> SA now marches with a bold, firm tread.
> Comrades shot by reactionaries and the Red Front—
> They march with us in spirit though they're dead. (61)

It is left to the viewer to make the connection between the paranoid
child murderer from Lang's 1931 film and the Hitler of 1939, between the sex criminal's blubbering about innocence and the intox-
icated masses whose collective madness expresses itself in their enthusiastic "Sieg Heil!" The hysteria of the people and the shocking
wretchedness of the captured criminal are related to each other in a
montage, but for what purpose? Is Hitler to be exculpated as a victim
of his drives? Are we to place the blame on the masses who shouted
for a "Führer"? Or is the hysteria of this scene supposed to evoke
the atmosphere of the era? Syberberg leaves the answer provocatively
open. He offers no interpretations but instead constructs experimental arrangements that circle the object: "For some, Hitler was a god
of light, for others a Jack-in-the-box and carpet chewer. Both interpretations receive the same weight and are juxtaposed with each
other in various forms."[24]
Hitler in Syberberg's film appears as "nothing," as Picard once
called him in his 1949 book *Hitler in uns selbst* (*Hitler in Ourselves*),[25] and at the same time as "everything:" "Hitler" means
nothing other than an empty vessel into which the most diverse

legends, anecdotes, and representations can be poured. According to Syberberg, Hitler served the Germans as a screen onto which they could project all their wishes, anxieties, and hopes. That is the point of the film's central monologue, given to Hitler:

> After all, there was no one else who would, who could take over my desired role. And so they called upon me. First, the bourgeoisie, then the military, rubbing their hands in bliss and dirt, and also to defend their honor, do you imagine I did not notice? Then, industry, to drive out Bolshevism, from whose Lenin I learned so much and whose Stalin could be venerated secretly. Then the petty bourgeois, the workers, for whom I could bring forth so much, and youth, to whom I gave a goal, and the students, who needed me, and the intellectuals, who were now liberated from the Jewish Mafia of their friends and foes, yes, and other countries, which were glad to have a pacified Europe again, strength and solemnity. And one should consider to how many people I gave something worth being against. And just compare the lives of so many people—listless, empty. I gave them what they put into me, what they wanted to hear, wanted to do, things they were afraid to do. I made and commanded for them, for it was all for them, not for me . . . I was and am the end of your most secret wishes, the legend and reality of your dreams, so we have to get through. Finally. The final time? Nightmares? Not by a long shot. (127–129)

Who is speaking? This is one of the many voices in which Syberberg lets Hitler speak, that is, defend himself. Essentially it is Hitler back from the dead who, ironically, is judging those who have assembled in order to judge him. Hitler appears as the goal of the Germans' "most secret wishes," as the object of their desire for subjugation, and as the executor of everything they yearned for collectively. Syberberg obliquely asks the taboo question of why fascism attracted such a broad following, even among the elite. After decades of traditional research that explained fascism in moral or economic terms, it was only in recent years that the obvious fascination and the aesthetics of fascism have been openly acknowledged: fascism seemed to have elicited and fulfilled hidden wishes and desires of a people who, after the Versailles Treaty and the self-effacing politics of the Weimar Republic, felt deprived of their national pride and collective identity.[26]

The visuals provide additional dimensions to this scene. In a hallucinatory image, Hitler, risen from the dead, emerges from Richard

Wagner's open grave. Wearing a Roman toga, "he is the color of a corpse as he comes out of hell" (127), surrounded by ground fog. The viewer is helplessly ambivalent in the face of such a scene, spellbound by its visual power but also shocked by the audacity that uses such consciously naive stage magic, in a manner verging on the burlesque. And Hitler's politically provocative speech of self-defense, which the spectator instinctively feels challenged to refute, is made unreal by its context, the overly obvious theatrical play. His statements are transposed from the realm of argument into that of suggestion. "It's only fiction," the viewer thinks, but some doubt remains.

The style of a scene like this is reminiscent of the postmodernist theater performance style developed by Robert Wilson. In their collaborative work *CIVIL warS* (1984), Wilson and the East German playwright Heiner Müller deconstructed the traditional concept of a unified text and overruled all theatrical conventions. As with Syberberg, the actors no longer embody dramatic figures; at most, they quote them. In the fourth act of *CIVIL warS,* for instance, the accumulation of fragmentary quotations and literary ready-mades taken from the cultural history of all centuries no longer allow, in the last analysis, a reading that strives for coherence and communication. These productions require a new mode of reception in which the spectator no longer searches for a (given or hidden) meaning of the work, but instead analyzes the process of producing such a text.[27]

Clearly, Syberberg's "text" is not quite as arbitrary as it seems at first. It is constructed around certain clusters of themes and motifs— guilt, death, mourning, faith, imagination—which recur in manifold variations throughout the film but are not linked to a dramatic figure or to a narrative context. In the staging of these motifs neither Syberberg nor Wilson hesitates to use images of striking simplicity and childlike naiveté, which results in the "paradox of highly reflective infantility," as Hans-Thies Lehmann wrote in an essay about Robert Wilson's stagecraft.[28] An adequate postmodern reception of Syberberg's work, however, is hindered because his irrepressible didactic impulse often dominates the images and, in fact, functions as a counterpoint to all his postmodern fragmentation and ironic simulation.

The interweaving of evocation and instruction is especially noticeable in the use of puppets as mouthpieces for Nazi ideology. In the

German tradition of the Faust drama, which goes back to a sixteenth-century puppet play, Syberberg revives the use of puppets in his systematic fight against realism in film and theater. Unlike the human face, which expresses constantly changing moods, the masklike face of the puppet arrests time. Puppets' faces look rigid, lifeless, fixed for eternity; there is no interplay of glances and gestures, no psychology. Syberberg transfers the obvious physical and emotional traits of Joseph Goebbels, Hermann Goering, Heinrich Himmler, Eva Braun, Albert Speer, and Hitler onto puppets: an "unseemly alienation" in "our world of realism."[29]

Like Walter Benjamin, Syberberg discovers the lost childlike side of history: "That is why the entire Hitler film is a child's world of puppets, dolls, full of stars and music, the material for a child's huge nightmare, such as has never been dreamed, tormenting and light. One feels that all this really shouldn't be, certainly not with this theme" (22). But the representation of the Nazi leaders as puppets demystifies and miniaturizes them, making them look ridiculous: "Yes, that's what we'll make of him: Adolf, the degenerate puppet from the Punch and Judy show . . . that's progress from Germany, the puppet-clown as Führer. Yes indeed, the Führer as a puppet-clown; that's it, the vengeance of hell, that they now have to live as puppet-clowns" (70). As puppets they have no life of their own, but are dependent in their movements and words on the person who animates (and manipulates) them and who puts words in their mouths. They are nothing but mouthpieces; we speak through them: "They can do nothing *we* don't want. They are in *our* hands. What would this Hitler be without us? without all of us?"[30]

In order to evoke the "Hitler in us," Syberberg tries to reduce the distance between ourselves and the historical person. In his earlier semi-documentary film about the cook of Ludwig II, *Theodor Hirneis oder: Wie man ehem. Hofkoch wird* (*Ludwig's Cook,* 1972), Syberberg had already made the servant's view, the view from below, the center of interest in order to gain knowledge about those "up there." In *Hitler* we have the figure of Karl-Wilhelm Krause, Hitler's valet from 1934 on. Helmut Lange plays Krause as the proverbial servant who is as conscientious as he is pedantic. His memories, recited dryly into the camera for an entire half-hour, give an unusual view of Hitler as private person. The meticulous notation of the course of a day, which to Krause was the same, day in, day out, shows Hitler from a pedestrian perspective that allows the temporal distance between him and the viewer to disappear for moments at a time. For instance, Krause describes the breakfast ritual: "The breakfast always consisted of the same things. Two cups of mouth-warm whole milk, as many as ten pieces of Leibniz zwieback cookies, and then a third to a half of a bar of bittersweet chocolate broken into small pieces . . . For his bath he used pine-needle tablets" (143). In our everyday lives we are all identical. In the cycle of our humdrum routines there is no change from yesterday to today; time itself seems to dissolve in an endless present. Precisely because of his commonplace daily life, because of his quaint little idiosyncrasies, his ludicrous likes and dislikes—"Isn't it possible for the Führer of the German people to get a pair of decent socks?" (151)—and his all too human dependence on moods and emotions, Hitler becomes "one of us." Roland Barthes spoke of this pleasure in the petty details of daily private life as a "singular theater: not one of grandeur but one of mediocrity (might there not be dreams, fantasies of mediocrity)?"[31]

With an obsessive precision of language and a frighteningly flat voice, the valet also describes Christmas Eve of 1937, when he and Hitler—"stretched out on the carpet" (155)—wrapped presents and drove incognito in a taxi through the streets of Munich. The private Christmas spirit of the petit bourgeois from Braunau is juxtaposed in the film with the political situation on Christmas 1942. The soundtrack that accompanies the valet's nostalgic description of Christmas of 1937 features the famous radio broadcast on December 24, 1942, which brought together German soldiers from all fronts across the globe. Sentimentality and aggressiveness, Christmas spirit and imperialist war blend into one:

> We ask you, comrades, to sing once more the lovely old Christmas carol "Silent Night." . . . All stations will now join in with this spontaneous greeting by comrades deep in the south, on the Black Sea. Now they are already singing in the Arctic Ocean off Finland, and now we are switching in all the other stations, Leningrad, Stalingrad. And now France as well. Now Catania. Now Africa. And now they are all singing together: . . . Sleep in heavenly peace . . . (155)

The radio recording, in original sound, documents a technological innovation, a simultaneous broadcast that symbolized Germany's expansion into all corners of the world. The recording dates from the same year as the German defeat at Stalingrad. In the film this recording is superimposed over Krause's monologue; he continues speaking, but the radio broadcast ultimately drowns him out. Associative links are suggested between the unbroken loyalty of the valet to his Führer and the fate of millions of German soldiers who died at the front out of loyalty to their Führer, and also between the administrative tone in which Krause talks about the human side of Hitler and the rational administrative ingenuity that was required to send 300,000 soldiers to Stalingrad—a link that Alexander Kluge had already explored with incredulous fascination in his documentary novel *Schlachtbeschreibung: Der organisatorische Aufbau eines Unglücks* (*Description of a Battle: The Organizational Construction of a Disaster*) in 1964. "The quality of Syberberg's film," said Michel Foucault in his review of the film, "consists in its statement that horror is banal, that banality in itself has dimensions of horror, that horror and banality are reversible."[32] Not only the madness of anti-Semitism but also the narrow bureaucratic diligence of a banal person like Krause was necessary to organize the assembly-line mass murders "effectively" and in an administratively "correct" way.[33] The end of the scene, however, suggests a different, more ambivalent reading of Stalingrad. Heavy snow starts falling down on Krause, who is quite obviously standing in the middle of a studio, and gradually covers him. Krause's face finally freezes, an emblematic embodiment of the trapped and freezing German army outside of Stalingrad. The Germans appear as victims of their high conception of duty: like Krause, they obey the Führer.

The private, petit-bourgeois idyll of daily life described in detail in Krause's monologue is counterpointed throughout the scene by huge background projections of Hitler's two residences, the Reich Chancellery and the teahouse on Obersalzberg. These grainy films, mostly taken with a hand-held camera, create the impression of a simulated environment through which Krause wanders like a tourist. At times, especially when the film shows extreme close-ups of Hitler's furniture, Krause appears dwarfed. The documentary film plays independently of the private story, as silent witness of a greater history. But while the valet loses himself further and further in a thicket of trivialities, something unexpected happens in the silent film behind him. First we see stills of Hitler's office, then, shot from the same angle, its total destruction in 1945. This cut dramatizes the instantaneous reversal from pomp and glory to ashes and ruins, undermining the valet's happy memories and silently contradicting his grotesquely limited view of history. A further layer of associations is added to this scene through a musical collage that combines march music and motifs from Wagner's *Rienzi*.

The vertical structure of this scene is a product of the layering of various linguistic, musical, and visual codes. Its simultaneous effects can only be approximated in a nonspatial medium like writing. Private and political, fictional and authentic, trivial and world-historical matters are intertwined and evoked at the same time. And the ensuing scene, added through an abrupt cut, puts all in question again: the close-up of the valet's head, covered with ice and snow, and the radio broadcast from Moscow in February 1943 announcing the defeat at Stalingrad are followed by a projection (a still) of William Blake's *Shrine of the Imagination*, in front of which André Heller sits, instructing us about the cosmos: "Astronomers at the University of California, Berkeley, have discovered the farthest known galaxy. This tremendous structure of over a trillion suns is more than eight billion light-years away. The light now reaching us from there was sent out at a time when our sun and its planetary system did not even exist" (157).

Susan Sontag compared this cut from Hitler's daily routine and the defeat of the German army at Stalingrad to the unreal idea of light-years with Stanley Kubrick's spectacular cut from the bone hurled into the air by cavemen to the space station in *2001*.[34] This dramatic shift of perspective from Hitler's private life and German history to the history of the cosmos is extremely problematic because it relativizes everything, suggesting that from the perspective of eight billion light-years, *all* world events seem trivial. Yet Syberberg does not stop there. Before a projected image of icebergs, Caspar David Friedrich's painting *Das Eismeer (The Frozen Ocean)*, Heller reads a passage from Adalbert Stifter's story of the Jew Abdias and his blind daughter Ditha: "If there are people on whom such an abundance of hardship falls from the clear blue sky that they finally stand there and let the hailstorm wash over them: then there must also be nations and stars, at least entire continents, that are so willfully afflicted by misfortune that it seems as if the natural laws were reversed so that only they can meet with disaster" (158–159). This passage in turn sheds new light on the two previous scenes: Germany's history (epitomized by Hitler and Stalingrad) is interpreted as a fate that is as incomprehensible as it is inexorable: a destiny "in regard to which we sometimes feel as though an invisible arm were reaching down from the clouds and doing the incomprehensible with us before our very eyes, for which we become guilty" (159). Through montage and association, the film here suggests a nature myth as an explanatory model for National Socialism—and not for Judaism, which of course was at issue in Stifter's novella. In Syberberg's work the postmodern joy of quoting from all sources succumbs time and again to the danger of false appropriation. In the postmodern spirit of "anything goes," the filmmaker presents himself as an ironic, detached "combiner"[35] who weaves a quotation meant to elucidate the fate of the Jews into a context where it suddenly seems to explain the history of the German nation.

Even this (certainly most dubious) cosmic model only approximates what Syberberg calls "the whole." He is obsessed by the insight that Hitlerism cannot be explained by a single thesis. He circumnavigates his theme with different voices, actions, recorded memories, and quotations from novels, poems, military reports, autobiographies, speeches, songs, pictures, melodies: all ways of approaching the secret center, Adolf Hitler, a subject that becomes concrete and comprehensible only in the distorting mirror of others, a hollow center that is filled to the degree that we project ourselves into it.

This indirect approach that circles the center and works by implication becomes most obvious in André Heller's reading of possible scenarios in the fourth part, introduced by the frequently repeated word: "Imagine . . . ," followed by a detailed verbal description of scenes we do not see. "Let me read from the notes for this film" (211), Heller says, sitting in front of a screen on which amateur documentary films from the Nazi period are projected, films sent to Syberberg by various individuals after he advertised in a newspaper for unknown footage from the Nazi era. Anonymous history, in the form of these amateur films, unreels silently and ceaselessly, like a nightmare, with grainy and often completely unintelligible images, while in the foreground stories are read, but not staged. We literally witness a film that is in the raw state of becoming. Every utterance is tentative, provisional. The words read by the actor are privileged over the image—a minimalist approach that stands in stark contrast to the striking tableaux of the first half of the film. There were, of course, financial reasons for this. Syberberg said that his nearly seven-hour Hitler film (shot on a shoestring budget of half a million dollars in four weeks after five years of preparation) was "like the draft of a film that was possible but not realized, that should have been made, with more time and more means, but time and money were not available at that point; that it could be made at all was miracle enough."[36] The economy of means creates a strong alienation effect and favors a dramatic structure that produces not reality but rather allusions to something that cannot be presented, only imagined.

Myth and Identity

I am not far from believing that, in our own societies, history has replaced mythology and fulfills the same function, that for societies without writing and without archives the aim of mythology is to ensure that as closely as possible—complete closeness is obviously impossible—the future will remain faithful to the present and to the past.

CLAUDE LÉVI-STRAUSS

Myth is once again in vogue, especially in West Germany. A glance at the scholarly and popular discussions of the last decade shows the fascination that mythological thinking has attracted.[37] Not only the Enlightenment but Western logocentrism in general has become suspect. Manfred Frank, in his published lectures on the New Mythology, speaks of the contemporary "reestablishment of the mythic-religious context of meaning,"[38] and Karl Heinz Bohrer pursues myth in its relation to modernity in a 600-page collection of essays.[39] In theater, literature, and painting we increasingly find elements of a mythic understanding of German history. Particularly the paintings of Anselm Kiefer (for instance, *Varus*, 1976; *Brunhilde Sleeps*, 1978; *Ways of Worldly Wisdom—Arminius's Battle*, 1978-80) explore ancient national myths in provocatively nonironic ways.[40] New theater productions of Kleist's *Hermannsschlacht (The Battle of Arminius)*, staged by Claus Peymann, and Hebbel's *Nibelungen*, staged by Frank-Patrick Steckel, also examine mythic perceptions of German history and reinterpret nineteenth-century nationalist myths in light of Germany's most recent history. Heiner Müller's scenic collage *Germania Tod in Berlin (Germania Death in Berlin, 1977)* and

Harald Mueller's play *Das Totenfloss (The Raft of the Dead,* 1984) make use of mythic motifs, as do recent novels and plays by Peter Handke, Botho Strauss, and Michael Ende.[41] Furthermore, films by Werner Herzog, with their romantic-visionary myths of destruction— for instance, *Fata Morgana* or *Herz aus Glas (Heart of Glass)*[42]— the enigmatic films of Andrej Tarkowskij (such as *Nostalghia),* and Godfrey Reggio and Philip Glass's *Koyaanisqatsi* go beyond a critique of civilization and revolve around magic and ritual, the incomprehensible and uncontrollable.[43] It seems that the cinema has a particular affinity for the neomythic tendencies of the present, because its nonverbal language of images appeals directly to the subconscious.

Several years before the now-fashionable debate about myth, Syberberg had spoken of his films *Ludwig: Requiem for a Virgin King* (1972) and *Karl May* (1974) as "positive mythologizings of history through the devices of cinema" (12). For him both Ludwig, the unworldly late-nineteenth-century King of Bavaria who built fairy-tale castles and was a patron of Richard Wagner, and Karl May, the popular writer who, without ever leaving Saxony, let his literary imagination roam to bring distant lands like the American West to millions of Germans, are symbols of the German search for a lost paradise. Ludwig II and Karl May both embrace archaic myths and utopias as a compensation for the increasingly hostile world of industry and commerce. The films devoted to them express the ambivalent attitude of the modern period toward myth. In *Ludwig,* for instance, Wagner's music is regularly interrupted by pop and folk music; *Karl May's* sentimentality is undermined by irony and the campy use of excessive Art Deco kitsch. Nevertheless, both films are serious attempts to come to grips with the mythological dimension of German history. Syberberg's Ludwig film in particular experiments with an aesthetics that translates myth into visual images, thereby anticipating *Hitler, a Film from Germany* by five years.

> My Ludwig film begins with the first E-flat major chords of the *Rhinegold* and ends with the conclusion of the *Götterdämmerung,* in whose last ray of light little Ludwig, old and bearded, steps out of the mist of Erda's grotto as a sadly smiling child. The myth of the Nibelungs presents the frame for my film. In the film the interrelations between allusions to Ludwig and to Wagner shuttle back and forth, creating an inextricable associative deepening of an epic cosmos in which we can recognize our-

selves and perhaps celebrate ourselves in the tragic mode. For the theme is the destruction of a utopia in the face of a person looking for a lost or artificial paradise.[44]

Ludwig's flight from the realpolitik of the Bismarck era into Wagner's mythic world of art has itself become a myth, or more precisely, a myth that soon degenerated into fantastic triviality thanks to tourism and the souvenir industry. The trivial myths surrounding the mysterious king of the fairy-tale castles are mercilessly illustrated at the end of the film. A rear-projection of a documentary showing hordes of American tourists jostling their way through his Neuschwanstein castle on a guided tour is superimposed over Ludwig, who sits at a table, his head buried in grief. The tourists look like phantoms from a nightmare. The projection makes it clear to what extent the romantic myth of the solitary artist, bewitched by beauty, is currently marketed as kitsch. Syberberg's *Ludwig* sheds light on both the origin and the trivialization of the myth of the royal dreamer. The same motif of the marketing of myths occurs in the Hitler film: against the background of the Obersalzberg, the director of tourism and the mayor formally open a new Hitler museum, a "German Disneyland," featuring Hitler as an international star "with genuine box-office appeal" (228).

Karl May shows us the world "of the last great German mystic in the age of the decline of the fairy tale."[45] Hitler is said to have been an enthusiast of May's fantasies of artificial paradises. Hitler himself appears as a character in the film, as an asocial young man who was present at the last public reading by Karl May in Vienna around 1912. Syberberg has Hitler, already a fanatic, announce his own platform: "What we lack in weaponry to achieve our freedom, we must make up for in our strength of will."[46] In *Karl May* Syberberg presents us with a psychogram, a mental history of fin-de-siècle Germany to explain Hitler's rise to power. Like Karl May, Hitler seems starved for idealism, willpower, loyalty, and heroism in a world increasingly dominated by economic values; like Karl May, he yearns for noble heroes, wide-open spaces, exotic landscapes. Even more than *Ludwig*, *Karl May* deals with the soil in which the Third Reich grew and took shape, a soil saturated with trivial literary myths. Ernst Bloch was one of the first to recognize Karl May's importance for the emotional and spiritual life of the Germans in the early twentieth century.[47] Syberberg uses a series of tableaux to show how Karl May (and, by association, Hitler as well) transcended his banal, hypochondriac, neurotic private life through art (and in Hitler's case, through politics misused as art).

The telos of both *Karl May* and *Ludwig* is Hitler, who, according to Syberberg, accomplished what Ludwig had not. Numerous interconnections make the three films a single text, a trilogy,[48] whose unspoken goal is to discover the unchanging mythic structures behind the historical figures and events, the structures that, in Roland Barthes's definition of myth, turn history into nature.[49] Syberberg seeks to fathom the characteristic unalterable nature of the romantic German soul that yearns for artificial paradises and falls victim to fantastic delusions in its search for paradise. The beginning of the Hitler film illuminates this. As in the classic science fiction film *Star Wars,* we soar through the darkness of outer space, watching the stars flying toward us. Hearing the noise of static and Mozart's Piano Concerto in D Minor, we read the projected words: "We all dream of traveling through space—into our inner self. The mysterious path goes inward, inward into the night" (26).

These words evoke a well-known aphorism by the German Romantic poet Novalis: "The secret path goes inward." That allusion, along with the associations of dream and night and the visual quotation from *Star Wars,* connotes the never-ending longing for other worlds that links German Romanticism to modern fantasies of space travel. The sudden shift of perspective from outer space to the path inward is meant to make us pause, to let our sense of reality falter for a moment, so that we might see the private world mirrored in the cosmos and the cosmos in the private world. Then a romantic, exotic landscape slowly emerges from the darkness, a picture of a tropical paradise from the time of Ludwig II, with high mountains, palm trees, and a lake. We hear the prelude to *Parsifal,* and a voiceover says: "And if I had in one hand the gold of business, the full beer belly of the functionary, happiness, and all the playthings of the world, and my other hand held fairy tales and the dreams of fancy, the yearning for paradise and the music of our ideas, then everybody would blindly choose paradise, even if it was false, greedy for sacrificial blood, ready to give their best, involving our hopes with the greatest cruelties for the sake of moonstruck triumphs of the human soul" (26).

Superimposed over the projection of the paradisiacal landscape, thick block letters, broad and cracked, form first the words "Der Gral," followed by "Le Graal" and "The Grail." The letters then fuzz out to a white blur. In Christian mythology the word "Grail" means a utopian, secret, and sacred object which brings its possessor earthly or heavenly joy but which only the pure at heart, the elected one, can find. The story of the Grail is told in legends and poetry from the European Middle Ages, by Chrétien de Troyes, Wolfram von Eschenbach in his *Parzifal,* and in the collection *Les Comtes del Graal.* According to Ernst Bloch, the Grail has an astral, mythical origin: "Whether they were lured by the golden apples of the Hesperides to the west or, as was mostly the case, by the marvels of India to the east, the strange unity of gold and Fleece, gold and Grail, gold and paradise always remained operative. Both the legendary dream-journeys and those that were actually carried out used it as a navigational guide, in the hope of loot and marvel, all at once."[50]

The original title of the Hitler film was "The Grail." For Syberberg the word means the power of myth to transcend reality, the mountain-moving belief in paradise. But in the film's opening sequence, the image of paradise upon which the block of letters appears suddenly rips in half from top to bottom—the screen itself seems to tear apart. In the resulting gap the stars appear again, as at the beginning. This trompe-l'oeil effect reveals the myth of paradise as a deceptive, brittle image, as a vanishing *fata morgana* that exists only through the illusion generated by cinematic projection.

For Syberberg, film itself functions as a myth-making medium, a kind of compensation for the pervasiveness of technological and economic rationality in this century. The demythologization by science, he says, finds an answer in "a remythologization that only film can accomplish in the sensory immediacy of its images and sound."[51] The myths that were overthrown in the Age of Reason return in the twentieth century as cinematic myths. Thus Claude Lévi-Strauss, the foremost scholar of myth, proposed in a 1964 interview in *Cahiers du Cinéma* that special movie houses be built in each of the world's large cities in which classic films would be shown on a permanent basis, providing "something like a museum of modern myths."[52]

The film medium since its beginning has used myths to express and shape national identity. D. W. Griffith's *The Birth of a Nation* (1915) and Abel Gance's *Napoléon* (1927) are the most obvious examples. Fritz Lang's two-part film on the Nibelungen myth, *Siegfried (Siegfried's Death)* and *Kriemhilds Rache (Kriemhild's Revenge)*, made in 1923–24, served as a means of redefining German identity after the defeat of World War I. Just as Siegfried was stabbed in the back by Hagen, Germany was betrayed by its enemies from within. And just as Siegfried was avenged, Germany, it was implied, had to be avenged. Goebbels and Hitler were not mistaken in their appreciation of Lang's suggestive film version of a seemingly timeless myth that could be refunctionalized and politicized in a contemporary context.

If myth is a principal means of defining and securing the collective identity of a nation, as Ernst Cassirer has pointed out,[53] then an understanding of the National Socialist arsenal of myths is indispensable. In Syberberg's *Hitler* there are many visual and acoustic references to such myths. Passages from Wagner operas, especially *Rienzi, Götterdämmerung,* and *Parsifal,* recur again and again as leitmotifs, as do musical phrases from the funeral service for those who fell in Hitler's putsch of 1923. We also hear expositions of ice cosmogony (130-137), one of the more bizarre theories of the Third Reich's pseudo-philosophy; we learn of the Darwinian doctrine of subhumans (164-165), and of the end of the world in the recitation of the *Muspilli* (40). The mysterious special-effect fog, the flags with swastikas, and the horror posters, as well as the trivial myths of the Third Reich—a replica of Hitler's favorite dog, a Volkswagen, the Reich's eagle, and Anton Graff's famous painting of Frederick the Great that hung in Hitler's bunker—all are significant clues to the manufactured mythical universe of the Hitler regime. Deprived of their functions and context and through their sheer accumulation, these Nazi myths seem emptied of meaning, almost ridiculous because of their pomposity. But the ironic close-out sale of historical mythologies at a carnival (97-106) reflects just one side of Syberberg's concept of myth, the critical side.

Syberberg's critique of the Enlightenment and of rationalism also bears out his serious resolve to reconstruct myth. "Think about our people, dominated by facts and figures, in this mythless time, with their great worship of Enlightenment and their dance around the golden calf of materialism."[54] The sober, soulless materialism that Syberberg decries in the Federal Republic is, of course, itself only a reaction to the intoxication of myth under Hitler. In a dialogue with a Hitler puppet, against the musical background of Haydn's "Emperor Quartet," which later became the German national anthem, André Heller says to Hitler: "You took away our sunsets, sunsets by Caspar David Friedrich. You are to blame that we can no longer look at a field of grain without thinking of you . . . The words 'magic' and 'myth' and 'serving' and 'ruling,' 'Führer,' 'authority,' are ruined, are gone, exiled to eternal time. And we are snuffed out. Nothing more will grow here. An entire nation stopped existing, in the diaspora of the mind and the elite" (242).

Because Hitler unscrupulously used for his own purposes German myths and the anti-Enlightenment strands of German Romanticism, they had to be denied after 1945; they seemed contaminated by their contact with the taboo world of the Nazis. Hitler had carried the myth of Germany itself to an absurd extreme: "Germany is Hitler. Hitler is Germany." Not only the National Socialist myths of Germany but the national myths as well seemed to have perished, irretrievably lost, at the end of the Third Reich. What remained, according to Syberberg, was a land without a national identity, full of neurotic uncertainties about its own myths that define and sustain identity. André Heller continues in his dialogue with the Hitler puppet: "You occupied everything else and corrupted it with your actions, everything, honor, loyalty, country life, hard work, movies, dignity, Fatherland, pride, faith. You are the executor of Western civilization, democratically self-elected, voluntarily, with the victory of money, of materialism over us. The plague of our century. The wretched artist as a hangman degenerating into a politician, voluntarily, cheered as no man ever before" (242).

The mythic dimension of German history seemed forever devalued through Hitler's misuse of it. The memory of the power of the medieval German empire and the dream of the return of the mythic Barbarossa, the often-evoked honor and loyalty of the Nibelungs, and the charisma of such leaders as Arminius and Frederick the Great—all had been appropriated by Hitler and integrated into the national myth of the Third Reich (itself a mythic idea). According to Syberberg, Hitler killed German identity at its roots by stealing and soiling all national myths. In Syberberg's film, however, the loss of German identity gives way to a vision of apocalypse:

> After the journey into this world, who is closer to God than the guilty man? But what about a time without God, when we have deposed him

ourselves? Thus spoke the devil. Ultimately cynical and moral or rather something human in one of his roles: about a twilight of the gods without gods, the Armageddon of progress, the end of time through the ecological death of the human species in the lower vermin of the insects, or the soul death of an ice-age society, the Universal Judgment without jurists and hence just at last, infinitely dreadful. Making room for the next generation, on the next star, after this one becomes definitively self-annihilating, due to the human species. (242-243)

Syberberg's allusion to a time without myths and gods that ends in apocalypse and human self-destruction anticipates the literature of the 1980s with its evocation of catastrophe.[55] But opening the horizon to the end of time and global destruction points to a controversial aspect of Syberberg's work: it evokes once again the "grand perspective" from which the crimes of the Hitler government seem negligible. Miniaturizing the leaders of the Third Reich into puppets does serve to make them less demonic, but it also makes them, and by extension their crimes, harmless and insignificant. Except for the scene in which Himmler's victims appear to him as visions of horror (164ff), the film neglects the perspective of the millions of physical victims; it seems to assume that the spectator already knows the extent of Nazi crimes and dwells more on the damage Hitler did to Germany than to his victims. As important as it is to take the public's fascination with fascism seriously and to understand the connections between aesthetics and fascist politics, this is, after all, only one side of Nazism; the fear and terror that Nazism inflicted on its victims is the other side, a side for which the film finds no images. Instead, the sins Hitler committed against the German people—murdering their language, falsifying their national myths, destroying a proud national identity—are catalogued in detail.

The end of the myth of Germany is expressed in the pervasive mythologizing of death: the original recordings of the National Socialist funeral service for the victims of Hitler's putsch on November 9, 1923, are used regularly as a leitmotif on the soundtrack. To the solemn beat of drums, the names of those who gave their lives for the movement resound. "Forward over graves! The dead are more powerful armies than we on the land, than we on the sea. They stride ahead of us" (189), said Goebbels in a speech given on Christmas of 1944. Syberberg intensifies and totalizes the mysterious collective death wish, characteristic of the National Socialist ideology, into a global longing for the end of the world that can only be grasped through myth. All crimes against humanity, including the extermination of the Indians, which the film also mentions, and the annihilation of the Jews, become mere symptoms for the fatal disease of the moribund West. Even before the titles appear on the screen, the film announces its position in a voice-over: "Dances of death, dialogues of the dead, conversations in the kingdom of the dead, a hundred years later, a thousand years, millions. Passions, oratorios . . . leftovers of a lost civilization and of a lost life, our Europe before the collapse. Farewell to the West. *Sub specie aeternitatis* and everything on film, our new chance. The story of the death of the old light in which we lived, and of our culture, a remote singing"(32).

The cultural pessimism of such passages allows the concrete guilt of the Germans to dissolve in the general malaise of *post-histoire* and the anticipation of the end of the world. Before the great mythical eye and against the horizon of the apocalypse and of eternity ("sub specie aeternitatis"), "rational" distinctions between henchmen and victims, between violence and suffering, lose their meaning and even their justification. For Syberberg, the real enemies are the Enlightenment, materialism, and the belief in progress.

Irrationalism Reclaimed

Art is the social antithesis of society.
THEODOR W. ADORNO

In 1918, shortly after the end of the First World War, Max Weber gave a lecture, "Science as a Vocation," in which he decried an increasing *Entzauberung* (disenchantment, loss of magic) as a result of the "rationalization" and "intellectualization" of modern industrial society.[56] This disenchantment, together with the crisis in all traditional values brought on by World War I, led, by way of compensation, to an unprecedented upsurge of irrational movements in the 1920s. Barefoot prophets traveled through the land and preached about future kingdoms of the spirit; intellectuals discussed Buddha and Lao-Tse; religious and irrational interpretations of the world captured the popular imagination.[57] Hitler himself belonged to this eccentric group of reformers and prophets, whose revolutionary solutions were seldom taken seriously. But there was no doubt that the rapid tempo of modernization in economic, social, and cultural areas created a growing reservoir attracting everything that did not fit into the picture of rational, technological reason—a reservoir that would sooner or later burst its dams and inundate the country. The more Weimar politics appeared as meek and "unsensuous," the more the support for the National Socialists grew. More than any other political party, they knew how to appeal to the collective imagination and satisfy the need for the irrational with their nocturnal torchlight parades, uniforms, and archaic rituals. Already in the late 1920s, Ernst Bloch, a Marxist, correctly pointed out the mass appeal of irrational elements in National Socialism and warned about the consequences of ignoring these potentially explosive forces.[58] Irrationalism had always been present in German culture as the "dark side" of Reason; in 1933 it became, logically enough, the basis for a secular state religion.

It is not surprising that the irrational currents that embodied the "German spirit" during the Hitler era fell into disrepute at the end of the Third Reich. What remained, according to Syberberg, was "the bulwark of a new rationality; for feelings and ideals lead to disaster, so they had been told" (6). Syberberg himself, born in Pomerania in 1935, son of a landowner, lived in the German Democratic Republic until 1959;[59] thus, unlike writers and filmmakers in the Federal Republic, he remained untouched by the "Americanization" of German culture. He claims to be "conservative in a Prussian sense, of the classic school, without chewing gum and pinball, not for nothing raised in the age of Stalin."[60] While the postwar culture of the Federal Republic became more and more dominated by American mass culture, a development running parallel to West Germany's incorporation into the Western economic and defense bloc, East Germany insisted with unusual vehemence on maintaining the classical German tradition.[61] But Syberberg's emphasis on the irrational elements of German culture—very much in the tradition of the conservative cultural criticism of the Weimar era[62]—puts him also at odds with the rationalistic-Marxist conception of culture in the GDR. His reproaches are thus directed against Germans from both West *and* East:

> In the course of assiduous lessons in rationalism and materialism, they repressed one of their most important traditions, the accursed main strand of their nature, pinning it all on the Nazis without a demurrer, putting

the curse of Fascism upon the long history of irrationalism and what relates to it. Hence everything that is mysticism, *Sturm und Drang,* large portions of classicism, the Romantic period, Nietzsche, Wagner, and Expressionism, and their music and parts of the best things they had, were surrendered, relocated, repressed . . . Germany was spiritually disinherited and dispossessed; anything that could not be justified by sociology and social policies was hushed up . . . without irrationality, no *Räuber* by Schiller and no fairy tales and no folk songs and no Runge. Give everything to Hitler and Goebbels? And is Caspar David Friedrich right-wing and Fascist? Is irrationalism right-wing or left-wing? . . . *We live in a country without a homeland, without "Heimat."* (6-7; emphasis mine)

Syberberg wants to use film to find a way back to the spiritual home of the Germans, which he believes has been lost to materialism and rationalism. His project is paradoxical: irrationalism, which the Hitler movement had appropriated and exploited, is to be wrested away from its National Socialist associations by means of a film that celebrates irrationalism as the essence of German identity. The attitude necessary for this task simultaneously constructs and demolishes, enchants and disillusions, hypnotizes and alienates: hence the contradictory union of stylistic models from Brecht and Wagner, and the vacillation between affirmation and criticism in the presentation of the fascination exercised by fascism. "Hitler is to be fought," Syberberg says, "not with the statistics of Auschwitz or with sociological analyses of the Nazi economy, but with Richard Wagner and Mozart" (9).

Syberberg's basic thesis, that Germany without irrationalism is "nothing but dangerous, sick, without identity, explosive—a wretched shadow of its possibilities" (9), led him to champion an irrationalism based on the substitute religion of art that has its roots in German Idealism. For Syberberg, art is "the only true and total opposition" to the rationalization of our lives; his film as art is a "refuge from the German misery" (7). The realm of art is far removed from politics; it is the place where utopias and paradises are designed and dreams and myths are born, where pathos, irony, and play reign in aristocratic freedom.[63] Film, according to Syberberg, can translate inner worlds and irrational impulses into a *Gesamtkunstwerk,* uniting opera, theater, painting, literature, historical reality, and scholarly analysis. In this power to shape the world lies the "Faustian global ambition of the artist," who can succeed in realizing "the shattered political illusions in the art of illusions" and who thus touches on "the taboo of the desire to dominate the world," as we know it "from Hitler and his Reich, the demonic artist of total war."[64]

Such fantasies of artistic omnipotence, which do not shy away from comparing the process of making a film to Hitler's own exercise of power[65]—Syberberg is without equal in his self-estimation—stood out strangely in the cultural scene of the late 1970s. Both Botho Strauss and Peter Handke had already adopted a generally elevated tone and had begun to touch on the mythic in their works, but they lacked Syberberg's provocative tenor and missionary zeal, his aggressive and maverick conservatism. Syberberg's own high aspirations for his Hitler film made its failure inevitable: he wanted to perform therapy on a nation, to accomplish the "work of mourning"; he wanted to give the Germans a chance to overcome Hitler by repeating and working through the past in the theater. His film, which *explored* irrationalism and the fascination of fascism, was accused of being irrational itself. It was brusquely and scornfully rejected in the Federal Republic, which had reason to be sensitive about irrationalism. Syberberg felt that this only proved once again the continuing German inability to carry out the work of mourning.

The idea of the "work" of mourning, of *Trauerarbeit,* was popularized by Alexander and Margarete Mitscherlich in their book *Die Unfähigkeit zu trauern (The Inability to Mourn,* 1958). They took as their point of departure Freud's thesis, expressed in his 1915 essay "Trauer und Melancholie," that the individual can overcome the loss of a loved person only by doing *Trauerarbeit,* that is, by undergoing a repeated, painful process of remembering.[66] Although Hitler was a beloved object for millions, after the loss of the Führer—that is, the collective ego ideal with which millions of Germans had identified— there was no opportunity to openly acknowledge this loss. Instead most Germans, as is well known, identified with the victors and plunged into the reconstruction period. In 1985, the year of the planned ceremony of reconciliation at the SS graves in Bitburg, Margarete Mitscherlich-Nielsen noted in her speech, "Rede über das eigene Land: Deutschland" ("Speaking about One's Own Country: Germany"): "But when denial, repression, derealization of the past replace the process of working through it, a repetition compulsion is unavoidable, even if it is concealed. It is not the content of a system that is repeated, but the structure of a society. Nazi symbols and

Nazi associations can be banned. But it is not possible to drive Nazi structures out of the world of education, of behavior, of social manners and modes of thought, without the work of mourning."[67]

In a similar way, Syberberg's filmic work of mourning challenges the present. Hitler, according to the film, lives on in terrorism, in modern totalitarianism, in the pollution of the environment, in the ravaging of life through the entertainment industry, in the quantitative, art-hating mass democracy. "Hitler himself is the theme and center of this past, which we must penetrate, this past so wounded and painful, yet so identifiable" (3). According to Mitscherlich-Nielsen, not until the Germans are able to take leave of their lost ideals and values will they become able to think and perceive in a new way.[68] Syberberg also poses the question: "Can and should a film about Hitler and his Germany explain anything in this respect, rediscover identities, heal and save?" (3). For him the question is rhetorical, because the dramatic structure of the film points the way from mourning to "salvation," from the confession of guilt to "healing." His film ends with the chorus, "Ode to Joy," from Beethoven's Ninth Symphony playing behind a visionary tableau dominated by the black stone from Dürer's famous engraving *Melencolia*. The film's last images fade into a science-fiction simulation, as at the beginning of the film: through a huge tear we see the starry sky with the silent girl, dressed in white, in the foreground, an allegory of innocence. She is holding her stuffed dog with Hitler's face, which she first kicks away and then picks up again and plays with, "turning away and yet taking it" (247).

Hitler is allegorized, aestheticized, and made an object of kitsch in this film; such stylistic means of estrangement provoke conflicting responses about the "appropriateness" of such representation. The traditional filmic patterns of reception no longer function; instead a condition of abeyance is generated that cannot be resolved by the use of reason. An "uneasiness" arises, as described by Saul Friedländer: "Attention has gradually shifted from the reevocation of Nazism as such, from the horror and the pain . . . to voluptuous anguish and ravishing images, images one would like to see going on forever. It may result in a masterpiece, but a masterpiece that, one may feel, is tuned to the wrong key; in the midst of meditation arises a suspicion of complacency. Some kind of limit has been overstepped and uneasiness appears: It is a sign of the new discourse."[69]

The Federal Republic rejected Syberberg's provocative presentation of irrationalism, his reminder of the irrational dimension of German culture, the Wagnerian excess and the aestheticization of the Third Reich, his advocacy of myth and his tendency to absolutism. All of that was enthusiastically greeted abroad, however, especially in France.[70] The French had long cherished ideas of the romantic, torn, irrational, Faustian German nature. As early as 1810 Mme de Staël had compiled these ideas in her book *De L'Allemagne,* and they recur, for instance, in Michel Tournier's novel *Le Roi des Aulnes (The Ogre,* 1970)[71] and most recently in Brigitte Sauzay's book *Le vertige Allemand* (1986). With such ideas in mind, the French naturally see Syberberg, who declares the irrational as the essence of Germanness, as an archetypal German, and his Hitler film as a continuation of the Faust tragedy, "Faust III."[72] Even an analytic critic like Christian Zimmer, writing in *Les temps modernes,* speaks of the "'metaphysical heat' of Germany"[73] and defends Syberberg against critics who reproach his neglect of the material basis of Nazism. Predictably, Zimmer emphasizes the religious-metaphysical, irrational, mythological, in short, "German" ground on which Hitler's self-destructive fanaticism rested. In this view Syberberg's film, which takes this spiritual ground of the German Reich seriously, corresponded to the mythical, romantic image of the "German nature" that had been firmly lodged in the minds of the French intelligentsia for 150 years.

The recognition that Syberberg received in Paris and New York— Susan Sontag's famous eight-page discussion of the Hitler film in the *New York Review of Books* is full of admiration for the symbolist and neosurrealist aesthetic of the film, with less to say about its political and "German" side[74]—was denied him at home. His image of an idealistic, visionary, irrational Germany, which he seems to have adopted from the French, can daily be disproved and shown to be an illusion by the reality of the Federal Republic; everywhere Syberberg looks, he sees banal materialism, rationalism, and intellectual stagnation. Thus his verdict on postwar Germany, like Fassbinder's, Sanders-Brahms's, and Reitz's, is unmitigatedly negative: Germany is "a dead land," a "joyless society," a "consumer democracy"[75] in which repressed irrationalism discharges itself in terrorist paroxysms. *Hitler* in fact reminds us of this nexus between irrationalism and terrorism with its closing title: "20 October 1977, the day after Mogadischu—Stammheim—Mulhouse." For Syberberg, the terrorist attacks, the prison deaths, and the murders of Autumn 1977 were merely outbreaks of the subterranean, suppressed irrationalism.

Syberberg places himself in the long tradition of German writers and artists—Lessing, Goethe, Hölderlin, Nietzsche, Wagner, Tucholsky—who designed an imaginary, idealized Germany in order to contrast it with the unbearable real Germany. The gulf between the fictional and the actual Germany is incessantly measured and endlessly described. No other country in the world has produced so much in the way of fantasy and images about itself. No other country ever had so many emigrants among its intellectuals, emigrants who—like Thomas Mann and Brecht in exile—still passionately indulged in fantasies of Germany. Syberberg, whose love of the German cultural tradition stands in sharp contrast to his distaste for the national, political, and economic systems of power in the Federal Republic of today, likes to see himself as an emigrant in his own country, alienated, speaking another language, homeless. It was no accident that it was a foreign film journal that asked him to comment on Edgar Reitz's attempts to reconstruct the lost homeland in *Heimat*. Syberberg wrote: "What is possible in the art form of the film seems lost in reality, for the answer in reality to the question about our ability to feel and find our 'Heimat' must be a sad one."[76]

3

THE PRESENCE OF THE PAST

Rainer Werner Fassbinder's
The Marriage of Maria Braun

"I am an expert in matters of the future."
—Hanna Schygulla and Elisabeth Trissenaar
in *The Marriage of Maria Braun*

The effacement of memory is more the achievement of an all-too-wakeful consciousness than it is the result of its weakness in the face of the superiority of unconscious processes. In this forgetting of what is scarcely past, one senses the fury of the one who has to talk himself out of what everyone else knows, before he can talk them out of it.

THEODOR W. ADORNO

I tell you all my secrets
But I lie about my past.

TOM WAITS

The arrow of memory is not poisoned, but the social body it hits seems to become more vulnerable the more it rears up and contorts itself so as not to show its vulnerability.

ANDRÉ GLUCKSMANN

The Politics of Private Life

Rainer Werner Fassbinder was found dead in his Munich apartment on June 10, 1982. He was thirty-seven years old. The epitaphs in all the world's major newspapers bear witness to the esteem he had gained for himself and for the New German Cinema. His oeuvre of forty-three films and television productions, many of which received prizes and awards, together with his uncompromising, provocatively bohemian lifestyle, won him an undisputed reputation as the "heart" of New German Cinema.[1] In the eyes of the foreign press, Fassbinder's critical view of West German reality qualified him as a reliable (because incorruptibly critical) chronicler of the Federal Republic. His films provided "information about Germany."[2] According to the conservative newspaper *The Daily Mail*, he acted as the "conscience of his nation."[3] Colette Godard began her front-page epitaph in *Le Monde* with these words: "Rainer Werner Fassbinder represented the passionate rage of the German film, the rage of a young generation that opened its eyes in the 1960s and learned what its elders had left behind: the destruction of German identity through National Socialism."[4]

Especially outside of Germany, Fassbinder seemed to embody the

West German postwar generation that grew up in the fifties during the so-called "economic miracle" and, in the sixties, revolted against parents, teachers, and the state. This is the generation of Andreas Baader (born in 1944), Gudrun Ensslin (1942), and Rudi Dutschke (1940), but also that of Peter Schneider (1942), Werner Herzog (1944), and Wim Wenders (1945). Unlike the generation of Syberberg or Kluge, born in the early 1930s, this generation did not directly experience the Third Reich, Hitler, and the war. Those born in 1945, like Fassbinder, were given the German past as an unwanted legacy.

It was a legacy that was taboo in the 1950s. The older generation had, consciously or unconsciously, banned all questions about the most recent German past. By the mid-1960s, shortly after the Eichmann trial in Jerusalem and the Auschwitz trial in Frankfurt, as the postwar children began to question their parents about their involvement in the Hitler regime, an acute crisis developed in the relations between the generations in West Germany. No matter what justifications and excuses the parents had, the younger generation's judgment knew no mercy: their parents, now polemically called the "Auschwitz generation," were guilty. Their pride in having transformed Germany from rubble and ruins to one of the most affluent countries in the world seemed to their children merely an evasive tactic meant to divert attention from the unatoned crimes committed by them in the name of Germany.

This long-repressed hatred toward the older generation, the "generation of culprits," exploded in 1967, intensified by worldwide protest campaigns against the Vietnam War, against the new state emergency laws passed by the Bundestag, and against the right-wing mass-circulation newspapers controlled by the press baron Axel Springer. It also fed on the students' discontent with the ossified educational system and the hierarchical structure of the university. As part of an international youth culture, the so-called Woodstock generation, a movement also arose in the Federal Republic that radically altered the consciousness of the postwar generation. For the first time in the West German democracy, the students (and many others) took a stand against the state and institutional authority. The protests, most of them successful at least initially, were full of anarchic power and utopian idealism. All this revolutionary energy that galvanized politics as well as culture must have affected Fassbinder deeply. It is not a coincidence that his career began exactly in 1967, at the height of the student rebellion in West Germany. He never departed from the radical utopian-anarchic ideals of this period; they form the horizon against which the reality (and integrity) of his heroes and heroines is measured. Not surprisingly, all of Fassbinder's films thematize the failure of these uncompromising ideals and the final shattering of illusions. They explore oppressive power relations and dependencies, melodramatic emotions, hopeless compromises, double binds, and inescapable situations that often end in suicide.

Fassbinder started out as an actor and theater director in Munich's vibrant underground theater scene. He met many of his collaborators there (for instance, Peer Raben, who wrote the scores to virtually all of Fassbinder's films) as well as many of the actors (among them Hanna Schygulla, Irm Hermann, Kurt Raab) with whom he worked for the next ten years, in the style of a small repertory theater. This working arrangement accounts in part for the remarkable speed with which Fassbinder was able to make his films and for the easily identifiable look of a "Fassbinder film." He became interested in filmmaking in 1967 when Jean-Marie Straub, whose minimalist 1965 film adaptation of a Böll novel, *Not Reconciled,* was one of the first critically acclaimed films of the New German Cinema, made a film with the *antiteater,* Fassbinder's experimental theater group in Munich. Straub's experimental short film, *Der Bräutigam, die Komödiantin und der Zuhälter (The Bridegroom, the Comedienne, and the Pimp),* took months of intensive rehearsal. Fassbinder learned a great deal in that time from Straub's controlled, self-reflexive, Brechtian use of film images. His own first films, *Liebe ist kälter als der Tod (Love is Colder Than Death)* and *Katzelmacher* (both 1969), show Straub's strong influence in both their filmic style and their dramatic structure.

In 1971 Fassbinder saw films by Douglas Sirk, the Hamburg-born Hollywood director, for the first time. Sirk had worked as Detlef Sierck for UFA and had made (among other films) the famous melodramas *La Habañera* and *Zu neuen Ufern (To New Shores),* starring the legendary actress Zarah Leander, before emigrating in 1937. Fassbinder was impressed by Sirk's ability to make commercially successful films with wide audience appeal without compromising a subversive, "European" sensibility and an idiosyncratic, personal style; he "adopted" the exiled German as his spiritual father, desperately wanting to be part of a tradition of German filmmaking.[5]

Sirk's great melodramas of the 1950s—especially *All That Heaven Allows* (1955) and *Imitation of Life* (1958)—follow the classical style of trivial novels in concentrating on the great emotions of little people and their unrealistic aspirations. His melodramas invariably deal with people doomed to failure in a hostile social environment. In Fassbinder's eyes, Sirk depicted unbridled passions in a distinctive manner, making filmic space itself signify through high-contrast lighting, through the symbolic use of everyday objects like flowers, mirrors, pictures on the wall, pieces of furniture, and clothing, and finally through careful compositions and a dynamic mise-en-scène— most of which harked back to Sirk's beginnings as a theater director.[6] Fassbinder's *Der Händler der vier Jahreszeiten* (*The Merchant of Four Seasons,* 1971) and *Angst essen Seele auf* (*Fear Eats the Soul,* 1973) consciously evoke Sirk's style, making use of melodramatic plots, "unrealistic" lighting, obtrusive camera movements, and artificial, highly stylized decor. Overly melodramatic music breaks the illusion, and a theatrical gestural language keeps the viewer at a critical distance despite the open display of strong emotions.[7]

Sirk's influence is also visible in Fassbinder's historical films, which appeared in rapid succession after 1977: *Die Ehe der Maria Braun* (*The Marriage of Maria Braun*), filmed from January to March 1978; *Berlin Alexanderplatz,* filmed from June 1979 to April 1980; *Lili Marleen,* filmed from July to September 1980; *Lola,* filmed from April to May 1981; and *Die Sehnsucht der Veronika Voss* (*Veronika Voss*), filmed from November to December 1981. All deal with the unfulfilled and unfulfillable desires of the characters, the exploitation and exploitability of their emotions, and the destruction they bring down on themselves. These melodramatic themes provide a continuity in Fassbinder's work from his first film to the last, regardless of whether they are set in today's Germany or in the Germany of the past. Apart from the adaptations of Theodor Fontane's *Effi Briest* (1974) and of Oskar Maria Graf's *Bolwieser* (1976), Fassbinder did not explore the historical dimensions of his socially critical themes until after the mid-1970s. In 1977, however, he began work on a ten-part television series based on Gustav Freytag's 1855 novel *Soll und Haben* (*Debit and Credit*), in which he planned to trace the National Socialist ideology back to the nineteenth-century German bourgeoisie. Although he had to abandon this project because of network objections,[8] he was still eager to explore the past as a (pre-)history of the present—if not in a large-scale television series, then in individual films.

The period that most fascinated Fassbinder was the postwar era, the time following the rupture of 1945 in which "everything" seemed possible. The Federal Republic was not yet firmly established, and utopian hopes still existed. "Our fathers," Fassbinder said in 1978, "had the chance to found a state that could have been the most humane and freest ever."[9] Confronting the founding years of the Federal Republic meant illuminating the dominant values and illusions of the period, as well as investigating its latent dreams and longings. The postwar era coincided with Fassbinder's own lifetime; at the age of thirty, he began to look back at his and the Federal Republic's early years with a critical eye. Like many other authors of his generation, he turned in the late 1970s to his own youth in the Adenauer era, albeit less autobiographically and nostalgically than, for instance, Jürgen Theobaldy in *Sonntags Kino* (*Movies on Sundays,* 1978) or Angelika Mechtel in *Wir sind arm, wir sind reich* (*We Are Poor, We Are Rich,* 1977).[10] Fassbinder's approach is a critical one; he had little interest in "the way it really was," but rather wondered how the thoughts, feelings, and actions of his contemporaries could be explained historically.[11] Like Walter Benjamin, he wanted to deal with the *constellation* of past and present, with the moment of recognition in which past and present mutually illuminate each other.[12]

A further impetus for his turning to history was the crisis of Autumn 1977, which Fassbinder's generation experienced as a watershed in the political development and self-understanding of the Federal Republic. In his 26-minute contribution to the collective film *Germany in Autumn,* Fassbinder reacted spontaneously to the intellectual atmosphere of that time by playing himself—the only one of the nine filmmakers to do so. In the film he appears beleaguered, literally locked up in his own dark apartment, linked to the outside world only by a telephone. We hear a police siren and steps on the stairs, noises that cause Fassbinder to panic. A furtive glance through the blinds shows someone crossing an empty street. Claustrophobia dominates as the camera peers into the private sphere of the controversial director whose life is surrounded by scandals. Fassbinder gives us a document of shameless self-revelation, a psychogram of his anxieties and aggressions. He intercuts the apartment scenes with an inquisitorial (scripted) interview with his own mother, who has appeared in many of his films. Scenes of radical, self-indulgent subjectivity alternate with scenes of analytical reflection. The striking disparity between Fassbinder the filmmaker, who is brought to the brink of a physical breakdown by the political situation, and Fassbinder the son, who fights with his mother about German traditions of state violence and political resistance, leaves a strong and highly disturbing impression.[13]

In the interview with his mother, the son insists on his democratic right to pursue open political discussions despite threats; anything less would mean a regression into dictatorship. His mother agrees; the current political climate reminds her "a lot of the Nazi time, when people just kept quiet to stay out of trouble."[14] Their dispute is about the freedom of opinion in times of crisis and the question of whether the law can be broken in the fight against terrorists. Fassbinder tells his mother that precisely because she lived through the Third Reich, she should have a more pronounced respect for democracy. Instead, however, she advocates a retreat from democracy: "The best thing now would be a kind of authoritarian ruler who is good and kind and orderly." Fassbinder condemns his mother for her authoritarian beliefs and her cowardice, while—and this is the dialectic behind his contribution— the camera captures those very same qualities in himself. We see him treat his mother and his gay lover in an authoritarian manner, almost sadistically. It is also clear that he does not exercise the right he demands, to take part in the public debate; instead, he withdraws from the outside world and dictates the shooting script for *Berlin Alexanderplatz,* his new film project at the time. The spectator alone must sort out these troubling contradictions.

What can a film like *Germany in Autumn* accomplish? In an interview at the end of 1977, Fassbinder said: "It can formulate anxieties. For others. If no one does that, we would retreat into a muteness in which we would soon become stupid. The film can encourage the viewer to continue to have an opinion and to express it."[15] But Fassbinder posed questions in *Germany in Autumn* that demanded a more complete answer. Following up on his interview with his mother, he planned to make another cooperative film about the older generation, called "The Marriages of Our Parents." Even though he was unable to secure financing, he did not want to relinquish this project, which, he said, would have been rich enough for an eight-hour film. Fassbinder therefore asked two professional screenwriters, Peter Märthesheimer and Pea Fröhlich, to reduce his unwieldy narrative to a conventional feature film length.[16] "The Marriages of Our Parents" thus became *The Marriage of Maria Braun,* a film that finally brought about Fassbinder's breakthrough to a mass audience both in Germany and abroad.

Coinciding with the film's premiere in February 1979, the weekly magazine *Stern* started to run a serialized novel based on Fassbinder's film, and even carrying the same title. Written by Gerhard Zwerenz, the novel more or less retold the film story and was illustrated with photographs from the film.[17] This multimedia marketing, common in the United States, was new in Germany and may have contributed to the film's commercial success. *The Marriage of Maria Braun* is the first part of Fassbinder's "BRD-Trilogie" (FRG Trilogy); it was followed by *Lola* (1981) and *Veronika Voss* (1982). All three films deal with the Federal Republic from the mid-1940s to the mid-1950s as seen from the perspective of the late seventies. When asked about the function of these historical films, Fassbinder responded:

> We didn't learn much about German history in Germany, so we have to catch up with some basic information, and as a filmmaker I simply used this information to tell a story. That means nothing more than making reality tangible. I see many things today that again arouse fear in me. The call for law and order. I want to use this film to give today's society something like a supplement to their history. Our democracy was decreed for the Western occupation zone; we didn't fight for it ourselves. Old ways of thinking have lots of opportunity to seep in through cracks, without a swastika, of course, but with old methods of education. I am astonished how quickly the rearmament came about in this country. The attempts by the younger generation to revolt were quite pitiful. I also want to show how the 1950s shaped the people of the 1960s. How the establishment clashed with the engaged youth, which was pushed into the abnormality of terrorism.[18]

Fassbinder is obviously as much concerned with the present as with the past. The stories he tells in the FRG Trilogy—unlike Syberberg, Fassbinder loves to tell conventional stories with a beginning, middle, and end—take place in the founding years of the Federal

Republic, but indirectly always refer to the present. They provide snapshots of German misery as Fassbinder understood and felt it at the end of the 1970s: the subjugation of emotions to mercenary material greed in the reconstruction years (*The Marriage of Maria Braun*); the ubiquitous corruption one had to accept in the years of opportunistic conformity (*Lola*); and the neurosis about one's own past and traumatic memories that had to be exorcised (*Veronika Voss*). The films show that the combination of economic miracle and collective denial of the past caused a potential for conflict that built up in the fifties and exploded ten years later.

Fassbinder's films on Germany do not present large-scale politics and economics directly. Instead they operate within the "micropolitics of desire,"[19] showing the hopes, aspirations, and frustrations of people in concrete historical situations. The protagonists in Fassbinder's FRG Trilogy are all women, for he believes that women are, as dramatic characters, more interesting, less predictable, and less conformist than men: "Men in this society are much more forced to play a role than women, who have a role but can break out of it much more easily or can deviate a step or two from the path."[20] Fassbinder's female protagonists shape their epoch as much as they are shaped by it. In their politically unaware private lives, they contribute to, and parabolically mirror, the dominant mentality of their time.[21] Fassbinder's films supplement official historiography with a psychological dimension, delving into everyday life and the private sphere; they show how politics is negotiated "from below."

To give an example: in a scene in *The Marriage of Maria Braun* in which Maria is visiting her relatives, the radio is turned on and Adenauer is giving a speech. "I do not want an army," we hear him say in an original sound recording, "we've had enough deaths ... One need only recall the fact that in Germany today there are 160 women for every 100 men" (93–94).[22] As Adenauer speaks, we see Maria and her relatives eating, commenting on the potato salad and exchanging recipes. No one listens to the radio speech, in which Adenauer vehemently opposes the rearmament of the Federal Republic. The radio voice brings a political dimension into the private family sphere, but it is ignored. Fassbinder uses this scene to illustrate dramatically the deficient political awareness of most Germans during the reconstruction period, when food was more important than politics. Toward the end of the film we hear another original recording of a radio broadcast, this time from 1954. Adenauer now advocates equally emphatically the rearmament of the Federal Republic: "We have the right to rearm—as much as we can, as much as we want" (145). It is unclear whether Maria Braun, who is eating alone in a restaurant, hears this speech with its complete about-face on the question of rearmament, but she suddenly gets up, stumbles, and vomits. The action seems to comment on the radio speech; the tension in this scene between image and sound allows Fassbinder to correlate public and private sickness, to show an extreme private reaction to what he considers a fatal development in German political history.

At regular intervals public history (*Geschichte*) breaks into the private stories (*Geschichten*). The history of the German nation from the end of the war to the so-called economic miracle of the 1950s punctuates and expands the story of Maria Braun. Political history enters the fictional frame in various forms. For instance, at the beginning of the film we hear a monotonous radio voice reading off the names and identification numbers of missing soldiers about whom information is available. The theme of searching and reunion is mirrored in public discourse: as Maria Braun looks for her husband, the state looks for its scattered subjects.

Visiting Germany in 1950, only five years after Germany's *Stunde Null* ("Zero Hour"), Hannah Arendt observed: "Everywhere one notices that there is no reaction to what has happened, but it is hard to say whether that is due to an intentional refusal to mourn or whether it is the expression of a genuine emotional incapacity."[23] Fassbinder's film reproduces this mood, in which practical survival and accommodation take precedence over the work of memory and mourning. (The camera emphasizes people's greed for simple pleasures like cigarettes or coffee through frequent, often obtrusive close-ups.) At the same time Fassbinder shows the beginnings of a re-emerging nationalist feeling. In the midst of a landscape of ruins someone clumsily plays a flawed version of the German national anthem on an accordion as the camera pans across destroyed buildings. Voices interrupt the street musician; someone starts singing "Deutschland, Deutschland über alles," stops, starts over, and breaks off in the middle. The dissonant, interrupted national anthem in this context stands as a sign for the half-devastated, crippled nation. The ragged singing of the anthem in the midst of ruins must be read as Fassbinder's sarcastic comment on the willed ignorance of those who do not want to admit that "Deutschland" has perished.

Historical Narration

There is always a purpose when one is talking about history.

ALFRED DÖBLIN

"History consists of wisps of narratives," says Jean-François Lyotard in his *Instructions païennes* (1977), "stories that one tells, that one hears, that one acts out; the people do not exist as a subject but as a mass of millions of insignificant and serious little stories that sometimes let themselves be collected together to constitute big stories and sometimes disperse into digressive elements."[24] Writing history would then consist of weaving together many individual narrative threads into a "text" (in the sense of the Latin *textum*, something woven). The way in which the narrative threads are intertwined attaches a certain meaning to the historical event, which by itself has an infinite multiplicity of potential meanings. Thus Karlheinz Stierle writes: "With respect to events, history writing is a reduction. This reduction follows a direction that can be called 'the superimposition of an ideal line' (Simmel). The 'ideal line' constitutes the basic narrative relations of the story which serve to integrate the elements of the event."[25]

The narrative pattern that Fassbinder uses in his FRG Trilogy is the biography of a woman who makes her way alone through the German postwar era as an adventuress and female picaro. Less vagrant than Defoe's Moll Flanders but similarly unscrupulous when it comes to her own advantage, Maria Braun moves through the period between 1945 and 1954. *The Marriage of Maria Braun* is a densely woven text that consists of a great number of isolated small stories subordinated to the central narrative, the story of the rise and fall of Maria Braun. The life of the film persona Maria Braun is structured "like a movie": narrative and images follow the pattern of the melodramatic films of the 1940s and 1950s, which in turn had generously drawn on motifs from the popular novel of the nineteenth century. Fassbinder adopts these clichés but defamiliarizes them by multiplying, exaggerating, and accentuating them (often with the accompaniment of melodramatic musical chords). He also undercuts the conventions of the genre; thus the film does not end with a marriage but instead begins with one.

Maria weds the infantryman Hermann Braun in the last year of the war, in the middle of a bomb attack, but their marriage lasts only a single night and half a day, since Hermann has to return to the front. She waits for him and trades on the black market in order to support herself and her mother. The film carefully reconstructs the historical ambience, with scenes of returning soldiers, women picking up the rubble, and black marketeers.[26] When Hermann, believed dead, suddenly appears in the doorway—the returning soldier is a classic motif in twentieth-century German drama[27]—he surprises Maria with her lover, a black occupation soldier who is an acquaintance from an off-limits bar where she works. Mr. Bill, the GI, is presented as attractive, shy rather than aggressive. Fassbinder shows Maria's fondness for him in idyllic scenes, an unusual and provocative counterimage to the negative image of the American liberators, for instance, in Helma Sanders-Brahms's *Germany, Pale Mother* and Edgar Reitz's *Heimat*. Hermann's return is all the more shocking because he bursts in on a love scene. The two men fight, and Hermann, weakened by the long journey home from the war, is about to lose when Maria, as if in a trance, hits Mr. Bill over the head with a bottle. The GI dies. Hermann, touched by Maria's loyalty, pleads guilty in court and goes to prison in her stead. Maria promises him that their "real" life will begin upon his release. In the meantime, on her own again, she pursues a single goal: economic success. Love and emotion, her whole private life, are deferred. She holds fast to the dream of a great eternal love even when she meets Oswald, an elderly emigrant and owner of a textile factory, who falls in love with her. She takes him as her lover and rapidly rises to a leading position in his firm.

In this film Fassbinder gives us a portrait of the reconstruction period of the Federal Republic, when the decline in human values is shown to correspond directly to the increase in profit rates. "Is that how it is between people outside? So cold?" (108), Hermann asks when Maria visits him in prison and tells him that she has strictly separated business and emotions. She answers: "It's a hard time now for feelings, I think." She has become affluent and has bought a luxurious villa; now she waits for Hermann: "Our life will start again when we're together" (80). But after he is released, to Maria's puzzlement, Hermann first goes abroad, only to reappear suddenly after Oswald's death. Maria (and the viewer) do not learn about the true state of affairs until Oswald's will is read in the last minutes of the film. Oswald, his death approaching, had feared losing Maria when Hermann was released. He visited Hermann in prison and made a deal with him behind Maria's back: Hermann was to receive half of Oswald's fortune for allowing Oswald to enjoy Maria until his death. Essentially, Hermann agreed to sell Maria to Oswald. When Maria learns about this secret deal, she suddenly understands that her utopian dreams of a future "real life" have been betrayed. She realizes that she was never in control of her own destiny, which she had thought she was manipulating so masterfully. Instead, she finds herself as a mere object of exchange in a business transaction between two men. The illusion that gave her life meaning shatters completely. A gas explosion, half-consciously caused by her, blows up the villa and Maria and Hermann with it.

The film does not hesitate to reproduce the classic narrative motifs of Hollywood melodramas from the late forties and fifties—love and murder, loyalty, betrayal, yearning for an absent lover, suffering, and death—in a film *about* the forties and fifties. It elaborates on these motifs in the various subplots that cluster around the story of Maria. As in the novels of Walter Scott and the tradition of the classical historical novel, political history and personal stories interact so that the individual private stories always contribute to and illustrate general history. As Maria Braun's own story unfolds, it touches other stories, joins with them, intervenes in them.[28] Maria's life is reflected in the life stories of the people around her; even peripheral figures are granted time to speak about their lives and shed new light on Maria's. For instance, a Red Cross nurse at the train station tells Maria that when her husband fell into a mountain crevice during the war, the army as compensation sent her a mass-produced oil painting of an *ocean*, with the inscription: "They died that Germany may live" (43). This one sentence succinctly illustrates the contradiction between the cynical official distortion of history and the private experience of suffering. It also epitomizes a motif that runs through the whole film: the antagonism between private and political history. Each of the numerous miniature life stories, sometimes shown and sometimes narrated, enrich Fassbinder's portrait of the times. These life stories, these wisps of narrative threads constitute the text of history, *Geschichten* making up *Geschichte*.

The viewer comes to a double awareness of how strongly political history determines private stories and how little the subjects of history understand that relationship. "From a private perspective," a German critic said in a review of the film, "political history appears as nothing but a series of hurdles that must be overcome."[29] The characters in the film neither discuss nor reflect upon such major historical events as the founding of the Federal Republic, the final division of Germany in 1949, or the uprising in East Berlin in 1953. West Germans of the 1950s believed that thinking about politics or the most recent past would only have impeded or slowed down reconstruction.[30] All that counted was the future; everything else was deferred.

The film presents elaborate stock images of the period, first the so-called "food wave," when Germans only seemed to have eating on their minds, then their preoccupation with clothes, furniture, and travel. Fassbinder dwells on these details, which do not advance the plot but deepen our understanding of the forces determining the characters' actions. Still, the telos of the film corresponds to the dynamics of the reconstruction period. Maria Braun embodies the idea that economic success is a function of keeping one's eyes on what is coming. At one point she calls herself "an expert in matters of the future" (101).

The film consists of a dense network of fictional private stories that give us insight into how the Germans of the fifties lived and experienced their lives. This proliferation of narrative strands leads to more information than is necessary to understand the main story. But it is precisely this excess of minor characters that fosters a realistic historical effect, an illusion of authentic history. The realistic effect also results from the fact that the historical fiction of *Maria Braun* seems to unfold as a story without a narrating subject; until the final scenes it is not clear who is telling the story. The elimination of an enunciating subject is one of the conventional devices to achieve the effect of "historical realism."

In the history film this effect is produced not only by the "pluralization" of the narration but also, and primarily, by the choice of images. In *The Marriage of Maria Braun* the detailed, accurate reconstruction of the visual world of the period guarantees the veracity of the historical fiction. The faithful reconstructions, from the postwar train station to the living room decor of the fifties, from the Allied uniforms to the women's hairstyles, evoke historical time between 1944 and 1954 through visual motifs well known from old photographs and newsreels. Images, for instance, of grizzled and haggard soldiers returning home, of women in head-scarves clearing away rubble, of well-fed American soldiers and their German war brides, all carry a high recognition value. Over the years they have become conventional representations of the immediate postwar years in Germany, engraving themselves on the collective memory as the "correct" representation of this era. Fassbinder uses them almost as one might use stock footage clichés to persuade the viewer to accept the film as a historical film. The realistic historical effect thus also depends on the visual memory of the audience. Because the historical film by definition refers to a past reality known to most viewers prior to the film, either from experience or from representations, they enjoy the effect of recognition ("That's just the way it was, that's what I remember having seen before"). This extra referent, which appeals to historical knowledge (and knowledge that exists outside of the film's fictional sphere), produces an additional level of meaning and increases the meaning potential of the film. Although the historical material loses its historiographic, factual status by being absorbed within the fiction, it remains discernible as a result of the viewer's historical knowledge, which the film activates. For instance, the documentary Adenauer speeches become part and parcel of *Maria Braun's* fictional space. At the same time they are experienced as "real," as "historical" in the sense that the sound recordings of Adenauer's speeches used in the film also exist outside of this fictional space. They are verifiable; they are not inventions or fabrications. The viewer senses, even if unconsciously, the unresolvable dual status of historical narratives, as document and fiction, authentically true and at the same time used within a freely invented story.[31]

Fassbinder's montages of sound and images became increasingly complex after 1978. That complexity corresponds to the multilayered historical subject matter of his last films, which contain diverse and stratified languages, conflicting voices, and different representational modes. His notion of film as the locus of diverse stylistic unities recalls M. M. Bakhtin's idea of "heteroglossia," a term describing the conflicting plurality of voices in the discourse of the novel. "The novel," Bakhtin says, "must represent all the social and ideological voices of its era, that is, all the era's languages that have any claim of significance; the novel must be a microcosm of heteroglossia."[32] Fassbinder tries to achieve this diversity in his historical films by an accumulation of different voices. The sheer mass of simultaneous messages, referring to one another, contradicting and mirroring one another, leads to stratified sound collages with up to four layers: music, dialogue, radio, sound effects. At the end of *Maria Braun*, for instance, as Oswald's will is being read aloud, the radio is on with the live broadcast of a soccer game, and at the same time Maria is talking to Senkenberg. This density of simultaneous acoustic signs makes it almost impossible for the viewer to follow the denouement of the story. Public and private voices intermix inseparably with one another.

The Marriage of Maria Braun is also a story about the labor of storytelling, of fabricating fictions. Maria Braun herself is the film's best storyteller. She purposely conceals, feigns, and prevaricates, lies when it is expedient, and manipulates others through her skilled self-presentation. She is an expert at pretense and disguise, the basic figures of narration. When asked why she tells different stories to different people, she answers ironically: "Because I am a master of deception. A capitalist tool by day, and by night an agent of the proletarian masses. The Mata Hari of the economic miracle!" (110). The unpredictability of Maria Braun's behavior determines the structure of the film. The narrative resembles the picaresque novel in its accidental meetings, sudden partings, coincidences, and unexpected reunions. Maria Braun adapts to each new turn of fate with skill, opportunism, and a strong belief in her own success. "I'd rather make the miracles than wait for them" (104), she says at the height of the career that has led her from poverty and unatoned murder to riches and public recognition.

The Marriage of Maria Braun is constructed around the memory of a marriage that lasted one night and half a day. This marriage is the secret center and at the same time the vanishing point of Maria's story. It legitimates her ambition, her accumulation of wealth, and her obsessive planning for the future. A growing tension between past and future that devalues the present makes her distracted and forgetful. Finally the tension between remembering and forgetting, which underlies her whole story, is compressed into a scene lasting only a few seconds. Remembering or forgetting suddenly becomes a matter of life or death. As Maria Braun takes a cigarette from the pack, she hesitates, looks at the pack, asks her husband for a match, and then goes into the kitchen, where (as we remember from an earlier scene) she has forgotten to turn off the gas. Fassbinder deliberately leaves it ambiguous as to whether she simply forgets or chooses not to remember. He sets the price of forgetting high: both protagonists die in the explosion. Maria Braun's hope for the ideal to be realized, her waiting for utopia, ends in catastrophe.

History as Trauma

Comment être encore un Allemand?

MARGUERITE DURAS

Several years before embarking on *The Marriage of Maria Braun,* Fassbinder had already attempted to deal in a more direct way with the German problem of forgetting and repression. However, his attempts to explore the most sensitive area of German memory, the memory of anti-Semitism and systematically planned and executed genocide, all failed. Two of his film projects were rejected, and the play *Der Müll, die Stadt und der Tod* (*Garbage, the City and Death*) was produced neither in 1976, when it was written, nor in 1985, when it was again proposed. Nonetheless, the searing debates surrounding these unrealized projects showed with shocking clarity that the relations between Germans and Jews in the Federal Republic are still far from normal.[33]

Garbage, the City and Death, written in 1975–76, was based on the Frankfurt novel *Die Erde ist unbewohnbar wie der Mond* (*The Earth Is as Inhabitable as the Moon,* 1973) by Gerhard Zwerenz. It became Fassbinder's most controversial project. The play's central figure, a sympathetically drawn Jewish real estate speculator who is called Abraham in the novel, appears without a name in the play. Instead, Fassbinder, employing an anti-Semitic stereotype, calls him the "Rich Jew" in his published script.[34] The play was hastily written, a comic-strip tirade of hatred from the perspective of prostitutes and pimps, triggered by the ruinous redevelopment of the Frankfurt West End. "And the city turns us into living corpses, horror figures without an adequate chamber, subway people with streets which poison us,"[35] one of the prostitutes says. Fassbinder intended his play to be an indictment of the city fathers who use and exploit the figure of the "Rich Jew" for their own purposes. The Jew in fact serves the corrupt politicians as a shield, because "today, you can't say anything against the Jews"—an insidious anti-Semitic statement in itself, as Adorno had already pointed out in 1964.[36] Fassbinder thematizes the cynical instrumentalization of the problematic relationship between Jewish and non-Jewish Germans by letting his characters make statements that are clearly anti-Semitic—and meant to be that way because they are supposed to define (and implicitly criticize) the dramatic character. The utterance of anti-Semitic stereotypes by a fictional character in a play is obviously used to portray him or her as anti-Semitic; it can never mean that Fassbinder identified with everything his characters say. Still, to hear anti-Semitic language used on a German stage in the 1970s—no matter if it is Fassbinder's or a stage character's thoughts that are expressed—was shocking and justifiably called for a reaction. The danger that the play might confirm still existing anti-Semitic prejudices or create new "misunderstandings" could not be ruled out.[37] "I do not think that Fassbinder was an anti-Semite," Henryk M. Broder argues, "but I am sure that his play served as a catalyst for plenty of anti-Semitic reactions."[38] In 1976 the city of Frankfurt denied funds for the production of the play and was relieved when Fassbinder consequently resigned from his position as the controversial director of the Theater am Turm, which he had held for less than a year. The public storm of protest broke when the printed text was published by Suhrkamp early in 1976.[39] An article by Helmut Schmitz in the *Frankfurter Rundschau* of March 12 pointed out the play's anti-Semitic tendencies. A week later, Joachim Fest took up the matter and wrote a vitriolic attack on Fassbinder's play in the *Frankfurter Allgemeine Zeitung,* calling it a prime example of leftist fascism and anti-Semitism.[40] In the same week the publisher stopped distribution of the play in order to avoid "misunderstandings." Siegfried Unseld, director of the Suhrkamp Publishing House, justified the decision as follows:

> The charge that the author is anti-Semitic and a leftist fascist cannot be maintained; it is unfounded and must be rejected. Like Fassbinder, we believe that we must discuss how certain groups in Frankfurt, consisting of Jewish groups and individuals, were able to change the city to the disadvantage of its citizens and what role the city government played in these events. But reader reactions show us that the text of this play is serving less the investigation of the state of affairs than the release of undesirable emotions. In fact the play can create misunderstandings for those who did not experience this period of German history. The play

quite correctly attacks a taboo. But Fassbinder's undifferentiated rough-hewn style does not avoid the danger of reproducing dangerous clichés for a public burdened by German history, clichés which the play and its author wish to oppose.[41]

Considerations of "a public burdened by German history" came to the fore again in 1977, when two similar projects by Fassbinder were rejected. Plans to film Zwerenz's *The Earth Is as Inhabitable as the Moon* failed because of the objections of the Project Commission of the Film Subsidy Board (Filmförderungsanstalt). And a planned ten-part television series based on Gustav Freytag's novel *Soll und Haben* (*Debit and Credit*), a projected critical history of the nineteenth-century German bourgeoisie, raised objections among German media officials and was blocked despite a year's preliminary work. In both cases, suspicions arose that Fassbinder was using, as he had in his play, figures and motifs that could be interpreted as anti-Semitic.[42] How can Fassbinder's relentless obsession with this topic be explained?

In Freytag's infamous anti-Semitic novel *Debit and Credit,* Fassbinder thought he had found the roots not only of National Socialist ideology but also of the social order of the Federal Republic. In addition, Freytag's style offered the kind of lurid appeal and melodramatic pathos that would be effective on film. In March 1977 Fassbinder wrote an article for *Die Zeit* describing this project as part of his coming to terms with the prehistory of the Nazi period: "It is precisely the sordid parts of *Soll und Haben*—the political consciousness of its author that seems false to us, which if it didn't produce the horrors to come, at least it covered them up literarily, and with rather slight literary ambitions at that—which force us to come to terms in one of the most important ways possible with our stories and our history, with the nineteenth century, our social ancestors and ourselves. The film, with the help of television, is capable of accomplishing this."[43]

In Fassbinder's view, *Debit and Credit* tells how the bourgeoisie of the mid-nineteenth century, after the failed revolution of 1848, developed not only virtues like industry and respectability but also values inextricably bound to the "German character," so that the German bourgeoisie constantly had to define itself "in relation to the proletariat and the nobility at home, in relation to everything foreign abroad, and especially in relation to a world view of objectivity, tolerance, and humanity, which was denounced as Jewish. The values attributed to the 'German character' found their way without difficulty into the National Socialist ideology of the Third Reich, but— and that is the decisive reason compelling us to come to terms with this novel—they have also survived in today's society."[44] Fassbinder's goal in his planned television series was an archaeology of German bourgeois ideology, which he held responsible for producing anti-Semitism as well as the dictatorship of the Third Reich, and which he saw—and here he violated a taboo—as continuing right up to the present. He wanted, in other words, to bring *Debit and Credit* up to date.

Fassbinder's project would have had to illuminate and probe Freytag's unquestionably anti-Semitic motifs in terms of their origin and consequences. But since film must *show* things, there was clearly a danger that, for instance, staged scenes of ghetto life might unintentionally contribute to the perpetuation of anti-Semitic stereotypes. That was the view of Friedrich-Wilhelm von Sell, director of the West German network WDR, who claimed in 1977 that using Freytag's novel to "come to terms with the historical phenomena of anti-Semitism and anti-Slavism is subject to too many risks and misunderstandings."[45] His reservations led to a protest by more than thirty German filmmakers, including Volker Schlöndorff, Peter Lilienthal, and Wolfgang Staudte.[46] Fassbinder was embittered. He believed that with this novel as a starting point, he could "present the entire history of the German bourgeoisie from the middle of the last century to the outbreak of National Socialism—and do the exact opposite of what Joachim Fest did in his Hitler film, which is terribly reactionary and really only the attempt of a bourgeois to free himself of guilt."[47] It seemed especially ironic that it was Joachim Fest who chastised Fassbinder for being an anti-Semite.[48] Fest's film, *Hitler: A Career,* had been publicly criticized for condensing the persecution and annihilation of the Jews by the Nazis to 2½ minutes in a two and one-half hour long film. Fassbinder responded:

> Calling me an anti-Semite is just an excuse, because what I wanted to show is how anti-Semitism comes into being. It may be that Freytag's novel is anti-Semitic, but that very fact makes it useful for a description of anti-Semitism—and Freytag is certainly not anti-Semitic in his descrip-

tion of life in the ghetto and the hopeless situation of the Jews, in which they had to behave in a negative way in order to survive. The best way to describe the oppression of a minority is to show what errors and misdeeds a minority is forced into as a result of that oppression.[49]

Fassbinder's complicated logic—"A film of *Soll und Haben* will be historically 'correct' when it proves false what Freytag, his figures, and his readers thought was 'correct'"[50]—demands a dialectically schooled viewer who would not blame the Jewish population for any "misdeeds" that would have to be shown, but rather would see them as the doings of the true guilty party, the German tormentors. Freytag's novel abounds with the anti-Semitic stereotypes that have been passed down through centuries and are part of a literary tradition. Fassbinder wanted to defuse those stereotypes by historicizing them and subjecting them to a dialectical process. Freytag's anti-Semitism itself would have become an object of investigation: the Jews were to appear in his film as an "ostracized group that cannot behave differently because it is not permitted to."[51] The Jews were granted, for instance, the "right" to be moneylenders, an occupation that ran counter to the bourgeois code of honor; for that reason, according to Fassbinder, they were hated. He continues:

> The bourgeoisie needed the Jews in order to stop despising its own atti-
> tudes, to be able to feel proud, important and strong. The final result of
> such subconscious self-hatred was the mass annihilation of the Jews in
> the Third Reich. It was really an attempt to weed out what people didn't
> want to acknowledge in themselves. This relationship means that in some
> way the history of the Germans and the Jews is linked for all time, not
> just during the period from 1933 to 1945. Something like a new original
> sin will be passed on to people who are born and live in Germany, a sin
> that is not the less weighty because the sons of the murderers now wash
> their hands in innocence.[52]

Fassbinder's main concern is the illumination of the relationship between "bourgeois ideology" and recent German history. At issue is the "guilt remaining in the subconscious" and the "danger of a renewed perversion of bourgeois ideology." Fassbinder wants to pierce the heart of German ideology, not only because it created the conditions that made murderous anti-Semitism possible, but also because, in his view, the soil that nourished anti-Semitism is still fertile. He sees continuities where others see rupture; he makes the system of bourgeois values itself responsible for the crimes of National Socialism. Brecht once said that fascism is "the fruit of all the centuries";[53] similarly for Fassbinder, anti-Semitism has roots that reach back for centuries.

Although Fassbinder speaks about "guilt remaining in the subconscious" and a "new original sin" with respect to the crimes of the Third Reich, he repeatedly makes use of old anti-Semitic narrative patterns and visual motifs in what he intends as a radical critique of anti-Semitism. This is not only the case in his play *Garbage, the City and Death*, which was made into a film in 1976 by Daniel Schmid, a friend of Fassbinder's, in a revised version under the title *Schatten der Engel* (*Shadow of Angels*), with Fassbinder playing the lead;[54] it is also, and especially, true in his later films, in *Veronika Voss, In A Year with Thirteen Moons,* and most clearly *Lili Marleen*, a film that Anni Goldmann in *Le Monde* polemically compared with Veit Harlan's *Jud Süss*, the well-known anti-Semitic propaganda film of 1940.[55] In these films the Jewish characters do not appear as oppressed victims; nor do they appear as caricatures of perfidy and immorality, as in *Der Stürmer*, the anti-Semitic Nazi periodical. Instead they are shown as privileged intellectuals or affluent businessmen who feel superior to the Germans. "The taboo," Gertrud Koch writes in her essay on the Jewish figures in Fassbinder's films, "the law forbidding contact, the shutting out from the everyday consciousness, can all be located in Fassbinder's Jews: his own coldness and distance is projected onto the Jews as an intrinsic quality. They are the ones who are untouchable, cold, aloof, unapproachable, arrogant, taking themselves for something better."[56] The victim's suffering is repressed. Instead, Koch sees Fassbinder's Jewish figures in the ambivalent position of being "judges over life and death."[57] Fassbinder aggressively turns the feelings of inhibition, guilt, and helpless shame, which the postwar generation must have felt (and still feels) in the face of the genocide their parents' generation organized, against those who gave rise to those feelings. He directs these emotions not only against the parents, the "Auschwitz generation," but against the victims as well, who seem—in his perverse logic—also responsible for the suffering that German history has caused him. In his play, one character says: "The Jew is guilty because he makes us guilty by simply being there."[58]

Fassbinder set himself the task of showing German Jewry not, as he put it, "philo-Semitically," as noble victims, since philo-Semi-tism—and here he follows Robert Neumann—is nothing more than anti-Semitism in reverse.[59] His provocative and, as usual with Fass-binder, radically spontaneous opposition to this philo-Semitism com-pletely disregarded the potential consequences and effects of his pro-vocative stance in a concrete historical setting. Yet the reaction to his well-publicized Frankfurt play must have made him aware that he was in danger of being misunderstood either as someone who unknowingly repeats anti-Semitic stereotypes or as someone who knowingly elicits anti-Semitic sentiments for the sake of deconstruct-ing them. It is a questionable tactic, and Fassbinder may have known the thin line he was walking when he specified in his will that the play could be premiered only in Frankfurt or New York.[60] However one interprets this strange clause, it is evidence, along with the ad-versarial stances taken with respect to Fassbinder in the debate on anti-Semitism that has gone on since 1976, of just how taboo-laden the post-Auschwitz "negative symbiosis" between Jews and Germans is,[61] how deeply the wound of Auschwitz festers not only in Fassbin-der's awareness but in that of his entire generation.[62]

In a letter of 1946 to Karl Jaspers, Hannah Arendt wrote that the guilt Germans had placed upon themselves for the mass murders at Auschwitz could not be assuaged through the legal process, because there were no punishments appropriate for such monstrous crimes. This guilt, she wrote, "transcends and crushes any system of law . . . There is no human, political way to deal with a guilt that is beyond crime and an innocence that is beyond good or virtue."[63] To translate this guilt onto film would exceed the limits of what can be presented, unless one proceeds as Herbert Achternbusch did in his film *Das letzte Loch* (*The Last Hole*, 1981), staging the incomprehensible as a grotesque farce and thus violating all the "rules" of traditional filmmaking (and of conventional decorum). His protagonist, Nil, insists on personally atoning for the murder of the Jews. His doctor gives him a prescription: for each murder, for each one of the six million dead, he is to drink one glass of whiskey in order to forget. The absurd calculation serves to symbolize the fact that German guilt can neither be forgotten nor cured. The surreal nature of the pre-scription presents the work of mourning as a helpless, hopeless, futile gesture.[64] This enigmatic film, vacillating between the grotesque and the melodramatic, ends with Nil's suicide. Full of revulsion toward

Germany as the "land of mass murderers," he plunges into the Sicilian volcano of Stromboli, as Empedocles once did, with these words: "I am committing suicide because then I will belong to the charnel house of the victims. I do not want to belong to the charnel house of the self-righteous Germans."[65]

Fassbinder no less than Achternbusch suffered because of Germany. His suffering moved him to work on the German past and propelled his work forward. In mid-1977, Fassbinder contemplated emigration to Paris, New York, or Hollywood. Tabloids and foreign news magazines reported his plans in detail, and a parliamentary deputy of the Christian Democratic Party even demanded that the government "take a position on the accusations made by film director Rainer Werner Fassbinder . . . who explained his move to the United States in terms of increasing censorship and 'less freedom' in the Federal Republic."[66] But Fassbinder abandoned those plans the very same year. He realized that only in his own country could he hold up a mirror to its faults and follies; he did not know any other country well enough, and no other country had done so much to shape him. Like Peter Schneider's Lenz, he decided to "stay here." In October 1980, an interviewer asked Fassbinder whether he was not acting like his own character Lili Marleen, the artist who did not care about the source of her money, even if it came from Hitler. Fassbinder responded: "I would say that I too live in a state whose structure I reject. Even though God knows the FRG is not comparable to Hitler's Reich. And although I can imagine a different government, this is where I do my business."[67] This antagonism toward the state is a feature in all of Fassbinder's films; his historical films especially are "counter-analyses"[68] of the present order in the Federal Republic.

The End of Utopia

The disaster is related to forgetfulness—forgetfulness with memory, the motionless retreat of what has not been treated.

MAURICE BLANCHOT

The career of Maria Braun was read, especially abroad, as an allegory of the Federal Republic during the economic miracle. As Jean de Baroncelli wrote in *Le Monde*: "The fate of the heroine actually parallels, point for point, the fate of Germany, conquered and reconstructed. Maria Braun not only symbolizes Germany; in Fassbinder's eyes she obviously 'is' Germany. What has become of Maria, what has become of Germany? In cynical and horrid images, Fassbinder gives the answer: a creature dressed in obviously expensive clothes that has lost its soul; a 'winner' whose head has been turned by fortune and who has courted disaster."[69] Fassbinder supports this reading by linking the history of Germany to Maria Braun's own story at the end of the film. Just as Maria Braun's utopia was betrayed, the film implies, the German nation was betrayed when Adenauer made secret deals to rearm Germany despite the painful memories of militarism and war.

As the private story of Maria Braun comes to a melodramatic end in a gas explosion, the public sphere intrudes in a live radio broadcast of the 1954 world soccer championship finals between West Germany and Hungary. The escape from private history—in the original screenplay by a conscious murder and suicide, more ambivalently in the film by a half-conscious accident—is ironically undercut by the West German team's unexpected victory. The last seven minutes of the match coincide exactly with the last seven minutes of the life of Maria and Hermann Braun. For seven minutes narrative and narrated time, fictional and "real" time are identical. The original sound recording of the sports broadcast accompanies, and at times drowns out, the fictional denouement: the reunion of Hermann and Maria Braun and the reading of Oswald's will. The rejoicing at the goal that decides the match blends into the noise of the explosion. As the final whistle blows, Herbert Zimmermann, the well-known sports announcer, screams hysterically: "Time's up! Time's up! Germany is world champion!" (Weltmeister—literally translated, "master of the world"), while the villa and its inhabitants go up in flames. The private story, as Fassbinder sees it, is over, but not the public one. One person's utopia disappears in rubble and ashes, but the nation "is somebody" again. The hopes for a radical new beginning were buried with the rise of Germany from the pariah of 1945 to the proud victor and "world champion" of 1954. The chances for utopia were lost.

The last images of the film are projected over the sounds of the soccer broadcast and the explosion. They consist of full-screen black-and-white negative portraits of West Germany's chancellors, projected, like still pictures in a slide show, one after the other, without commentary: Konrad Adenauer, Ludwig Erhard, Kurt Georg Kiesinger, and Helmut Schmidt, during whose term of office the film was made. This gallery of photo-portraits catapults us out of the fictional space. The flagrant anachronism suddenly confronts the viewer with the specific time when the film was made. The black-and-white negative still of Schmidt then changes to a positive; the change dates the fictional events, openly identifying the narrative as the construct of a later era. From the perspective of Helmut Schmidt's chancellorship (1974–1982), Fassbinder looks back on the first ten years of the Federal Republic, the period of rapid economic and military reconstruction in West Germany. By the late seventies the price of this "reconstruction" had become apparent.

The pictures at the end lead the viewer back to the very first image of the film: a framed painting of Hitler that falls off the wall during a bomb raid and crashes to the floor. The film itself is thus framed by pictures of German chancellors, suggesting some sort of continuity between Hitler and the postwar chancellors of the Federal Republic—an allusion that is more irritating than provocative because of its unhistorical superficiality. The picture of Willy Brandt, chancellor between 1969 and 1974 and the first Social Democratic chancellor since the founding of the Federal Republic, is pointedly absent from the gallery of portraits. Asked why Brandt had been omitted, Fassbinder answered: "I have the feeling that Willy Brandt's time was a hiatus, that Brandt tended to encourage self-questioning . . . leaving basic features of the government open to criticism. I just have the feeling that (what Brandt did) was something that not everyone agreed with. I see democracy as something that works like a kaleidoscope, that doesn't mean permanent revolution but rather permanent movement, the permanent questioning of premises by every generation."[70]

The idealization of Willy Brandt (who had emigrated during the Nazi era) goes back to Fassbinder's central experience, the protest movement of the mid- and late sixties. Intellectual and cultural life was strongly politicized at that time—Günter Grass, for example, campaigned extensively for the Social Democratic Party—and major reforms seemed imminent. The antifascist resistance fighter Willy Brandt stood in the eyes of Fassbinder and his generation as a symbol of this new direction in German politics, and he became the rallying point of a younger generation's hopes. The Great Coalition of December 1966, formed when Fassbinder had just turned twenty-one, had created the first political crisis of postwar West Germany because it eliminated any parliamentary opposition. The intellectuals felt called upon to assume this role outside of parliament. Hans Magnus Enzensberger warned: "The end of the second German democracy is in sight."[71] He feared that the Great Coalition also signaled the end of German literature as an oppositional, educational institution "whose goal it has been since 1945 to balance out the structural flaws of the Federal Republic with its poor powers."[72] But this opposition, consisting, in Enzensberger's self-critical view, of "belated liberals, good Social Democrats, moralists, socialists without clear ideas, antifascists without a plan for the future," no longer sufficed in 1968. "In fact, what we now need," Enzensberger wrote, "is not communism but revolution. The political system of the Federal Republic is beyond repair."[73] Fassbinder adopted this uncompromising attitude toward the Federal Republic, and, in principle, it remained his attitude for the next fifteen years. The events that occurred after 1968—the passage of the state emergency laws (under Willy Brandt), the persecution of terrorist sympathizers, the job blacklisting, and the constant attacks on Fassbinder in the Springer press—only strengthened this conviction.

Fassbinder was one of the very few among the 1968 generation to maintain his resolute radical utopianism throughout the seventies. In March 1982, three months before his death, he described himself as "a romantic anarchist."[74] For Fassbinder, anarchy meant radical independence from parties, leftist and rightist philosophies, and personal or political ties. There is an inherent utopianism in his belief that unlimited individual and national freedom could be the product of democracy correctly understood. "With the concrete utopia of anarchy in my head," he considered himself an "extreme representative of democracy":

> It's hardly permissible to say that today, that part about anarchy, because we've learned through the media that anarchy and terrorism are synonymous. But on the one hand there is the utopian idea of a nation without hierarchies, without anxieties, without aggressions, and on the other hand a concrete social situation in which utopian ideas are suppressed. A few people flipped out, understandably, and a certain dominant class wanted that, maybe on an unconscious level, in order to define itself more concretely.[75]

In his film *Die dritte Generation* (*The Third Generation,* 1979), Fassbinder settles accounts with the prevailing terrorism: terrorists of the third generation, he feels, were making common cause with the surveillance and security industries. The film demonstrates that there was little ideological difference between leftist terrorists and the rightist state. The terrorists of the first generation, Meinhof and Baader and Ensslin, had represented to him political content and an idealist utopia that had gone awry; those motives were now missing. *The Third Generation* is a film about the cynicism of modern terrorism and its disregard of human life. The film itself becomes an assault; its deafeningly aggressive soundtrack (constant radio announcements are layered over the dialogue) and its disorienting cuts (which serve to erase distinctions between terrorists and victims, pursuers and pursued) frustrate the viewer in the extreme.[76] Utopia no longer appears as even a vague possibility.

The exhaustion of utopian energies, which Jürgen Habermas considers a sign of the seventies, left its mark on Fassbinder's late films as well. Habermas writes: "Today it seems that utopian energies have been fully consumed, as if they had withdrawn from historical thinking. The horizon of the future has shrunk and, as a consequence, the spirit of the times, as well as its politics, has changed utterly. The future has negative connotations."[77] The loss of Maria Braun's private utopia, which confronts her as a shock at the end of the film, corresponds to the loss of the great utopian designs in the public sphere of the late seventies, when the film was made. More than other filmmakers of the time, Fassbinder reflects the dissolution of the dreams of 1968. In December 1977, after *Germany in Autumn* and just before filming began on *Maria Braun,* he was asked by an interviewer where he got the strength to keep on working. He answered:

> From utopia, the concrete longing for this utopia. If this longing is driven out of me, I will not do anything else; that's why as a creative person I have the feeling of being murdered in Germany, if you would please not mistake that for paranoia. I believe this recent witch-hunt, which, I think, is just the tip of the iceberg, was staged in order to destroy individual utopias. That means also to let my fears and my feelings of guilt become overpowering. If it comes to the point where my fears are greater than my longing for something beautiful, then I'll quit. And not just quit working.[78]

"You'll quit living?" he was asked. "Yes, of course. There's no reason to live without a goal."[79]

The total destruction of all the "bourgeois illusions" that we see at the end of *Maria Braun* is reminiscent of the final sequence of *Zabriskie Point* (1969). Antonioni's film about the sixties ends with the hallucinatory explosion of a nouveau-riche villa, repeated several times in slow motion. These radical endings in both films betray a helpless aggression against the "system" as a whole: what can no longer be saved should be blown up. In the negative utopia of *Maria Braun*, the explosion that occurs in 1954, at the beginning of West German rearmament, recreates the landscape of ruins of 1945. The idea of a "Zero Hour" proved illusory; the film begins and ends with an explosion. Nothing had changed. Germany's unique chance for a radically new beginning in 1945, was, in Fassbinder's view, missed once and for all. Instead, the old capitalist ideas of property and greed and all the traditional bourgeois values were restored. The will to reform had all too soon exhausted itself.

In *Lola*, the second part of his FRG Trilogy, Fassbinder chooses a resigned rather than a violent end. The city planner, who initially exhibits moral and personal integrity, becomes vulnerable to black-mail through his love for a woman. As a consequence he gets more and more deeply implicated in the already corrupt politics of the city. But his awareness of the corruption does not lead to an explosion at the end. He accommodates himself, is "realistic," and thus becomes an accomplice.

The end of the third film in the trilogy is equally cynical and resigned. *Veronika Voss* is the story of a drug-addicted film star from the old UFA days who wallows in her memories. She is murdered, and the journalist who covers the story is led deeper and deeper into the morass of the city. He abandons his investigation at the end when he recognizes that the guilty doctor is protected by high officials, including the police. The film's ending implies that it is useless to try to expose the corruption in private and public affairs that Fassbinder considered typical of the fifties. As in *Lola*, there is no explosion of stored-up hatred of the "system"; instead the characters carry on, very much aware of inescapable moral corruption.

In principle the story in *Maria Braun* also continues after the violent exit of the protagonists. At the very moment when the explosion ends the lives of the private individuals, the rise of Germany as "world champion" begins. "We're somebody again," the Germans said proudly during the reconstruction period. This famous slogan is indicative of precisely the attitude of complacency and amnesia that Fassbinder wanted to destroy—a terrorist act that included self-destruction.

4

IN SEARCH OF GERMANY

Alexander Kluge's *The Patriot*

"Given this history, being a patriot is something of a contradiction."
—Hannelore Hoger in *The Patriot*

For the people, history is and remains a collection of stories. It is what people can remember and what is worth being told again and again: a retelling. The tradition flinches at no legend, triviality, or error, provided it has some connection with the battles of the past. Hence the notorious impotence of facts in the face of colorful pictures and sensational stories.

HANS MAGNUS ENZENSBERGER

When crises occur, one searches the depths of one's memory to discover some vestige of the past, not the past of the individual, faltering and ephemeral, but rather that of the community, which, though left behind, nonetheless represents that which is permanent and lasting.

SAUL FRIEDLÄNDER

If we want to approach our buried past, we have to go about it in the manner of someone who is digging.

WALTER BENJAMIN

Nomadic History

"We must begin to work on our history. I mean something very concrete by that; we could even start by telling each other stories."[1] Alexander Kluge made this statement in his Fontane Prize acceptance speech in September 1979; it announced a program that he himself wanted to fulfill in his film *Die Patriotin* (*The Patriot*), which premiered in the same month.[2] Although the original conception of the film goes back to the fall of 1977,[3] it had lost none of its relevance two years later. On the contrary, at the beginning of 1979 the American television series *Holocaust* had reignited interest in German history. And a film entitled *The Patriot* seemed to answer those critics of *Holocaust* who wanted German history to be represented not by American television specials but by *German* films. Kluge had indeed intended to make a German film about German history, and to counter *Holocaust* in every respect. In its treatment of history as well as in its way of dealing with stories and images, *The Patriot* differed radically not only from the Hollywood television series but also from the classical narrative cinema. Kluge's aversion to the conventional narrative film, apparent since his first feature film of 1966, *Abschied von gestern* (*Yesterday Girl*), shaped *The Patriot* as well.

In fact, none of Kluge's films (with very few exceptions) tells a continuous, coherent story. Like the Austrian novelist Robert Musil (and later the postmodernist Jean-François Lyotard),[4] Kluge relinquishes the "narrative thread" that holds all the strands together in a logical order. In his film, fragments of several stories seem to lie around, isolated parts of different puzzles. It is up to the viewer to piece together the various parts, a process that liberates the imagination but also demands considerable associative aplomb and a willingness on the part of the viewer to collaborate in the construction of meaning. Unlike *Holocaust* and innumerable other conventional history films, Kluge's films do not reconstruct the past as a backdrop for stories of love and suffering; nor do they relate tales and historical events in the past tense. Instead, his films deal with history from the perspective of the present, shedding new light not only on the past (as a prelude to the present) but also on the present itself in its historical dimension.

Ferreting out this dimension calls for the strength of memory as well as an investigative energy. In *The Patriot,* Kluge employs the device of a fictional character who is involved in exploring and researching German history.[5] Hannelore Hoger, a well-known stage actress, plays Gabi Teichert, a Hessian history teacher who harbors an obsession with German history that goes far beyond her official responsibilities.[6] As an amateur archaeologist, she searches for traces and vestiges of the German past. In her expeditions through two thousand years of history, she digs up so many contradictory things that she can no longer make sense of them. History becomes a mere jumble to her. The more she grows suspicious of the linear, radically reductionist explanations of history found in schoolbooks, the more she questions a job that calls on her to teach German history in neat 45-minute segments. When Gabi Teichert shows interest, for instance, in the hundreds of little everyday stories that have been excluded by the "official" historiography, she deals with German history in the spirit of Kluge's project: "And what else is the history of a country but the vastest narrative surface of all? Not *one* story but *many* stories."[7]

Alexander Kluge himself is many things: a writer as well as a filmmaker who has won many prizes; moving spirit and signatory of the Oberhausen Manifesto of 1962; a tireless and skillful strategist, promulgator, and activist of the New German Cinema; a lawyer, teacher, scholar (mostly in collaboration with the philosopher Oskar Negt), media theorist, and essayist. Born in 1932, he belongs to a generation that felt the impact of German history more strongly than succeeding generations. Other members of this generation include the novelists Günter Grass and Martin Walser (both born in 1927), the poet, playwright, and essayist Hans Magnus Enzensberger (born in 1929), the novelist and essayist Christa Wolf (born in 1929), the playwright Rolf Hochhuth (born in 1931), the filmmaker Edgar Reitz (born in 1932), the novelist Uwe Johnson (born in 1934), and the filmmaker Hans Jürgen Syberberg (born in 1935). This generation grew up under Hitler and lived through the Third Reich and the war as children and adolescents. They were old enough to experience National Socialism in school, if not at home, but too young to be actively involved in the regime of terror and to be guilty themselves.[8] But all of them were victims of the war. At age thirteen, at the very end of the war in April 1945, Kluge watched American bombers attack his hometown and witnessed the bombardment and destruction of his parents' house in Halberstadt.[9] He barely escaped death himself. The image of the burning city must have engraved itself indelibly on his consciousness; he returns obsessively to the motif of the individual's helplessness in the face of "attacks from above" in almost all of his works.

Kluge's first literary works, the collection of stories entitled *Lebensläufe* (*Curricula Vitae,* 1962) and the documentary description of the German defeat at Stalingrad, *Schlachtbeschreibung* (*Description of a Battle,* 1964), can be seen as a rehearsal of the main theme that he explored continuously in text, image, and theory over the subsequent two decades: private lives in collision with history writ large, for which war is a symbol. Kluge's first feature film, *Abschied von gestern* (*Farewell to Yesterday,* in English known under the title *Yesterday Girl,* 1965/66) is based on one of the stories published in Kluge's 1962 collection. It deals with the life of the young woman Anita G., daughter of Jewish parents, who leaves the German Democratic Republic in 1957 for the Federal Republic. We see her as she wanders, suitcase and purse in hand, from job to job, from lover to lover, never finding a foothold in West German society. Her past makes it impossible for her to fit in. The camera tracks her pointless journeys, exploring the reality of West Germany in the late 1950s with a critical eye—the calcified conditions in the political and educational institutions and in daily life as well as the patriarchal terms of interpersonal relations. Anita's role as outsider makes her a sharp observer of the dominant mentality, a seismograph of West German society under Adenauer.[10] Fifteen years later Kluge used a similar dramatic structure in *The Patriot*. An independent and impulsive woman, a teacher who thinks of herself as a patriot and likes to teach German history in its "patriotic version" (59),[11] Gabi Teichert becomes an outsider by virtue of her independent spirit and stubbornness. From that position she is able to see West German society, particularly its educational system, in a critical light. The more deeply she digs in search of the roots of German history, the more alienated she becomes from her colleagues, her students, and their parents. She is accused of being disorganized, undisciplined, and insubordinate. The viewer recognizes all this as the necessary consequence of her serious preoccupation with German history.

A few short scenes showing Gabi Teichert digging with a spade for German history first appeared in *Germany in Autumn*. These scenes recur in *The Patriot,* where digging for Germany's buried history serves as the film's central metaphor. Kluge once again took the figurative phrase "digging for the treasures of the past" literally, illustrating it through the concrete image of Gabi Teichert digging into the frozen earth.[12] What results is a kind of image-pun in the tradition of Luis Buñuel or Karl Valentin, which has the effect of distancing the audience. The viewer is obviously asked to respond to the eccentric actions of Gabi Teichert not with empathy, but with a critical, ironically detached skepticism. Similarly, when she wants to translate the knowledge contained in thick historical tomes into sensory experience, the film shows her taking apart and "working on" history books with saws, drills, and hammers and dissolving the pages in orange juice in order to swallow them. She thus "bores her way into history," she "makes history a part of herself," she "digests" it, and so on—all figures of speech which, translated from their Heideggerian literal meaning, generate surrealistic dream images. As an amateur archaeologist, she participates in illegal excavations at the city wall in the hopes of finding prehistoric everyday objects in order to "grasp" (*be-greifen*) the past; only when she can touch it does she understand it sensually.

Gabi Teichert collects fragments of the German past, a "form of practical remembering," as Walter Benjamin once put it.[13] Like the piles of shards gathered by archaeologists, her finds are amassed before her: images (illustrations and documentary film clips) of political history from Napoleon to Stalingrad; curiosities from the history of everyday life, ranging from the wish list of twelfth-century peasants to the price of geese in Silesia in 1914; references to the history of the imagination, from Grimms' fairy tales to comic strips; a plethora of anecdotes and life stories; quotations from the history of music, painting, and film. The accumulation of heterogeneous fragments, typical of the postmodern understanding of history, resists all attempts at systematization.[14] The multifarious, the marginal, and the idiosyncratic all sabotage general categories of order. The film takes a stand against abstraction: Gabi Teichert's "greatest difficulty," according to Kluge, is that she appears to be unable to "learn history from the small print of thick books."[15] Gabi Teichert's conception of history, based on sensory experience, the joy of discovery, and active personal involvement, underlies the whole film. *The Patriot* is itself, as a film, an illustration of a practical, robust attitude toward history.

Kluge's technique for dealing with history is both nomadic and analytic. His plan to scout unsystematically through two thousand years of German history runs counter to the traditional linear, chronological approach that characterizes historical narratives. Like Brecht in his historical novel, *The Business Affairs of Mr. Caesar,* Kluge draws a sharp line between past and present; only if the reconstruction of the past is itself made the object of inquiry can the past be seen in a critical light.[16] By recognizing the past as something foreign, something to be actively searched for and selectively reconstituted in the present, he is able to lift events, persons, texts, and images from their historical contexts and to use them as quotations. Benjamin's maxim, "Writing history means quoting history,"[17] describes Kluge's approach exactly.

The numerous anecdotal life stories embedded in the fictional space of *The Patriot* seem like case studies from which lessons can be drawn for the present. The experimental arrangement is seldom so clearly emphasized as in the sequence introduced by the written title, "The Relation of a Love Story to History." After a short montage of documentary photographs from fascist Italy of the 1930s, we see a long, static shot of a newlywed couple observing each other silently in front of a mirror. The voice-over gives us details: they are a German officer named Fred Tacke and his wife Hildegard, née Gartmann, who happen to be honeymooning in Rome in August 1939 shortly before the outbreak of World War II. Suddenly the scene shifts to the pair frantically packing their suitcases and leaving the room. The abrupt cut is explained by the voice-over: "September 1. He has to join his regiment" (111). These scenes are followed by shots of Tacke's activities at the front and of his wife at home waiting. Then the off-screen voice comments on a photograph which shows an elderly couple: "In 1953 Tacke returns from Russia, where he was a prisoner of war. Now the two are supposed to continue the love story of August 1939" (112). The story, radically reduced to major plot reversals, demonstrates to the viewer the irreconcilable antagonism between personal and public history, between subjective happiness and the demands of the state. The destruction of private life by politics—the classic conflict between private and public history—is compressed into a 10-minute miniature film within the film. It is a conflict that recurs as the central narrative in several other films from this period: in Helma Sanders-Brahms's *Germany, Pale Mother* as well as in Fassbinder's *The Marriage of Maria Braun*.

The Patriot presents German history not only from the perspective of the living but from that of the dead as well: as a patriot, Gabi Teichert takes an "interest in all the dead of the Reich" (50). An off-camera voice speaks in the name of those who died for Germany. In another of Kluge's bizarre conceits, the voice identifies itself as the knee of a certain Corporal Wieland, who fell at Stalingrad on January 29, 1943. The image comes from Christian Morgenstern's grotesque poem, "The Knee":

In war one time a man was shot,
They shot him through and through.
His knee alone was in one piece,
As if it were a holy relic.
Since then: a knee walks lonely through the world.
It's just a knee, that's all.

With the use of this image, Kluge has found a perspective that allows him to criticize the history of the living. "I must clear up once and for all," the voice-over says, accompanied by pictures of Stalingrad, "a fundamental error: that we dead are somehow dead. We are full of protest and energy. Who wants to die? We speed through history, examining it. How can I escape the history that will kill us all?" (58). Kluge focuses on the critical perspective of the dead on the living, because history, as Benjamin says, has always been written by the survivors, the victors: "*Even the dead* will not be safe from the enemy if he wins. And this enemy has not ceased being victorious."[18]

In terms of conventional narrative structure, the idea of having a knee represent the dead belongs to the realm of the fairy tale: it is odd, naive, silly. The knee, anatomically nothing more than a joint that makes movement possible, can in this context also be read literally, as a concrete image for the "between." It functions here as an allegory for montage and *Zusammenhang*— a central category for Kluge, which can be rendered only approximately as "seeing things in their interconnection."[19] Just as the knee links the upper and lower leg and is itself only the "articulation" between the two, the knee as commentator mediates between the past and the present, the dead and the living, memory and anticipation, the dream world of history and the waking world of the moment.

Gabi Teichert and the knee of the soldier who died at Stalingrad— both narrative roles of the implied author—assume an investigative attitude toward history, exemplifying the attitude of constant searching and questioning that the viewer is meant to adopt in relation to history. Because *The Patriot* gives the process of mediation the same weight it gives to what is mediated, it has an open, dialogic, discursive form, allowing viewers to test their own experiences against those offered by the film. The numerous breaks and "gaps" in this film imply and, indeed, demand viewers who are willing to fill in the blanks and draw connections between their stories/histories and the history seen on the screen.

The Constructivist Method

> The method of this work: literary montage. I have nothing to say. Only something to show. I will not appropriate any ingenious formulations, will not pilfer anything of value, only the rags, the rubbish: I will not describe them, I will show them.
>
> WALTER BENJAMIN

Kluge's films erect dams to stem the flood of images. In one of his earliest essays, entitled "Die Utopie Film" (1964), he agrees with Adorno in his claim that the flow of film images naturally tends to hinder rather than to stimulate the critical faculties of the viewer:

> The film is aimed at mature and immature people. Even mature people cannot maintain the continuity of their thoughts and their critical attitude in the face of a film's shock effect. The film superimposes its own sequence of associations on theirs. Walter Benjamin says: We do not watch films in a concentrated frame of mind . . . The viewer will normally not assume a critical attitude toward a film, and it is also not appropriate to the film medium. The film must rather *anticipate* the critical attitude of the viewer and his right to be treated as an enlightened person.[20]

Kluge's awareness of the manipulative power and the magic spell of images, all too well known from the films of National Socialism, and his fear that viewers will yield without resistance to the seductions of visual pleasure caused him to take radical preventive measures. Compared to the Hollywood narrative cinema, his films seem consciously unfilmic. In order to enable, if not to force, the viewer to maintain the critical distance Kluge demands, his films systematically violate the conventions of representation established by traditional feature films. Kluge uses the film medium, but he resists its suggestive power. "I like to go to the movies; the only thing that bothers me is the picture on the screen," Theodor W. Adorno is supposed to have said to his student Alexander Kluge, exaggerating only slightly.[21] Kluge himself talks about the "annihilation of images" necessary to "move human beings."[22]

Like Godard, Kluge draws on Brecht's epic theater and demands that film become "literary": verbal elements (in the form of writing and commentary) are given the same importance as the visual ones. The words do not heighten the impression of reality created by the sequence of images, as is usually the case in the classical narrative film; language does not emerge "realistically" from the story. Instead, voice-over commentary, texts projected on the screen, and intertitles (as used in silent film) are juxtaposed with the film images in an openly "unrealistic" manner. This technique recalls Brecht's experiments at making the theater "literary" in the 1920s—attempts that in turn drew from the silent film and its mixture of images and written text. In his "Notes to the *Threepenny Opera*," Brecht writes:

> The screens on which the titles of each scene are projected are a primitive attempt at literarizing the theatre. This literarization of the theatre needs to be developed to the utmost degree, as in general does the literarizing of all public occasions.
> Literarizing entails punctuating "representation" with "formulation";

gives the theatre the possibility of making contact with other institutions for intellectual activities; but is bound to remain one-sided so long as the audience is taking no part in it and using it as a means of obtaining access to "higher things."

The orthodox playwright's objection to the titles is that the dramatist ought to say everything that has to be said in the action, that the text must express everything within its own confines. The corresponding attitude for the spectator is that he should not think about a subject, but within the confines of the subject. But this way of subordinating everything to a single idea, this passion for propelling the spectator along a single track where he can look neither right nor left, up nor down, is something that the new school of play-writing must reject. Footnotes, and the habit of turning back in order to check a point, need to be introduced into play-writing too.[23]

In *The Patriot,* representation is "punctuated" repeatedly by projected texts and intertitles, by still photographs or illustrations. These islands in the midst of the stream of images allow us to stop for a moment and reflect; they foil the temptation to be swept along by the continuous narrative flow. The juxtaposition of different kinds of sign systems—moving images, interposed written texts (aphorisms, short poems), and still pictures—also destroys the illusion that the film reflects some self-contained historical world "out there." Kluge's Brechtian approach to film emphasizes at all times that representation is a construct.

The voice-over commentary provides a counterpoint to the images and has the function of both engaging and distancing the viewer. It gives the viewer the sense that there is an authority present who has arranged the images and stories in a definite, often ironic way. The off-screen voice is Kluge's; here, as in most of his films, he makes comments about the images from outside the fictional space, even though he slips into different roles. This same voice introduces the pictorial material, summarizes it aphoristically, and sometimes communicates directly with the viewer about what is being shown; it even goes to the extreme of undermining its own omniscience: "At this point I wanted to say something more about the collapse of the army corps, but I forgot what I wanted to say" (176).

This dialogic relation between the commentator and the viewer results in irony; it also affects the relation of the viewer to Gabi Teichert. The voice-over describes in short, often dry and witty sentences what the protagonist is doing and why. During long stretches of the film, the disembodied *male* voice speaks for the female character; she, as a consequence, seems naive, often clownish, and child-like (not unlike Alice in Wonderland) in her inappropriate reactions and her literal misunderstandings.[24] Since the analytical off-camera voice offers a perspective beyond that of the characters—a perspective that cannot be perceived by them—the viewer can easily feel superior to the characters of the film. Even a viewer who is unaware that the voice is Kluge's could reasonably relate the off-screen voice to an authorial consciousness that selects the images, controls what is shown, tries out experimental arrangements, and tests new combinations. This running commentary, a didactic gesture which is sometimes parodied through exaggeration, creates a distance from the fictional space of the film and undercuts identification.

Kluge uses montage as a technique that allows him to link, through a quick cut, two images or sequences that at first glance seem unrelated, thereby producing new interconnections that are "realistic." In his *Ulmer Dramaturgien,* Kluge writes:

> If I conceive of realism as the knowledge of relationships, then I must provide a trope for what cannot be shown in the film, for what the camera cannot record. This trope consists in the contrast between two shots, which is only another way of saying montage. At issue here are the concrete relations between two images. Because of the relationship which develops between two shots, and to the degree that movement (the so-called cinematic) is generated between such shots, information is hidden in the cut which would not be contained in the shot itself. This means that montage has as its object something qualitatively quite different from raw material.[25]

Montage, according to Adorno the cornerstone of all modern art,[26] figured centrally in early film theory until the end of the silent era. The "dialectical" montages in the tradition of Eisenstein and the Russian film of the 1920s were particularly influential for a political conception of filmmaking in the Weimar Republic. Kluge places himself squarely in this tradition: "I wouldn't be making films if it weren't for the cinema of the 1920s, the silent era. Since I have been making films it has been in reference to this classical tradition."[27] It is a tradition that became obsolete with the arrival of "realistic" sound at the end of the twenties. The classical Hollywood cinema, from the early days of D. W. Griffith, had always resisted the use of conspicuous montage effects, which draw attention to the film's construction and fabrication;[28] self-conscious editing was consistently played down so that the spectator might retain the *illusion* of being witness to a self-contained, continuous action, instead of one spliced together on the cutting table. For the sake of a semblance of reality, editing had to become more and more invisible. Kluge, in contrast, does not believe in this self-effacing "semblance of reality," which suppresses the marks of enunciation in favor of a seemingly self-evident story that somehow unfolds all by itself.[29]

For Kluge, montage becomes a means of taking issue with the world around us, an approach that no longer yields truth simply through representation. "In montage," Ernst Bloch notes in his *Erbschaft dieser Zeit,* "the context of the old surface is destroyed, a new context is constructed. This is possible because the old context reveals itself more and more as appearance, as fragile, as simply a surface."[30] In this sense the principle of montage is a form of protest that disrupts old coordinates of meaning and establishes new ones: "One would have to perceive the subjective splinters (of the old meaning), collect them, and use them to reassemble a world centered around human values."[31] To perceive, collect, assemble: the constructivist principle offers a critical counter-history, demonstrating the possibility of an alternative organization ("assembly") of reality and its experience.

According to Kluge, reality can always be construed alternatively and be changed. His view contradicts the idea that circumstances have an inherent inevitability. He contrasts his "dramaturgy of *Zusammenhang,*" based on principles of montage, association, and multiple interconnections, with the "dramaturgy of inescapable tragedy," which characterizes nineteenth-century opera. In his view, a plot whose action points to a tragic outcome should be interrupted by a sudden change of perspective, like the one made possible by montage. He believes that the tragic literature of the nineteenth century should be rewritten in this way. In Bizet's *Carmen,* for instance, Kluge suggests that, seconds before Don José stabs Carmen, the prompter should intervene and say, "This situation calls for an immediate discussion."[32] The sudden unexpected shift of perspective would allow for distance and a possible alternative. According to Kluge, the constructivist principle of montage is prefigured in the works of the German realist writer Theodor Fontane: "Fontane is absolutely not in favor of inevitable tragedy ... He is never infatuated with the terror of real circumstances; instead, he always looks for ways out, and one reason for montage-technique, for the 'novel of multiple voices' is precisely this search for alternatives ... Seeing things in context [*Zusammenhang*] always provides an alternative, a way out."[33] In *The Patriot,* Gabi Teichert constantly searches for *Zusammenhänge,* for interconnections in German history. Perturbed by the putative inexorability of historical events and circumstances, she constructs alternative *Zusammenhänge* in her mind. Thus, for instance, in the case of Gerda Baethe, who was buried under bombs in 1944, she imagines that it probably would have taken the combined efforts of "seventy thousand teachers working for sixteen years" (148) to have possibly prevented Gerda Baethe's fate.

The playful manipulation of the course of history corresponds to the idea of film as a "time machine" that can alter (stretch, shorten, fragment) any faithfully recorded action through editing and montage. "In each of its stages, (1) during filming, (2) during editing, (3) during screening, film is a mechanical construction for the production of temporal sequences that do not exist in this form in society. It is a machine for producing time."[34] This "machine" translates historical time into film time and consequently frees it from all contingencies. As if to remind us of the difference between film time and real time, Kluge shows banks of clouds floating over Frankfurt in time-lapse photography, an effect (also used in the 1983 film *Koyaanisqatsi* by Godfrey Reggio and Philip Glass) that illustrates how temporal sequences can be manipulated on film.

The splintering and disintegration of the narrative continuum in *The Patriot* follow from Kluge's conviction that two thousand years of German history cannot be grasped from the single perspective of a psychological, causal story. Even an individual historical event like Stalingrad, for instance, exists only as a multitude of perspectives, a point already exemplified in Kluge's 1964 book about Stalingrad, *Schlachtbeschreibung.*[35] History in this view no longer unfolds as a neat, self-contained narrative; instead we find a gigantic collection of heterogeneous texts, images, life stories, songs, statistics, and anecdotes, a plethora of fragments and scraps without center and without internal coherence. As a "bricoleur,"[36] the author picks up fragments, selecting and assembling them. Here art is no longer the expression or confession of a creator but a technique based on reflection and combination. As early as 1917, Viktor Shklovsky wrote in his pioneering essay "Art as Technique": "Poets are much more concerned with arranging images than with creating them. Images are given to poets; the ability to remember them is far more important than the ability to create them."[37]

Kluge's film also undermines the classic institutional distinction between documentary and fiction film. In his view, the strict separation between the two needs to be broken down for the sake of realism. To the extent that the documentary film limits itself to simply recording the visible surface and the fiction film abstracts from historical reality, neither is "realistic":

> Mere documentation forecloses *Zusammenhang*: objectivity does not exist without the emotions, actions and desires, that is, without the eyes and the senses of the people involved. I have never understood why the depiction of such acts (mostly they have to be staged) is called fiction, fiction-film. But it is equally ideological to believe that individuals could determine history and their story. Therefore, no narrative succeeds without a certain measure of authentic material, i.e., documentation. Such use of documentation establishes a point of reference for the eyes and senses: real conditions clear the view for the story. (41)

Montage places fictional and documentary parts in a dynamic and contradictory relationship; on the editing table new *Zusammenhänge* can be constructed, new connections arise. For instance, in *The Patriot* a squadron of bombers is shown in grainy newsreel footage, followed by a cut to a woman with two children in an air-raid shelter. The commentary says: "This is staged! These bombers are *not* authentic. That is, I do not know whether it was *this* bomber whose bomb hits the shelter. I do know the bomber is up there" (69). Kluge does not allow the historical material to speak for itself but instead works with it, shaping and manipulating it through editing and commentary. He calls this analytical activity "construction work, no different than the work of people who build railroads or bridges or who found cities, except that it does not operate with straight lines."[38]

Kluge's film is a hybrid of documentary and fiction that corresponds to the intermingling of facts and desires in the mind of the viewer.[39] This deliberate confusion between fact and fiction allows him to have a fictional figure take part in the documentary filming of a real event. The actress Hannelore Hoger, whom we know in the film as the fictional character Gabi Teichert, visits the Social Democratic Party Congress in Hamburg in the fall of 1977 and in her role as the Hessian history teacher interviews several deputies and delegates "live," including well-known party members, who were probably not aware that they played a part in a feature film. She asks them with a provocative naiveté how the "raw material" for the history lessons she has to teach could be improved. The presence of a fictional character undermines the unquestioned public spectacle of a Party Congress and makes it seem staged. Through this figure Kluge creates a critical perspective *within* the scene (not, as usual, by juxtaposition or commentary). Gabi Teichert, the scholar of history—and that means, in her own words, also being an investigator of the present reality (108)—would like to participate herself in "improving" history. She makes the following proposition to a deputy from Lower Bavaria: "I am a history teacher. I have come here because I would like to work with you to change history. What do you think of that?" (75). The reaction of the "historical" deputy, partly affable and partly condescending, is scrutinized by the sharp gaze of the fictional figure. Hoger, playing Gabi Teichert, also listens when a vote is taken and notes: "For three thousand years government has been arranged so that I can vote for what I want only if I also vote for what I do not want" (83). The democratic process and private wishes are shown to be incompatible.

Other documentary sequences of the film, shot as cinéma vérité, include the staged teachers' conference, where the headmaster says: "I have official notice that there is no such word as '*Berufsverbot*' ["professional proscription"—a government response to prospective state employees sympathetic to the terrorists of the late 1970s], even though the thing itself might exist" (119), and the police detail in the department store during the Christmas season, ironically summarized with the self-revealing description: "The purpose of the police detail is the disturbance of the Christmas peace in the department store by young men" (142). These sequences use a restless hand-held camera to record statements, gestures, and attitudes that betray a deficient understanding of democracy. In the context of the film, these partly fictional, partly documentary passages function as semiotic training grounds where split-second recognitions of authoritarian gestures and phrases are playfully tested and probed.

Kluge's work of deconstructing standard oppositions such as document versus fiction, history versus present, reality versus imagination, representation versus articulation resembles an expansive excavation and construction site with its continuous digging, building, razing, and reassembling. Thus many "building blocks" from *The Patriot* are found in Kluge's literary works *Schlachtbeschreibung* and *Neue Geschichten* as well as in his theoretical book *Geschichte und Eigensinn*. His films and literary texts, his numerous speeches, theoretical reflections, and interviews all have a dialogic, unfinished, and open character; all call for supplementation. The (de)constructivist principle that is derived from film montage has become the signature of Kluge's work in general.

Archaeology and Imagination

Prefer what is positive and multiple, difference over uniformity, flows over unities, mobile arrangements over system. Believe that what is productive is not sedentary but nomadic.

MICHAEL FOUCAULT

Once upon a time: that means, as in a fairy tale, not only something past, but also a brighter or happier somewhere else.

ERNST BLOCH

"The collector really lives as in a dream. For in a dream the rhythm of perception and experience is also changed in such a way that everything—even the most apparently neutral thing—thrusts itself upon us, concerns us."[40] Walter Benjamin's theory of perception, influenced by surrealism and its interest in Freud's work on dreams, can be applied to Kluge's filmmaking. In *The Patriot* Gabi Teichert collects fragments and *objets trouvés* from the German past and assembles them according to a principle that has more in common with dreams than with narrative logic. Everything in German history, even the incidental, abstruse, and obscure, seems to concern her personally. According to Benjamin, dreams open up a world "with special, secret affinities," in which things enter into "the most contradictory connections" and can exhibit an "indeterminate relatedness."[41] What is fixed and frozen dissolves in a dream, and persons, events, and things appear outside of their usual context and unconstrained by conventional logic and hierarchy, free to enter into new relationships.

Kluge calls cinema the "black communicative space of dreams, wishes, and unconscious images."[42] As in a dream, film can break up what has become congealed and encrusted, through the use of condensation, displacement, leaps, associations, and substitution. Kluge derives from this similarity a dramaturgy of movement specific to film. For example, in *The Patriot* the grainy, black-and-white, noisy documentary footage from the Social Democratic Party Congress is followed by sudden silence and a still color photograph. The contrast could not be greater. In the scene of the plenary session of the Party Congress, filmed with an erratic hand-held camera and accompanied by loud, often distorted original sound, the language is extremely abstract, dealing with legislative bills, the voting behavior of the majority, and such things as partial construction permits for energy plants. Suddenly a quick cut catapults us out of the political discussion and confronts us with a colorful, exotic picture from Hindu cosmology: seven elephants stand on a giant turtle; a snow-capped mountain rests on the elephants; golden stars shine against a violet sky. The voice-over says: "Human wishes assume many forms." Kluge remains quite aware of the effects of such editing:

> The viewer now hears this sentence—human wishes assume many forms—and sees more than just this image. Since the image is not realistic and cannot easily be made to fit into the context, it becomes an image that stays with the viewer. It has an after-image. In the film, the after-image is what matters. Before it, something has been emptied out, and after it there is an image that does not belong. I call that the subversive work of the cinema. Film can do that. Compared to that the written word is less effective.[43]

The cut from the unsteady cinéma vérité images to the motionless, brightly colored illustration creates a connection between the reality of everyday political life and the realm of human wishes. Things that normally belong to two radically different areas are brought into relation by a bold juxtaposition, as in a dream. This ability of film to join together things that are usually separate, distinct, and incompatible through abrupt cuts challenges the imagination and expands the perceptual boundaries of the viewer.

Kluge's "delight in the improbable,"[44] his enthusiasm for the world of fantasy and fairy tale, is directed against the ideologically established "main routes of experience," against suppressed and impoverished perception, and against a "logic of meaning" that robs everyday life of its wishes:

> When I point the camera at an everyday event and film it with "available light," I have curtailed the everyday by an essential element—by its wishes. The wishes that do not become reality in the everyday world but that are present in the mind and that cause our eyes never to see everyday reality as it actually is. Our eyes falsify reality through our wishes. They demand something else in a film. So in the following sequence I have to portray this everyday scene again but this time through the eyes of our wishes. Wishes give the everyday a completely different light.[45]

In *The Patriot* the "eyes of our wishes" point to an imaginary Germany seen across the centuries: pictures from the twelfth century (a sequence of medieval illustrations with the title: "Wishes in the twelfth century—something very simple"), followed by a poster of the 1941 Nazi propaganda film *Heimkehr* (*Homecoming*) by Gustav Ucicky, a film about the murder of a German minority group by Poles shortly before the outbreak of World War II; this, too, is an image of the fantasy production of the Germans. Next comes a drawing of an absurd plan proposed by the Nazi Organisation Todt to build canals over the Alps; then glimpses of paintings by Caspar David Friedrich, and pictures of the Brothers Grimm with shovels in their hands. The voice-over comments: "At the time of this emperor (a portrait of Napoleon I), the scholars Jacob and Wilhelm Grimm were digging intensively into German history. They dug and dug and unearthed the fairy tales. Their content: how a people deals with its wishes over a period of 800 years" (123).

History and fairy tale: imaginary wish production and the real experience of suffering supplement and comment on each other. Kluge's film assumes that collective hopes, dreams, anxieties, and disasters have left their traces in fairy tales over the centuries. As popular myths of Germany, they have come to terms with history in a special way. In an improvised documentary interview sequence, Gabi Teichert asks a lawyer and aficionado of fairy tales about the story of the seven ravens, in which the father wants to have his seven sons killed so that his only daughter can inherit the kingdom. "From a legal point of view there is nothing to say about this story," says the expert, who as a hobby analyzes fairy tales from a legal point of view. "The father has the *patria potestas* and is king here, absolute ruler. He can have his children killed with impunity" (126). Then there is an abrupt cut, and the camera pans over a map with names of cities like Verdun and Fort St. Michel. The voice-over comments: "Fairy tales have a historical core. And that tells of great disasters" (126). The viewer must make the connection in this sequence between the king in the fairy tale who can have his sons killed at his whimsy and the Kaiser who sent his subjects to death at Verdun in World War I. The montage establishes a constellation whose critical potential sheds new light on the circumstances of domination and the power over life and death in fairy tales as well as in history.

Fairy tales are history written from below—anonymous, ubiquitous, full of excessive, often hidden subversive energy. Their narrative simplicity stimulates the imagination. In addition, fairy tales have always been screens for the projection of the secret dreams of Germans, allowing them to measure the scope of the compensatory fantasy work that was necessary to balance out the historical misery of the people. "Anyone who laughs at fairy tales has never suffered" (129).

"L'imagination au pouvoir!" ("Power to the imagination!"), the French students wrote on the walls of the Sorbonne in May 1968, demanding a politics guided not by the reality principle but by free-floating imagination, and based on the pleasure principle. For Kluge, too, fantasy is "the most important productive force" when it comes to "people themselves determining their relations to their history, to their life, to the things they produce and to each other. In film, this power is at issue."[46] *The Patriot* shows the activity of the imagination as a form of historiography. The division between fiction and historiography, between imagination and the search for facts does not exist for Kluge. In *The Patriot* the imagination roams nomadically through past and future, through distant lands and imagined worlds, calling on the viewer's powers of association and memory, breaking up sedimented contexts and opening new realms of experience. "A constant shifting of perspectives," Kluge wrote in 1980, "is typical of fantasy. In fantasy I can transport myself to Africa without effort or I can imagine myself involved in a love scene in the middle of a desert—all this happens as in a dream. The obstacles of reality cease to exist."[47]

The film as dream. And history in this dream? It becomes a product of fantasy that illuminates connections, challenges perception, and correlates images and texts from different centuries and different cultures. It may well be that Kluge's associative approach to history ultimately denies the effect of objectively existing conditions (for instance, in the economic sphere) and actual consequences (for instance, in politics) by relativizing and "de-realizing" them in a loose network of free associations, intertextual references, and allusions. Kluge's "savage" montages (in the sense of Lévi-Strauss's "savage mind") dehistoricize images; torn from their original contexts, they are freely interpretable fragments, easily used for historical constructs that proceed associatively and ahistorically, with the license of a dream. In his "historical miniatures"—as he calls the intermittent montage sequences of illustrations, stills, film clips, and short commentaries—Kluge is obviously not much concerned with logical, rational explanations of history. He wants to plow up the "field of history" and turn over material to induce the viewer to grasp historical reality in a sensual and unmethodical way.[48] No other film depends so much on the disposition of the recipient for its eventual effect as the open, evocative, and polyphonically resonating film of Kluge's.

His work on the "expansion of the perceptual horizon"[49] demands from the spectator a mature capacity of association and memory, a readiness to establish connections between the film and one's own life experience. He believes that viewers can more easily relate their own experience to a film that is diffuse and has ruptures and mistakes than to a "perfect," aesthetically closed film.[50] For this reason even incomprehensible passages are included in his films: "When the knee speaks Latin," Kluge says, referring to a scene in which the voice-over switches to rapid Latin to explain a point, "I do not at all assume that anyone understands that, at least not anyone who interests me as a viewer."[51] The renunciation of meaning, which Kluge here propounds in an ironic exaggeration, is the final consequence of a realistic, "robust" attitude toward history, which should appear to us as something that remains unfamiliar, distant, not easily assimilated. The recourse to Latin also alludes to the learned language of the humanists, who for a long time restricted the knowledge of history to a small minority. At the other extreme, history today is totally "democratized" and socialized through the technical media of photography, film, and television; all foreignness has been driven out of it. Television in particular has trivialized history into easily accessible information bites or shallow entertainment; history no longer engenders experience.

A film like *The Patriot,* in contrast, demands effort, concentration, and active intellectual involvement on the part of the spectator. What Kluge said in 1984 about his film *Die Macht der Gefühle* (*The Power of Emotions*) applies even more to *The Patriot:* "One problem with the film is that it must be seen several times so that the individual images and the structure of their arrangement are retained in memory. The experimental attitude that the film advocates needs time to develop and is easily overtaxed. The more so since the film abstains from using crude means of orientation."[52] Kluge's films tend to overwhelm the viewer's imagination with heterogeneous signs, contradictory messages, and narrative motifs that are often merely hinted at, in order to keep all possibilities for association open; they definitely need imaginative and creative spectators.

To give an example, in one of the first montage sequences in *The Patriot* we see Gabi Teichert at the telescope of an observatory. We also see in rapid succession the image of a crescent moon; a factory with smoking chimneys; tall buildings by day; night shots of a fire in a high-rise (commentary: "This high-rise belongs to the industrialist Selmi. One evening it burns. The fire department's hoses do not reach to the top"); the birth of a child (commentary: "Frankfurt-North, 10 p.m."); and the picture of a puddle with raindrops falling on it (commentary: "A puddle has a history of three days"). Each part of the sequence lasts only a few seconds. One way of dealing with such a montage is to search for hidden connections beneath the associative flow of images. Thus the sudden shift in perspective from cosmic space to the birth of a human being and then to the image of a puddle might well be seen as an attempt to visualize the relativity of our concepts of time and history and to make this abstract thought accessible to our senses. But the centrifugal motifs in the images cannot be reduced to a single meaning. We are also prevented from falling back on the intention of the author. "I do not claim that I myself always understand their connections," Kluge writes in the foreword to his *Neue Geschichten.*[53] Ideally, we become stirred up and stimulated to relate the images that flash by with dreamlike alacrity to our own waking world. Kluge provides us with pictures which help us assemble our own films that are projected continuously in our imagination.

The New Patriotism

All my life I knew no Germany.
Just two foreign states forbidding me
Ever to be German in the name of a people.
So much history, to end this way?

BOTHO STRAUSS

It is strange to hear the German national anthem as a leitmotif in a film like *Germany in Autumn,* one of the few films of the New German Cinema not made with government money. It is as if the love for Germany could only be articulated when one felt free of the government. In the autumn of 1977, the German Left believed the government had thoroughly discredited itself with its massive use of police, with its hunt for so-called leftist sympathizers and its *Berufs-verbot,* and not least of all through the unexplained deaths of the terrorists in the maximum-security prison of Stammheim.[54] As distrust of the government mounted and old questions resurfaced (especially abroad) about whether the Germans were capable of democracy, a growing need was felt in the Federal Republic to reflect on the foundations of the state. Was the West German state worth saving if it could so easily be attacked and destabilized? Was there such a thing as a German identity? If so, what did it consist of? Many people posed these questions during the crisis of 1977, searching for points of orientation that promised historical continuity and stability beyond the fickleness of everyday politics.

Germany itself seemed to provide an answer: not Germany as a political entity—the Left had only contempt for that—but Germany as a place that validated individual identity, a place to which people were undeniably bound by birth and childhood, through their language and earliest experiences. The leftist love of Heimat, the yearning for a peacefully reunited Germany, was patriotic, not nationalistic. It was also opposed to the dominant politics, which, for instance, was very cautiously "realistic" with respect to the question of reunification.[55] Lothar Baier recently attempted to explain the origin of this new interest in Germany as homeland, tracing it to the domestic crisis of 1977:

> A strange little plant began to bloom in the shadow of the hideous German police state and its Stammheim Bastille. Above ground, life in this country was still running away from itself while underneath it had already put down roots in the warm, damp semi-dark. A strange, shamefaced, embarrassed love of homeland had begun to grow, disguised as sorrow at the destruction of some idyll or another that had seemed worth keeping. Where could it have found nurturing soil in these stagnant times? I believe it was in the crack that opened between state and society . . . Something like a "civil society" had divorced itself from the German state, a society that refused to follow the commands of the government machine, which continued to hiss and stamp . . . A new reality had emerged—the "people"—that was not yet the entire country, but somehow we belonged to it. But no one said it aloud. The new love of homeland bloomed, like any illicit passion, in secret.[56]

Baier's retrospective view of the "German Autumn" appeared in 1984 in *Abschiedsbriefe aus Deutschland (Farewell Letters from Germany)*, a collection of essays whose theme is the ambivalence of the new patriotism. A changing relationship of West German leftists to their own land had already been seen in the early 1970s. Peter Schneider's Lenz, the eponymous hero of the 1973 story, is asked what he plans to do after having grown disillusioned with the student activists and after a sobering visit with some Italian socialists. He answers decisively: "Stay here."[57] This half-resigned, half-optimistic renunciation of leftist utopias in the early 1970s coincided with the end of economic prosperity and a growing skepticism about progress and growth. It freed the Left from its fixation on the future and led it to consider questions of origin and identity.

Another factor in the 1970s was undoubtedly the intensified demands of the younger generation for emancipation from the American superego, the ersatz father who had by then assumed his own burden of guilt in the Vietnam War and who, the young Germans began to suspect, considered the Federal Republic primarily as a military outpost in the struggle against communism. And the widely publicized idea that Germany might well serve as the scene for a "limited" atomic war between the two superpowers caused Germans in the late 1970s to reconsider questions that had been ignored for good reason since the founding of the Federal Republic: questions about the "real" political sovereignty of the nation, its national identity, and its history.

A flood of books and articles, films, television programs, speeches, and public debates about Germany, its identity and its history, began to inundate the country in the late 1970s; it still continues.[58] Writers, filmmakers, artists, journalists, social scientists, and politicians discovered one common concern: their own country. Thinking about Germany became fashionable. Book titles proclaimed it to be a "difficult fatherland," a "two-headed child"; scholars spoke openly about the "German neurosis." In the weeklies, journalists speculated about why it seemed a burden to be a German, why the Germans are as they are, and why Germany wants to be loved more than other nations.[59] During the filming of *Die Blechtrommel (The Tin Drum,* 1979), Volker Schlöndorff claimed that, despite his Francophilia, as a German he could only make German films.[60] Likewise, the failure of Wim Wenders in Hollywood—which he dramatized in his film *Der Stand der Dinge (The State of Things,* 1982)—seemed to echo the maxim, "Stay here." Literary authors were no less preoccupied with the subject of their own country.[61] Germany has, after all, always been the place where intellectuals, in despair over the existing Germany, were obsessed with images of an imaginary Germany located either in the distant past or projected into the future. Kluge's *The Patriot* and the other films discussed in this book are part and parcel of this new (and, basically, old) debate about Germany and its identity. These films provide aesthetically complex and politically ambiguous answers to the unresolved question of a German identity.

Toward the end of *The Patriot,* a cryptic sentence from Karl Kraus appears as an intertitle in white print: "The more closely you look at a word, the more distantly it looks back at you." Underneath, in capital letters, the word "GERMANY" is added (165). Kluge looks so closely at Germany that the viewer's gaze becomes confused, and what has been familiar suddenly seems distant, strange, foreign. It is his project to dissolve any large and abstract conceptions of Germany and instead to emphasize concrete experiences. Like Edgar Reitz in *Heimat,* Kluge sees "Germany" first of all in its real, geographic dimension. *The Patriot* begins with traditional postcard motifs: rural landscapes, mowed fields, green meadows, blossoming cherry trees, a view of a castle in ruins, of woods and pastures. The voice-over is spoken by the knee: "It's said I'm interested in history. That's true, of course. I can't forget that I would still be part of a whole if Corporal Wieland, my former master, were still part of a whole, *part of our beautiful Germany.* And not in his bunker . . . As a German knee I am naturally interested, above all, in German history: the emperors, the peasants, blossoms, trees, farms, meadows, plants" (60).

In the filmscript the expression "our beautiful Germany" is set in italics, as if Kluge wanted it to be highlighted. Judging from the accompanying images, "our beautiful Germany" extends only to nature, to the cherry blossoms, which are shown in an unusually lengthy close-up, and to the historical ruins, which are so overgrown that they have become part of nature again. In 1928 Kurt Tucholsky, the famous social satirist, ended *Deutschland, Deutschland über alles,* his bitter diatribe against the Germany of the Weimar Republic, with a similar series of idyllic images of German landscapes. Tucholsky's book, after castigating in word and image (mostly through photo-montages by John Heartfield) German militarism and submissiveness, philistinism and obsession with authority, asserts in its final sequence of landscape images his basic love of Germany, which in the end transcends his contempt for its debased political culture.[62] Kluge's landscape shots of various German regions, emptied of people, are no less nostalgic; but he abruptly cuts from the tranquil color pictures of German scenery in spring to documentary footage of emaciated German soldiers awaiting their sure death in the winter of Stalingrad. As in Syberberg's Hitler film, a disparity arises, between Germany and Stalingrad, between home and far away, between peaceful nature and the hostile history "that will kill us all" (58).

Kluge finds numerous pictorial and textual metaphors that link German history with ice and winter, coldness, freezing, and death. After the "German Autumn," a German winter. At the beginning of the film we see images of Gabi Teichert digging in the frozen ground, followed by a picture of someone trying to climb a glassy ice slope to a castle, a nightmare image. This is followed by pictures of German soldiers freezing to death in Stalingrad. Toward the end of the film a scientist reports that at minus 273 degrees centigrade, matter has finally come to its most perfect order, an order, however, where there is no more life. Then there is a cut to documentary shots of the

Russian campaign in the winter of 1942, followed by an anonymous children's verse that summarizes Kluge's idea of German history:[63]

A little man who wasn't wise
Built his house upon the ice.
Said: O Lord, keep up the freeze
Or else my little house I'll lose.
But the little house sank down
And the little man did drown. (160)

Immediately afterward we see "Gabi Teichert in her car, driving through the city. She is crying" (160). The film's *Trauerarbeit* (work of mourning) surfaces mutely in the patriot's tears: mourning for the many war victims and for the lost fatherland; mourning also for the cold rigidity that keeps the society together. "Being a patriot with this history is something of a contradiction."[64]

Even in the earlier *Germany in Autumn,* Kluge did not hesitate to use music to express his love for Germany. Several times in both films we hear the instrumental version of the Haydn melody that has become the German national anthem. In *Germany in Autumn* we also hear an interpretation of a Schubert lied from the *Winterreise.* The most disparate juxtapositions of images are held together and united by music, mostly classical German pieces. The music indicates how deeply both *The Patriot* and *Germany in Autumn* are indebted to German Romanticism: in both films we find a tone that hovers between elegy and irony; a pleasure in fairy tales; a dissatisfaction with the present, which both films counter by dreaming their way out of it, either toward the distant past or into other imaginary worlds; a penchant for fragments and formal self-reflexivity. All these attributes clearly point to the German Romantic tradition, from Brentano to Heinrich Heine's *Deutschland: Ein Wintermärchen* (*Germany: A Winter's Tale,* 1844). Even the word "patriot" derives from the time of Romanticism; Prussian reformers adopted it from French in their battle against the usurper Napoleon Bonaparte. But Kluge also knows that "for the past 150 years the word has been the private property of the political Right" (342).

What images of Germany does Kluge show? Along with pictures of the landscape, there are repeated documentary shots of doomed German soldiers at Stalingrad, images of battlefields, air raid shelters, and falling bombs, pictures of tanks moving across the meadows, cannon frigates, and bombers. Kluge also used Allied newsreel footage of the execution of young German Nazis by the occupation forces in the spring of 1945 and documentary shots of American planes attacking a German city. We see the bomber pilots standing awkwardly beside their planes, grinning and joking. Kluge makes a sarcastic comment in the voice-over: "These bomber pilots have returned from their mission. They have not learned anything definite about Germany. They have just expertly shot up the country for eighteen hours. Now they are returning to their quarters to sleep" (172). In another sequence of the film we see documentary footage of bombs falling from an airplane, burning houses, and clouds of smoke. Commenting on these images, the voice-over says: "Let us not forget that sixty thousand people burned to death in Hamburg" (149).

Such statements reveal a highly ambivalent political agenda covertly at work in the film. Some of Kluge's comments, which in the late 1970s may have been intended to remind viewers about *German* suffering at a time when recent German history was equated with the Holocaust (or, more precisely, with *Holocaust,* the American television series), from today's perspective appear provocatively and even dangerously one-sided. Given the present danger of interested parties wanting to rewrite German history in order to relativize the crimes of the past, Kluge's film suddenly seems rather problematic.[65] The Germans are shown throughout his film as *victims* of crimes perpetrated against them; we see them endure war, bombardment, imprisonment, execution. It follows that, for Kluge, to be a patriot in Germany means to be mindful of all the many German victims. Thus Gabi Teichert, Kluge's protagonist, is introduced in the very first scene of the film with the following voice-over comment: "Gabi Teichert, history teacher in Hessen, a patriot, *that is,* she takes an interest in all the dead of the Reich" (50; emphasis mine). This introduction is followed by underlit, grainy war film footage that is difficult to localize: "It is either the time of the Seven Years' War or during the Wars of Liberation, but now we see an anti-aircraft cannon of 1943," states the script, playfully alluding to the basic sameness of all wars (51).[66] The music that accompanies the scenes of fallen soldiers is by Hanns Eisler; he composed it for Alan Resnais's film *La nuit et brouillard* (*Night and Fog*) of 1958, which was not shown on West German television until twenty years later, in January 1978.

Night and Fog is a memorial to the victims of Auschwitz, a documentary that blends historical photographs of concentration camp horrors with long, calm tracking shots that search the landscape for traces of the vanished barracks and gas chambers. Kluge uses the musical theme that functioned as a leitmotif for Resnais as an overture for his own film (but does not mention the source of the music, either in his published script or in the credits). This musical quotation may hint at a consciousness that does not want to exclude Auschwitz from the patriotic *Trauerarbeit*. But even those who can appreciate the subtle allusion to the leitmotif from *Night and Fog* are soon pulled back to the side of the *German* war victims because the music is combined with images of German soldiers at Stalingrad. The victims of the Germans at Auschwitz, Buchenwald, and many other concentration camps are not part of the picture.[67] Already the first images of *The Patriot* show that the film is concerned with a Germany that is haunted by the memory of its wars and strewn with dead bodies. The Reich has been broken up into innumerable fragments, like Kluge's film itself, and the idea of Germany survives today only as a memory, a myth, a wishful fantasy, a dream—and a film.

Kluge was one of the first speakers in the lecture series "Speaking about Our Country: Germany," held on Sunday mornings at the Munich Kammerspiel Theater beginning in 1983. In his lecture, he tried to give a precise definition of his notion of Germany. He began by saying that Germany could not be identical with the national entity that perished in 1945, the German Reich. "If what is called Germany could perish in 1945, then this Germany did not exist before that time ... If one thinks of Germany just as a national entity, then from the time the empire was founded in 1870–71 it has been something imaginary."[68] Germany is imaginary for Kluge not only in the sense of Cornelius Castoriadis, for whom national identity represents part of the social imagination,[69] but also in the literal sense that Germany cannot easily be defined in spatial terms. Even those boundaries that Hoffmann von Fallersleben named in the words to the national anthem, "From the Maas to the Memel, from the Etsch to the Belt," have never been German boundaries. "Germany never had fixed geographical boundaries. It must be understood in terms of its *lack* of boundaries. It is easier to understand that Germany was always absent, has never come into existence, and that therefore an unyielding desire for unity, for community crystallized around this word. Such longing, such expectations and desires indicate a temporal dimension: it is *a living being that is 2,000 years old.*"[70]

Germany is a "historical product" for which—according to Kluge's calculations—eighty-seven generations have worked themselves to the bone, and even died defending it. Germany can also be seen as a "factory of collective experience," a "concrete vessel of our memories."[71] In their theoretical treatise *Geschichte und Eigensinn* (*History and Obstinacy,* 1981) Kluge and Oskar Negt hold two contradictory notions of Germany: on the one hand, they consider Germany a "gigantic kitchen"[72] in which collective work has ceaselessly produced historical changes; on the other hand, they speak of Germany as an "illusion":[73] "Germany, always on the point of ruin, exists only as something imagined, as a collective prejudice with appended institutional structures."[74] Kluge and Negt postulate the "most bitter antagonism" between "the result of history, *this* Germany as it exists now, and *that* Germany for which people have indefatigably worked without achieving it."[75]

All the hopes and desires produced over the centuries in this "laboratory" called Germany were not bound by the actual reality of the existing nation. They always aimed far beyond it; they were "romantic." The collective wishes of German poets and thinkers for some "other" Germany remain unfulfilled, something that has become especially clear today. For this reason, Kluge defines his concept of Germany paradoxically as the "lack of Germany." It is precisely the absence of the imagined "other" Germany that determines our understanding of the existing Germany. Nonetheless, or perhaps for that reason, he ends his speech with a neo-patriotic appeal that is itself based on wishes and hopes:

> What we need is a structure, a community, a vessel, a laboratory, a social factory, it doesn't matter what we call it, that unites sufficient intensities, time spans, forms of good will, and if necessary evil will, in such a way that it is possible to make peace in an emergency, to defend what is worth my life, and to invest our thoughts, our feelings, and our work in it, as illuminated by the proverb: "If you don't give your life, you will never gain your life." This quasi-negative concept, the lack of Germany, the lack of such a community, is what ... I understand by the concept of Ger-

many—a challenge, something that would be worthwhile to reconstruct or to build.[76]

Quite appropriately, *The Patriot* ends on the last day of the year with a close-up of Gabi Teichert's face, "looking hopefully into the winter storm" (178). Kluge's voice-over comments: "Every year on New Year's Eve Gabi Teichert sees 365 days before her. Thus the hope arises that she can improve the raw material for history classes in high schools this year" (178). The open structure of the film does not permit a dramatic closure; the new year will bring new stories, new experiences, and new memories that will change Germany and its history. The march of time itself promises an exit from a fatal past and an entry into a possibly better present.

5

OUR CHILDHOODS, OURSELVES

Helma Sanders-Brahms's
Germany, Pale Mother

"Once hearth and home were demolished you became cheerful."
—Eva Mattes in *Germany, Pale Mother*

The past—whatever the continuously accumulating stack of memories may be—cannot be described objectively. The twofold meaning of the word "to mediate." To be the mediator between past and present—the medium of a communication between the two. In the sense of reconciliation? appeasement? smoothing out? Or a rapprochement of the two? To permit today's person to meet yesterday's person through the medium of writing?

CHRISTA WOLF

I look on memory as more than a haphazard thinking back . . . The work of memory situates experience in a sequence that keeps it alive, a story which can open out into free storytelling, greater life, invention.

PETER HANDKE

Autobiography and Memory

It has become a truism in German literary history that the rapid demise of the student movement and the concomitant political disillusionment in the 1970s were accompanied by literature's retreat into the private sphere.[1] According to this periodization, the political resolve to educate and agitate had spurred authors in the second half of the sixties to attack the institution of literature as elitist and to draw on pragmatic literary forms from the Weimar Republic, especially documentary literature and agitprop theater. Writing itself had become suspect; what counted was the immediate political impact, not personal expression. It was not until the early seventies that individual experience and the unique subjectivity of the writer regained their legitimate place. But the so-called New Subjectivity of the seventies cannot be so easily separated from the politically engaged literature of the sixties. Thus, for instance, the demand for authenticity and immediacy, so central to the literary programs of the sixties, was continued in the wave of autobiographies in the seventies. In addition, the interest in recent German history, which gave rise to such documentary dramas as *Der Stellvertreter* (*The Deputy*, 1963) by Rolf Hochhuth and *Die Ermittlung* (*The Investigation*, 1966), by Peter Weiss, continued in the seventies in the plethora of historical novels and biographies.

The process of dealing with the past, however, no longer centered on figures like Adolf Eichmann or Pope Pius XII; as political and moral ambitions became more modest in the seventies, so too did the scope of inquiry. Writers began to focus on their parents, on fathers and mothers who had lived through the Hitler period and were emotionally, if not physically, scarred by it. The psychological damage wrought by National Socialism became a strange and ambivalent source of curiosity for the generation born during the last years of the war or at its end. In the mid-1970s, approaching their midlife point and having children of their own, the postwar generation looked back on their childhood and asked, as Christa Wolf did in *Kindheitsmuster* (*Patterns of Childhood*, 1976), "How did we become what we are today?"[2] This retrospective look at one's childhood ultimately involved contradictory impulses. On the one hand, knowing the prehistory of the present helped one understand how the status quo came about, how it was the necessary and inevitable result of time and circumstance. At the same time, however, looking back at one's origins contained a utopian dimension because everything that seemed closed, rigid, and unalterable in the present suddenly appeared wide open, undetermined, full of potential. As people's belief in the future diminished, their nostalgia for the past, for a new beginning in innocence, grew. It is not surprising that children play a central role as identification figures in the cinema of this period, not only in Sanders-Brahms's film but also in Syberberg's *Hitler* and Edgar Reitz's *Heimat*. Children embody unrealized utopias, the joy of pure origin, an innocent state of nature.[3]

For those born in the early 1940s (Sanders-Brahms was born in 1940), the parent generation was the war generation. Questioning them meant interrogating the German past. For many years during the 1950s and early 1960s, no one had dared to ask their parents what they did during the war, how they lived under Hitler, and to what extent they collaborated with the regime, unwittingly or not. Not until the late 1970s did writers and filmmakers willingly take part in what Freud described as a process of "remembering, repeating, and working through."[4] They no longer simply pointed an accusing finger at their parents (as in the sixties) but made an attempt to understand and even to pity them. Especially the encounters with German fathers evinced a disquieting sense of moral ambivalence.[5] An autobiographical subgenre, the so-called *Väterliteratur*, emerged in the late seventies, dealing with fathers as representatives of the German past.[6] Now that most of the fathers were either dead or very old, questions arose that had never been asked before; memories of one's early childhood years were awakened. The authors of this *Väterliteratur* undertake a journey into their own past, to the beginnings of their lives in the midst of ruins, a journey back into a childhood dominated by parents who often were both culprits and victims. They remember their fathers with a mixture of sympathy and revulsion, love and rejection; they mourn them, but still condemn them as "Nazis."

One of the most disturbing filmic accounts of the ambivalent relationship between Nazi father and son is the semidocumentary film *Wundkanal* (*Wound Passage*, 1985) by Thomas Harlan, the son of Veit Harlan, the famous director of the Nazi propaganda films *Jud Süss* and *Kolberg*.[7] Thomas Harlan hired a convicted mass murderer to play his father's role and forced him to undergo sadistic interrogations that pushed the aging actor to the brink of a physical breakdown. Veit Harlan, acquitted of war crimes in a sensational verdict in 1949, is found guilty in a simulated trial in the film and receives a symbolic death sentence at the hands of his son thirty-six years later. Thomas Harlan's film, radical in form and uncompromising in tone, intermingles documentary and fictional modes; it also blurs the clear boundaries between victim and aggressor. This is the dialectic of the film: the more we become aware of the hatred and vindictiveness of the son, the more we pity the father; his vulnerability engages our interest more than the moral rigor of the son, whose violent revenge scenario proves ultimately to be self-destructive. *The Sons Die before the Fathers:*[8] Thomas Brasch's book title pinpoints the psychological trauma of these belated confrontations between Nazi fathers and their sons.

Less frequently we find mothers at the center of childhood memories. For instance, Karin Struck's novel *Die Mutter* (*The Mother*, 1975), Helga Novak's *Die Eisheiligen* (*The Ice Saints*, 1979), Elfriede Jelinek's *Die Klavierspielerin* (*The Piano Player*, 1983), and Waltraud Anna Mitgutsch's *Die Züchtigung* (*The Chastisement*, 1985),[9] despite their differences in narrative and style, all treat conflicts between mothers and daughters. They share similar themes as well: parting and separation, crippling dependence and liberation, and finally defeat and emotional hardening—on both sides. Ingmar Bergman's film *Autumn Sonata* (1976) could have been a model for the theatrical presentation of the feelings between mothers and daughters depicted in these autobiographical novels. As in *Autumn Sonata,* love can turn into hatred, affection into contempt, in a single moment. Emotional frigidity, depression, and thoughts of suicide often ensue in such constrictive mother-daughter relationships. Still, the daughter feels bound to question the mother to gain self-knowledge and a sense of identity. The retrospective look at one's childhood serves to explain and come to grips with the emotional wounds and sensitivities of the present self.

The film *Deutschland, bleiche Mutter* (*Germany, Pale Mother*), in preparation from 1976, had its world premiere at the Berlin Film Festival in February 1980. It is part of the literary discourse of the late seventies about childhood and parents, female identity and German history—but with a difference. The biting criticism of the mother in Jelinek or Novak has been softened to an empathetic evocation. In Sanders-Brahms's film the mother, Lene, appears as a victim, psychologically and physically, of the recent German past. Her psychosomatic facial paralysis at the end of the film externalizes the physical destruction brought about by German history. Like the mother in Peter Handke's *Wunschloses Unglück* (*A Sorrow Beyond Dreams,* 1972), Lene is the object of pity and mourning, but also of critical self-questioning from today's perspective. "I don't live any differently from my parents; I just live in other times" (11),[10] says Sanders-Brahms in the preface to her filmscript.

The times of her parents appear in the film's first shot: a gigantic swastika rippling on the waters of an idyllic lake. We do not see the flag itself but rather its reflection, which fills the screen. The black swastika against a red background, a symbol of Hitler's regime, not only locates and dates the events; it also symbolizes the power of the Nazi state over its subjects, an all-encompassing but not tangible power, present only indirectly as a reflection. While a rowboat glides into the frame from the left and cuts across the reflected image of the flag, a female voice-over comments: "I can't remember anything of the time before my life. I am not guilty for what happened before I was born. I wasn't around then. I began when my father saw my mother for the first time" (112). It is the voice of the daughter who comments off-camera from the perspective of the present, marking the temporal rupture between the staged past and the moment of speaking.

The voice belongs to Sanders-Brahms. At regular intervals she addresses the images, commenting on the motives, qualities, and disposition of her parents, played by two well-known stage actors, Eva Mattes and Hans Jacobi. She glosses the action and expresses what cannot be captured visually: her own memories, inner thoughts, subsequent opinions. The narrative structure of the film is that of an autobiography staged with the help of actors but accompanied and validated by an authentic "I."

Autobiographical narration in literature assumes the identity of a narrating "I" and a narrated "I," of the object and the subject of narration. Autobiography in film involves not only an imagined narrated "I" but also a staged one, that is, one that is played and dramatized.[11] The identity of the narrated and narrating "I," essential to autobiography, is thus split. Since the daughter (the narrating "I") cannot play herself as a child (the narrated "I"), the film takes recourse to actors. The actors and their dialogues, in the style of traditional film stories, create a closed fictional space. The story told in images has its own dynamics and presence and would, it seems, progress in the same way without the voice-over commentary. In comparison, Alexander Kluge's voice-over in *The Patriot* attempts (often ironically) to establish meaning in the confusion of different images and sounds by pointing out connections among the shards and fragments of German history. Sanders-Brahms's voice-over does not perform this playful gesture of searching and combining; instead, the daughter's voice personalizes the staged historical events through direct address ("This is *your* love story, Mother,' your love story, Father") (112) and through private acts of memory: "Lene, that's how we were. You and I, two witches" (113). This kind of dialogue involves two points in history: the past of the world of childhood, reconstructed for the film, and the present of the remembering adult, who judges her past with a blend of empathy and critical distance. The film provides both a political history of Germany between 1939 and 1955 and, at the same time, the prehistory of a narrating "I," who looks back over forty years.

The narration begins conventionally by introducing the main characters. "He was not the Nazi. That was the other one, his friend" (112), the omniscient authorial voice of the daughter assures us as her father appears on screen with a friend. From a boat, the men watch a dark-haired woman walking along the bank, the future wife of the father and the mother of the narrator. The camera shows her merely as the distant object of male gazes. They shout "Hello, Miss"; she does not respond. In a medium shot we see four men in Nazi uniforms behind her. Suddenly and without provocation, they set their German shepherd upon her. She silently defends herself. The camera does not exploit the opportunity to create "action" by cutting quickly to close-ups; instead it remains in the distance and simply observes the events. Several motifs that are developed in the course of the story are already foreshadowed in this initial scene: the role of woman as passive object of the male gaze and as the victim of male aggression, and the form of mute self-defense which is deemed valuable in the eyes of men: "She didn't scream. A German woman, a true German woman" (28). The long, almost static camera shots, the dark colors, and the autumn light generate a persuasive melancholic atmosphere, which is intensified by portentous music whose heavy chords presage future misfortune.

Germany, Pale Mother tells the story of the narrator's parents, Lene and Hans, who met in 1939. A love story, a marriage: "Happy, completely normal," says the voice of the grown-up daughter, looking back. "It's just that it happens at this time, in this country. The story of my beginning" (112). Shortly after their wedding, Hitler invades Poland. Hans, not a Party member, is drafted and sent to the front to fight for his country. An associative nexus develops, linking war, father, and fatherland.[12] During the six years of war, Lene and Hans see each other only during his brief leaves; feelings of alienation grow between them. Still, Lene wants to have a child, as a substitute for Hans. Their daughter Anna is born during a bombing raid. "When they cut me from you, Lene," the daughter comments in a voice-over, "I fell onto a battlefield. Yet so much that I couldn't even see was already destroyed" (113). Lene raises the child and survives the war and the postwar years with tenacity despite innumerable hardships. But when Hans returns from a prison camp, defeated, embittered, and alienated, the "war at home" begins.

While the fathers were away at war, the mothers had taken charge: they scavenged for food, cleared away rubble, raised their children. But with the fathers' return, the mothers' newly discovered strength was no longer needed. Lene, again imprisoned in the domestic sphere, begins drinking, and takes refuge in a sickness, her facial paralysis. She becomes mute and withdrawn, rejecting even her daughter's love. In the final scene Lene locks herself in the bathroom and turns on the gas in the water heater to commit suicide. A painfully long close-up shows the nine-year-old daughter crying and hammering on the door, begging her to come out. The mother stands behind the door, silent, her face distorted. She appears in the same pose and light used by Carl Theodor Dreyer to portray the suffering martyr in his 1928 film *La Passion de Jeanne d'Arc*. The voice-over tells us that this moment marks the daughter's definitive separation from her mother: "It was a long time before Lene opened the door, and sometimes I think she is still behind it, and I am still standing in front of it, and that she will never come out again, and I have to be grown up and alone. But she is still here. Lene is still here" (113).

Autobiographical, fictional, and historical elements blend together in a melodrama that is based on personal experience, free invention, and historical research. Sanders-Brahms's two-year-old daughter plays the child in the film, that is, she plays her mother as a small girl. "I am the daughter of my mother and the mother of my daughter," Sanders-Brahms said in a commentary to her film (115);[13] thus three generations of mothers and daughters join in the film. Its working title was *For Lene;* the final version carried a dedication to the director's daughter, because it was the birth of her child that enabled Sanders-Brahms to discuss her own childhood with her mother. She made the film, she told a French interviewer, to show her daughter that the history of her country consisted of more than just Hitler, concentration camps, and war.[14]

An essential attribute of autobiography is its claim to truth and authenticity. However, this did not prevent Sanders-Brahms from fictionally reshaping her life and that of her parents, condensing their lives and imparting to them a higher level of generality. "My history with Lene was not exactly as the film now shows it," Sanders-Brahms wrote in the afterword to the film. "Lene, as far as I know, was not raped, but she was terribly afraid she might be. As a child I once watched a rape and thought that it could have happened to Lene" (115). She also at times seems to mock the conventions of autobiographical truth in comments like this: "The facial paralysis really happened. But Lene thinks it was on the other side, so let me report that. Let me also say that the other characters who appear don't exist just as they are shown, but are usually composites of several people" (117).

Germany, Pale Mother is enriched by material that Sanders-Brahms gathered through the methods of oral history. It is a story "constructed of personal experiences and the experiences of many women, from whom I have taped interviews, notes, etc." (25). These interviews with women and mothers from this period commingle with the family history of Hans, Lene, and Anna, and help create the illusion of a "real" historical environment. The process of memory and historical appropriation itself, however, remains unquestioned. The subject who looks back at her childhood in Sanders-Brahms's film seems to have no self-doubts, unlike, for instance, Christa Wolf's narrator in *Patterns of Childhood*, who equates memory with forgetting, denying, falsifying, and repressing and unmasks it as unreliable and self-serving:[15] "One must forget a great deal and re-think and re-interpret a great deal before one can see oneself in the best light everywhere and at all times."[16] In Sanders-Brahms's film, the actual process of historical reconstruction does not seem to pose a problem; memory and narration run parallel. There are no "blind spots"[17] of memory here.

Fatherland, Mother Tongue

> I heard Aunt Barbara say: I don't know if I'll ever lose my inhibitions about saying the word "fatherland."
>
> ANGELIKA MECHTEL

"I am telling my parents' story because I am familiar with it, because it affects me deeply . . . and because this story is both individual and collective" (11). Sanders-Brahms's private story stands for the collective history of Germany; this explains her struggle to combine her autobiographical interest with the allegorical impulse toward abstraction. Perhaps reacting to the proliferation of confessional literature by women in the late 1970s, she seeks to go beyond "purely" private autobiography and show instead characters who symbolize something larger.[18] While an author like Christa Wolf makes a point of saying that her fictional character Christa T. has an "unexemplary life, a life that can't be used as a model,"[19] Sanders-Brahms emphasizes the universal, allegorical dimension of her characters. In contrast also to Fassbinder's *The Marriage of Maria Braun*, the allegorical intentions in Sanders-Brahms's film are undisguised. Maria Braun's story might stand as an allegory of the early days of the Federal

Republic, but this remains implicit. Sanders-Brahms, on the other hand, changed the title of her film from the original *For Lene* to *Germany, Pale Mother,* which clearly emphasizes the allegorical design. The title comes from a line of Bertolt Brecht's poem "Germany,"[20] written with uncanny foresight in 1933. Taking this line as the title of her autobiographical film also points to Sander-Brahms's literary ambitions.

The film opens with a voice-over reading of Brecht's five-stanza poem by his own daughter, Hanne Hiob. The text appears on the screen without accompanying images, radically reducing filmic enunciation to a written text and a voice. The poem opens up a fictional space in which, according to a tradition that goes back to the late Romantic poet Heinrich Heine, Germany appears as the mother:[21]

> O Germany, pale mother
> How you sit defiled
> Among the peoples!
> Among the besmirched
> You stand out.[22]

The poem's first lines imagine and allegorize the National Socialist terror as a family conflict in which the sons violate and shame mother Germany. The poem thus presents an image of Germany that evokes both fear and pity. The narrator distances himself from Germany ("When they hear the speeches issuing from your house, people laugh. / But whoever sees you grips his knife / As on seeing a murderess"), but at the same time presents Germany as a victim:

> O Germany, pale mother!
> What have your sons done to you
> That you sit among the peoples
> A mockery or a threat![23]

The sons' crimes have made Germany, the "pale mother," a victim who attempts to conceal the murderous deed ("And at the same time all see you / Hiding the hem of your skirt, which is bloody / With the blood of your / Best son."). The poem's language also has strong biblical undertones, alluding to the Old Testament's Book of Lamentations, in which the destruction of Jerusalem is poetically evoked and mourned.[24] Even in the last stages of his American exile Brecht did not abandon his ambivalent attitude toward the Germany of

1933, vacillating between rejection and sympathy, fear and affection, reproach and mourning. Unlike Thomas Mann, who in 1945 demanded harsh punishment for all Germans, Brecht made a distinction between the German people and the National Socialists when speaking about Germany's future.[25] Sanders-Brahms adopts this differentiation, already present in Brecht's poem of 1933, using gender-specific terms. The murderous sons of Brecht's poem are the National Socialists of her film, the fathers who go to war: Germany as the fathers' land. The German people, Germania, the "pale mother," on the other hand, appears as the victim of the sons' bloody deeds.

This allegorical construction is, to say the least, disputable, for women in the Third Reich were culprits and conformists as well as victims.[26] The allegory also works counter to the autobiographical attempt to present the characters in a differentiated, "realistic"—that is, contradictory—way. Thus the father is seen as a victim too, and in some scenes the mother appears as insensitive and cowardly. For instance, Lene as a young woman insists on pulling down the blinds when she and her sister see the Gestapo deport Rahel Bernstein, a school friend who lives across the street. Lene prefers not to see what happens outside her private sphere. "You can be so hard-hearted" (32), her sister says. Later in the film, the voice-over addresses the father with sympathy: "So they sent you off to kill people. You couldn't do it. Who can do it. My father. Fatherland" (112).

This conflation of abstract allegory and concrete autobiography leads to ruptures in the film, which were heavily attacked by West German critics.[27] In fact, the autobiographical project suffers whenever the personal and the private assume a contrived allegorical dimension. Thus after being raped by two drunken American soldiers in 1945, Lene says to her daughter, who watches in silence: "That's the right of the victors, little girl. They take the things and the women" (78). The allegorical logic of the film suggests that if the mother embodies Germany, then postwar Germany is the innocent victim of rape by America, a revisionist insinuation that the film—seen as allegory—implies.

The allegorical impulse also underlies the nearly twenty-minute sequence in which Lene tells her daughter the fairy tale of the robber bridegroom, taken in full length from Grimms' *Fairy Tales*. The story deals with a young girl sold by her father to a robber bridegroom. When she visits her bridegroom's house, she learns that he is a cannibal. "Turn back, turn back, you young bride, you are in a murderer's house," the birds sing, but the girl does not turn back. Instead, she watches from a hiding place as the cannibals hack a virgin to pieces. Soon afterwards, at the wedding feast, she tells the story of what she has seen, but she presents it as a dream. Thus we hear the story a second time, in the girl's narration, repeatedly punctuated by the sentence, "My dear, it was only a dream." The story of the cannibals and their innocent victim was so horrible that it could not be true; it could only be dreamed. But at the end of the story the bride suddenly holds up the severed finger of the murdered virgin, which had fallen into her lap while she witnessed the murder, to prove the validity of her story. "The robber, who had gone chalk white during the story, jumped up and was about to escape, but the guests captured him and turned him over to the court. He and his whole band were sentenced for their evil deeds" (96).

The fairy tale, the "mad monstrosity in the middle of the film," as Sanders-Brahms calls it (116), restates a central motif of Lene's own story: the violence of men toward women and women's fear of this violence. The fairy tale not only articulates "the primitive psychological fears that women have of men,"[28] it also associates marriage with death and self-destruction. The fairy tale refers to German history when the birds call out to the girl three times in the course of the story: "Turn back, turn back, you young bride, you are in a murderer's house." The images accompanying her narration support the association suggested by the fairy tale: that Nazi Germany is a house in which robbers kill people. Lene flees with Anna on her back through a forest. She comes to an abandoned factory, whose high chimneys and huge ovens evoke images of a concentration camp. They find the bloody corpse of a soldier in the bushes. This gruesome discovery is followed by a series of long, soundless aerial shots of Berlin's ghostly skeleton houses and documentary pictures of Hitler's burning bunker. These images, like the finger in the fairy tale, provide irrefutable evidence: if it were not for these documents, everyone would think that the story of Germany in the "Thousand-Year Reich" was a bad dream.

Precisely because fairy tales stand outside of history, they confront us directly with unconscious impulses and let us project into them our own wishes and fantasies. "Anyone who laughs at fairy tales has never suffered," says Alexander Kluge in *The Patriot*, where fairy tales also play a central role. Sanders-Brahms often alludes to fairy-tale motifs (for example, Lene pricks her finger—a dark foreboding—and, as in Sleeping Beauty, drops of blood appear; she is said to be the only black-haired daughter in a family with seven blond sisters; and so forth), and these allusions impart to the whole film a slightly unreal, artificial atmosphere, which is further enhanced by dark, gloomy music. Set in marked counterpoint to the fictional sequences of the film, documentary footage is used intermittently to dramatize air raids, to illustrate the desolate ruins of Berlin in 1945, and to remind us of the existence of *Trümmerfrauen,* the women who cleared away the tons of debris after the bombings ended. The powerful image of a forlorn little boy, who in the midst of rubble and ruins searches for his parents (a scene designed to contrast with the happy symbiosis between Lene and Anna), is incorporated into the reconstructed historical fiction. Sanders-Brahms has edited the clearly authentic sequence, which is taken from a 1945 documentary film in such a way (with shot/countershot and added dialogue) that it seems as if the boy from 1945 had carried on an imaginary conversation with the fictional Lene. The spectator notices the manipulation of the documentary footage and feels uneasy about the unquestioned appropriation of historical material into the fictional world.

Sanders-Brahms wants to present a picture of a country in which families are destroyed and children run around alone looking for their parents. In preparing *Germany, Pale Mother,* she again viewed documentary footage from the war and recognized that "That's how the war was. Those are the images that still appear in my dreams sometimes and that I am trying to control by making this film" (118–119). Experiences and fairy tales, film documentaries and dreams: to the extent that film repeats and works through historical experiences with the distancing effect of fiction, it may even have a therapeutic effect.

Structurally, the fairy-tale sequence serves as a bridge between the first part of the film (marriage and the father's battle at the front) and the second (the postwar era and the decay of the marriage). Sanders-Brahms gives us an extremely negative image of Germany under Adenauer. The father's Nazi friend, who survived the war by malingering, finds a niche for himself after 1945 much more readily than Hans, who, consumed with jealousy, carps at this "unfairness." And Uncle Bertrand in Berlin, air transport minister under

Hitler and now a deacon, speaks unctuously about religion and metaphysics, a caricature of the hypocritical opportunist. In the film's most polemical scene, we hear an original radio broadcast of a speech by Adenauer in the background while Hans and Lene have a party. Adenauer propagates Western ideals as the drunken men play an infantile game, hopping around and babbling. The contrast between the heralding of humanistic European values and the embarrassing spectacle of inebriated ex-soldiers could not be more shocking. Lene sits silently, as if absent, protesting through her speechlessness, refusing to participate in this society. She takes refuge in alcohol, disease, and finally depression and a suicide attempt. Lene's destiny provides a paradigm: a woman destroyed by the father/land.

Throughout the film, the camera follows Lene in tight close-ups or claustrophobic medium shots that emphasize her enclosure. The first close-up of Lene at the beginning of the film stylizes her serious, suffering face into the iconic image of a martyr. The camera takes in her features as the daughter speaks: "My mother. I learned to keep quiet, you said. You taught me to speak. Mother tongue" (112). The film begins and ends with woman as speechlessness incarnate. When her husband departs, Lene learns to speak for herself and teaches her daughter to speak as well. The daughter then feels called upon to speak for her mother after the father returns and the mother again retreats into silence, "speaking" only through her physical disease.[29] The silence of the one provokes the speech of the other. Julia Kristeva writes about female silence, using the image of all the silent women who have always stood mutely in the wings while men have staged history.[30] How this silent and hidden history comes to language is the project of Sanders-Brahms's film: "Our parents are looking for someone to tell their story. Not in a moralizing way, not with the undertone that it had to happen as it did; just so that they can recognize it and think about it again, not repress it deeper and deeper as the stories of the protagonists receive more and more elaborations" (10–11).

The memoirs and biographies of these "protagonists" have aroused great public interest over the years; Joachim Fest's Hitler biography and Albert Speer's memoirs became instant best-sellers. The culprits had an audience. They wrote history while the great mass of *Mitläufer,* that is, those who participated and "went along" without resistance or protest, declared the recent German past taboo and repressed their memories of it. They were not wrong to fear the moral judgment of the younger generation; even Sanders-Brahms feels compelled to say that she does not want to moralize when telling her parents' story (10). Edgar Reitz, too, made it his task to dig up the buried stories of common people between 1933 and 1945; instead of moral censure, his dominant tone is one of fascination, sympathy, and even nostalgia.

The project of rehabilitating, if not German *Geschichte* (history), then at least German *Geschichten* (stories), poses an insuperable problem: who, in the final analysis, carries the responsibility for the crimes committed during Hitler's regime? "It is true, and I believe them," said Sanders-Brahms, "they didn't want all that to happen. They didn't stop it, either. We reproach them for that, but with what justification? How are we better except that we have the advantage of being born later"? (11). The younger generation, it seems, had to reach a certain age and experience their own moral fallibility before they could understand, even excuse and pardon, parents who did not actively oppose the Nazi terror. Seen retrospectively, the survival skills of mothers, their independence, determination, and energy, even became objects of admiration: "This is the positive history of Germany under fascism, during the Second World War and afterwards. The history of the women who kept life going while the men were being sent to kill. It should have been told long ago. Now this generation of women, our mothers, is about 65 years old and not going to live much longer. Now it is time, high time, to write their history, their story, with images that we can still find in Berlin" (25).

Germany in 1945: 3.5 million men had been killed, hundreds of thousands crippled by the war. About 12 million soldiers remained in prison camps. Sixty-five percent of the population were women. These statistics take on life only through the stories and reports of people who lived through this time. By the late 1970s the survivors of the Third Reich were beginning to die out and the living traces of this time were gradually disappearing. A new, often nostalgic interest in the war generation and its experiences arose, resulting in numerous historical studies about the everyday lives of women in the Third Reich and the postwar era.[31]

Starting in the 1970s, as oral history became more popular and workshops for the study of local, everyday history sprang up across West Germany, women's experiences also came under closer scrutiny.

It is not surprising that the recent focus of women's oral history has been less on the Hitler period than on the time afterward, the reconstruction period. The title of a 1984 collection of interviews indicates the upbeat tone of these attempts to write a "positive history of Germany": *How We Managed All That: Unmarried Women Report on Their Lives after 1945.*[32] Sanders-Brahms wants to lend her voice to the generation of forgotten women who picked up the rubble in the first years after the war; there were 50,000 of them in Berlin alone. She wants to evoke memories in her viewers, memories that have been long buried. Rejecting the latter-day glorification of male heroism in a film like Fest's *Hitler: A Career,* Sanders-Brahms concentrates on the private, hidden stories of those

> who made the protagonists possible. Who elected Hitler. Or maybe didn't even vote for him but didn't protest, didn't join the underground, the resistance movement, weren't sent to a concentration camp, didn't emigrate, but instead wanted a simple life, love, marriage, a child, in the midst of the twilight of the gods, in the midst of the immense staging of the male dream of victory or annihilation, of triumph and the void, those millions of chorus members in the great opera whose last act portrayed the gigantic self-sacrifice of the protagonists and the chorus as well as the destruction of the stage set, finale, and ending.[33]

The revalorization of the simple, apolitical life of common people continues in Edgar Reitz's *Heimat.* Here, in *Germany, Pale Mother,* it functions as a gender-specific determination of historical experience. To the extent that history is made by men, according to the logic of the film, women must see themselves as the victims of this history.

Feminist Historiography

> The task to be accomplished is not the conservation of the past, but the redemption of the hopes of the past.
>
> MAX HORKHEIMER / THEODOR W. ADORNO

Is there a historiography from a feminist perspective? Judith Mayne argues in her essay "Visibility and Feminist Film Criticism":

> The task of rendering ourselves visible has, for feminist historians, entailed a process of re-reading the very notion of history: not as a series of Grand

Events in the public domain, but as a constant interaction of the realms of private and public life. For women have always participated in public life, although most frequently through the mediation of domestic life. "The personal is political" has by now become a truism for feminists. Yet we are only beginning to realize the extent to which the so-called "personal" areas of existence are shaped and shape in their turn the nature of social relations.[34]

In her film, Sanders-Brahms dramatizes this dialectic between the public and private spheres. But dialectic for her means setting up contrasts. Thus she intercuts documentary footage of bombs falling from airplanes with a realistically staged sequence of Lene giving birth; the images show the chasm between the private and the public realm through the critical opposition between life-giving and life-destroying activities. In addition, the scene refers to the different ways of experiencing the war at home and on the front. Women did not experience the war as a time of heroism; they experienced it "differently, more objectively," Sanders-Brahms writes in her preface to the filmscript: "Heroism was a matter of indifference to them, they would have preferred to have their men at home" (26). The private realm is played off against the political in a particularly provocative way when the film insists that Lene and Anna have their happiest moments in the midst of war, without a roof over their heads, surrounded by ruins. "Once hearth and home were demolished you became cheerful. We began to have good times after everything was destroyed" (113). The film implies that the physical destruction of the bourgeois-patriarchal household creates the freedom necessary for the mother to develop as an independent personality. After her husband returns from war—and with him the old patriarchal order—the conventional division between the private and public spheres is reinstated, and the mother is once again trapped in the home: "The stones we pounded were used to make houses that were worse than those before. Lene, if we had known. Lene, if we had only known . . . That was the return of the living rooms. The war began inside, once there was peace outside" (113). Inside and outside: immovable walls separate the personal and private realm from the political and public sphere.

The specifically female experiences of German history provide the point of departure and the point of convergence for Sanders-Brahms's presentation of the past. She is convinced that women have their own history, which differs from male history. For that reason official history must be rewritten from the perspective of women, that is, from the perspective of those for whom life continued after the "immense staging of the male dream of victory or annihilation": "They had to clear away the debris, install themselves, forget, and once again, among the remnants of the drama that had been played out, start living the simple life that they had wanted to lead from the start, just like any Frenchwoman, Italian, Englishwoman . . . Hitler in many films, a man. A film for my mother, thousands of women" (9–10).

As long as there are gender differences there will be gender-specific experiences that cannot be homogenized into a collective memory, into one single history.[35] "Women's writing," in Christa Wolf's words, exists to the extent that "women, for historical and biological reasons, experience a different reality than men. Experience reality differently than men and express it."[36] In keeping with this idea, Sanders-Brahms intentionally emphasizes experiences of reality in her film that are gender-specific and that do not occur in the male version of history: the significance of a birth, maternal care for the child, the fear of rape, the physical reaction of women to violence and psychological harm, and finally the relationship between mother and daughter, which is particularly important for the establishment of female identity.[37]

From the very beginning of the film Hans, the father, stands apart. He looks significantly older than Lene; the voice-over offers an explanation: "You were as young as she, my father. But in my memory your face is always as old as it was when you came home from the war they sent you to" (112). From the child's perspective, the father's very appearance is associated with "war." In his daughter's memory, he was outside of the family, somewhere out there where one fought for the "father-land." During his brief visits, the camera observes him from Lene's and Anna's perspective, often in tight medium shots and close-ups, so that the viewer perceives his presence as disruptive.

The more Hans becomes aware that he is disturbing the idyllic symbiosis between mother and child, the more aggressive he becomes toward his wife and child. "What should I have done with a father?" the voice-over asks, remembering. "I preferred to be a witch with Lene in the fields of rubble" (113). After his return from war and incarceration, Hans appears embittered, disoriented, and hostile. He hits his daughter when she asks him a pointed question, an experience often recounted in the literature about fathers of the late 1970s. "His self-confidence," writes Christoph Meckel about his father, "had collapsed after the war and had to be produced anew every day, violently, at the expense of his family . . . His brokenness tormented the children (they did not know that his fatherhood—the disillusioned, helpless despot—was characteristic of a whole generation)."[38]

The fathers, made deeply insecure by their military defeat and the knowledge (not often admitted) of the grotesque futility of their personal sufferings and losses, were beaten as soldiers, held in contempt as Germans, humiliated by the "reeducation" program. They were also confronted with the destruction of all the values and ideals for which they had supposedly fought. These fathers compensated for their loss of authority in their harshness toward their wives and children. "Write neatly," her father yells at Anna. His desperate struggle for recognition at least at home meets with mute hostility from his wife and daughter.

The fathers who returned from war were irritable and short-tempered; Sanders-Brahms intensifies this to the point of an unfeeling brutality. When Lene starts to suffer from her facial paralysis, the doctor misdiagnoses the illness and advises that all her teeth be pulled. Hans gives the doctor permission to do this. The camera shows this process in an agonizing close-up, accentuating the sadistic side of men's "treatment" of women. Repugnant and indelible images illustrate how the war's inhumanity carries over into the relations between man and woman. Writing about this film in *frauen und film*, Helke Sander said that she had never before seen "the connection between private male violence and politically sanctioned violence" so clearly.[39]

According to Freud, male aggression directs itself against the father but does not surface for fear of the father's reprisal, especially because of castration anxiety. This aggression instead finds an outlet outside the family, most often against scapegoats. Women handle aggressive impulses in a different way, as Margarete Mitscherlich-Nielsen points out in her "Speech about her Own Land: Germany":

> Women also suffer from castration fantasies, but much less frequently than men. The fear of reprisal in the sense of physical destruction, that fear which so easily turns into violence, plays a much smaller role. The central fear of women is the fear of loss of love. In keeping with that,

they transform their aggression into masochistic self-sacrifice, guilt feelings, or a reproachful attitude rather than into a search for scapegoats on whom the violent aggression produced through rivalry can be discharged without fear. The rearing and the gender-specific development of women predestine them less to develop a basic structure of paranoia linked with violence, even though fear of loss of love makes them inclined to accept the role models, prejudices, and values of a male-dominated society. The way in which both genders are reared naturally depends on these "values." In other words, the witch hunts, anticommunism, anti-Semitism, the arms race mentality, all disastrous alliances of paranoia and violence, are more part of men than of women.[40]

Sanders-Brahms shows these gender-specific differences in confronting aggression in her portrayal of the recent German past. Hans releases his stored-up anger by mistreating his wife and child, while Lene masochistically acts out the part of the victim and escapes into sickness, alcohol, and attempted suicide. From the perspective of her feminist daughter in the 1970s, the stages of this fatal path toward self-destruction must be shown, but they must also be criticized. Consequently Sanders-Brahms diminishes the sympathy we feel toward her mother by having Lene appear in an increasingly negative light. Not only does she withdraw more and more from active life; we even see her, in a fit of helpless aggression, fling hot soup into her daughter's face. This scene stages a rupture between mother and daughter, as well as a break with the older generation's self-sacrificial attitude that produced these self-destructive symptoms. In phrases such as "I didn't marry. I unlearned that from you" (112), we hear the daughter's resistance to repeating her mother's story.

The search for female identity, the separation from the mother, the settling of accounts with the father, the gender-specific historiography, and the perspective of memory: these are motifs of the feminist film that did not emerge until the late 1970s. They recur also in Jutta Brückner's *Hungerjahre* (*Years of Hunger,* 1980) and Jeanine Meerapfel's *Malou* (1981). Brückner's autobiographical film *Years of Hunger* deals in a more open, essayistic form than *Germany, Pale Mother* with the oppressive, numbing domestic atmosphere in Germany during the economic miracle and the Cold War. The film's perspective is that of a thirteen-year-old girl, whose gradual alienation from her parents, her environment, and even her own body is recounted. The author's voice-over monologue, consisting of reflections, literary quotations, and scraps of personal memory, plays against a background of ascetic black-and-white images. The story, which ends with the girl's suicide attempt, is told nostalgically and at the same time despairingly from the retrospective viewpoint of the remembering subject. Brückner's film mirrors the hypocritical, repressive family structures of the Adenauer era, but, in contrast to *Germany, Pale Mother,* there is no allegorical reference to Germany as a fateful whole. The title alludes to the hunger of those years for life, love, experience, and meaning. Through a polyphony of images, sounds, poetic texts, and retrospective autobiographical commentaries, *Years of Hunger* gives a complex insight into the oppressive petit-bourgeois consciousness of the 1950s and a sense of the era's emotional barrenness.

The fragmentary nature of its structure and the analytical, dispassionate camera in Brückner's film keep the viewer at a greater distance than in Jeanine Meerapfel's unabashedly autobiographical *Malou.* Her melodramatic film uses flashbacks to show the identity crisis of a daughter and her tormented struggle with her mother, a woman shattered by a life spent in political exile. *Malou* also reflects the German feminist film of the early 1980s: the search for identity as a way back to one's own mother, the gesture of remembering and the coming to terms with a national past that is reflected and inscribed in personal biography.

The beginnings of politically engaged feminist cinema at the end of the 1960s had quite different goals.[41] It arose out of autonomous women's groups in the context of the student movement. A collective of women filmmakers formed who wanted to educate audiences about themes specific to women (especially paragraph 218, which deals with the abortion issue, equal pay, and equal rights) and to create female solidarity. These themes provided the focus of Sanders-Brahms's first films, *Angelika Urban, Verkäuferin, 24 Jahre (Angelika Urban, Salesgirl, 24),* her *cinéma vérité* documentary short of 1969 about a day in the life of a department store employee, as well as her first feature film, *Unterm Pflaster ist der Strand (The Beach under the Sidewalk,* 1974). These early, political feminist films consciously set themselves apart from so-called women's films:

> Unlike women's films, which are made about and for, but seldom by, women and which follow an affirmative, melodramatic concept, the feminist film is always made by women and is empowered by female political emancipatory engagement. According to the self-understanding of the

women's movement that arose in the 1960s, the feminist film promotes self-analysis and the raising of consciousness and is a call to action to dismantle discrimination and oppression. Favorite themes, therefore, are the effect of female socialization, role behavior, identity problems, the abilities and compulsions in the personality structure; the fateful psychological consequences of compulsory role behavior; analysis of male strategies of suppression.[42]

But the feminist cinema soon began to explore new issues. In the wake of Jacques Lacan, Julia Kristeva, and Luce Irigaray, but lagging several years behind, German feminists began to discuss more radical theories centered around the filmic construction of the female subject in general. The feminist film was no longer to be defined through its content and overt ideology (discussion of women's issues or the critique of patriarchal structures) but through its narrative form and its positioning of the male and female viewer.[43] New ways of storytelling and expression were sought. The influential essays by Claire Johnston ("Women's Cinema as Counter Cinema") and Laura Mulvey ("Visual Pleasure and Narrative Cinema") from the mid-1970s attacked especially the classical narrative cinema of Hollywood in which men are portrayed as active, as bearers of the look, while women are invariably shown as passive, the object of the male gaze.[44] In the Hollywood film the camera traditionally assumes a male perspective, so that even films critical of society perpetuate a stereotypical view of women. It was above all the male gaze of the camera that needed to be questioned and undermined first. According to Johnson and Mulvey, feminist films must become "counter-cinema": they must destroy the conventions of the filmic production of meaning if they do not want to invalidate new contents through old forms of presentation. "The most authentic thing," Helke Sander wrote in a similar vein in 1978, "that women today can express in all areas, even in art, does not consist in unifying and harmonizing the means but in their destruction. Where women are true, they break things."[45]

Feminist films that adopt this definition consider it their duty to disrupt conventionalized patterns of viewing, to unmask filmic signs as the vehicles of ideology, and to destroy the structure and coherence of the classic realistic film. This project of the "deconstruction" of the reigning codes creates affinities between the feminist film and the experimental and avant-garde film.[46]

Sanders-Brahms's *Germany, Pale Mother* adopts some formal elements of the new feminist film (the presence of an authorial speaking and listening voice, the unorthodox narrative economy in the fairy-tale sequence, the avoidance of the male gaze), but it goes beyond the gender-specific interests of the politically engaged feminist film in its focus on Germany and German problems. Sanders-Brahms anchors the traditional feminist themes (the relations between the sexes, the mother-daughter relationship, the critique of patriarchy) in the context of German history and thus historicizes them. This perspective reveals buried and obscured traditions and continuities, as well as missed opportunities and foiled developments in German history. During the war, when men were drafted, women lived on their own for a few years and gained "an awareness of their strength" (26). "After the war," Sanders-Brahms contends, "that strength in many cases was suddenly worthless. But we, children of that generation, who were born during the war, inherited it" (26). For the "children of the ruins," emancipation was the first experience of their childhood, an emancipation experienced in the midst of a battle for survival. Sanders-Brahms's memory of her mother as a *Trümmerfrau* gave her the courage to actualize the female self-realization that had been stultified in the early postwar years. In her search for origins, she found hope for the future.

6

GERMANY AS MEMORY

Edgar Reitz's *Heimat*

"We should no longer forbid ourselves to take our personal lives seriously" (Edgar Reitz).
—Marita Breuer in *Heimat*

"Our memories are neither objective notations nor filmic images. Our consciousness works with a thousand mirrors, each of which refracts a thousand times ... Our memories are personal, which merely means that they do not yield an image of the world but a puzzle of that image, created in our mental hall of mirrors, with our individual reflections, omissions, and additions. That may appear to be an image of the world and serves us as such; in truth, however, it is only a representation of our consciousness, as we usually call the refracting mirror of our brain."

Horn smoked and looked out the window.

"Am I boring you?"

CHRISTOPH HEIN

Scenes from the Provinces

Asked by an American interviewer about the meaning of "Heimat," the untranslatable German word for home and homeland, Edgar Reitz responded:

> The word is always linked to strong feeling, mostly remembrances and longing. "Heimat" always evokes in me the feeling of something lost or very far away, something which one cannot easily find or find again. In this respect, it is also a German romantic word and a romantic feeling with a particular romantic dialectic. "Heimat" is such that if one would go closer and closer to it, one would discover that at the moment of arrival it is gone, it has dissolved into nothingness. It seems to me that one has a more precise idea of "Heimat" the further one is away from it. This for me is "Heimat," it's fiction, and one can arrive there only in poetry, and I include film in poetry.[1]

Reitz made a sixteen-hour film about this romantic fiction called Heimat and struck a resonant cord. No fewer than 25 million West German television viewers saw at least one of the eleven episodes of Reitz's film on television in the fall of 1984; an average of 9 million viewers watched each episode.[2] *Heimat* was also presented as a 35-millimeter film (shown in two parts over two days) in major European and American cities; it won prizes at numerous film festivals. A subtitled version was shown on American television, first on Bravo cable in 1985 and then on PBS in the fall of 1987.

In West Germany, *Heimat* generated more debate than any other recent film (with the exception of *Holocaust* in 1979). The stories and images that the film invented about the Hunsrück region, a rural area in the southern part of the Rhineland, have since 1984 become part of the West German public memory; it is now hard to think of Heimat in West Germany without thinking of the film *Heimat*. At the same time, it is difficult to discuss the film without taking into consideration the multitude of connotations, overtones, and implications that the term "Heimat" has accrued in German history. The reception of *Heimat* clearly showed that more than the response to a film was at issue.

Reitz was one of the first directors of the Young German Film; along with Alexander Kluge, he had signed the Oberhausen manifesto in 1962. Both men were thirty at the time. Reitz may also be one of the last of the *auteur* filmmakers whose work retains its basis in the "real experiences of the author."[3] *Heimat* is at its core an autobiographical film. Born in a village in the Hunsrück a year before Hitler's rise to power, Reitz left the provinces when he was twenty, like the film's male protagonist, Paul, and did not return (again like Paul) until he was almost fifty. Then, for the next five years, starting in 1979, Reitz made a film about his homeland that dramatizes the tensions between "staying here," leaving, and returning.

This return to the native region, to the place of one's birth and childhood, coincides with similar tendencies in the literature of the late 1970s and early 1980s, a literature concerned with memory and autobiography. Sanders-Brahms's *Germany, Pale Mother* and Kluge's *The Patriot*—although completely different in style—belong to the same trend. Nonetheless, Reitz's radical regionalism, his peasant characters, his use of dialect, and his minute, often nostalgic descriptions of everyday life in the village have no equivalent in contemporary German literature or film. His film evokes associations of the "homeland" and "blood and soil" literature of the Nazi era—associations that must be regarded as dangerous. This interweaving of provincialism and homeland is a specifically German phenomenon whose historical dimension has continually been repressed and denied. Scenes of provincial life are never innocent in Germany.

"Man trägt wieder Erde" ("People Are Returning to the Soil")[4] was the title of an essay in the *Literarische Welt* of 1931, which criticized the new literary trend of rural themes and regional writing that was polemically opposed to the modern, avant-garde literature of the city. There was good reason for anxiety about the reactionary tendency of this new agrarian regionalism, for only a few years later its major motifs—love of hearth and home, hatred of anything foreign or urban—were easily assimilated into the fascist "blood and soil" literature of the National Socialists.

The high value placed on the simple life in the provinces "with their belief in law and order"[5] dates back to the Heimat movement of the 1890s, which had arisen in reaction to rapid industrialization and the concomitant shift from rural to urban living. In the ideology of this antimodern, antiurban movement, Heimat was precisely that which was abandoned on the way into the cities; from then on the word "Heimat" began to connote "region," "province," and "country." Since the era of industrialization, German literature has weighted this term with emotional connotations almost to the breaking point: Heimat means the site of one's lost childhood, of family, of identity. It also stands for the possibility of secure human relations, unalienated, precapitalist labor, and the romantic harmony between the country dweller and nature. Heimat refers to everything that is not distant and foreign. Ernst Bloch, at the conclusion of his three-volume *Prinzip Hoffnung* (*Principle of Hope*), describes Heimat as the utopian antithesis to alienation per se: "There arises in the world something which shines into the childhood of all and in which no one has yet been: homeland."[6]

From its beginnings in the late nineteenth century, Heimat literature attracted a wide audience not only because it met the needs of all those readers who had trouble following modernist literature, but also because it conjured up a rural, archaic image of the German Reich and a German community rooted in an ahistorical, mythic time. It promised order, permanence, and national pride. From this perspective, the city always remained the "Other"—the site of rootlessness, hectic activity, and transient, superficial values; a soulless, anonymous desert of concrete; the scene of international business, immorality, and decadence. All these images of horror figured in the Heimat movement, and they reappeared under National Socialism as a counterpoint to the idealized notion of Heimat. During the 1920s the concept absorbed agrarian-romantic, reactionary, and also anti-Semitic variants, which in turn were incorporated in the National Socialist "blood and soil" movement. After 1933 Heimat was a synonym for race (blood) and territory (soil), a deadly combination

that led to the exile or annihilation of anyone who did not "belong."
Under the National Socialists Heimat meant the murderous exclusion
of everything "un-German."

The concept of Heimat acquired new layers of meaning after World
War II, when millions of Germans had lost their homes or were
displaced from their homeland. Refugees from former German territories in eastern Europe encountered Germans whose own homes
had been destroyed. The places of childhood were in ruins, family
members had perished in the war, and the nation was divided among
the victors. The German Reich lay in ashes. Thus, in the first years
after the war, Heimat signified above all an experience of loss, a
vacuum that Germans filled with nostalgic memories. The many
Heimat films made during the 1950s reconstruction era portrayed
Germany as a rural, provincial homeland with which all Germans
could identify. These films concentrated on German landscapes such
as the Black Forest and the Lüneburg Heath that had not been
devastated by the war; on untainted, politically naive, and innocent
Germans; and on regional dress, customs, speech, and music. Hit
songs from the fifties like Freddy Quinn's "Heimatlos" ("Without a
Home") stylized the quest for Heimat into an inescapable fate: the
German as a sailor, far away, yearning for home. Like no other word,
Heimat encompasses at once kitsch sentiment, false consciousness,
and genuine emotional needs.

A similar, widespread feeling about Heimat suddenly reemerged in
the mid-seventies. The reasons for this are complex. On the one
hand, the political energies of the sixties, directed primarily at Vietnam, Cuba, and China, had exhausted themselves; on the other hand,
Germans were becoming aware of the rapidly increasing dangers
facing their own country. Poisonous industrial by-products had pol-
luted water, land, and air; acid rain had decimated forests; nuclear
power plants and NATO missiles posed a threat to survival itself.
Fears about the quality of life and the future caused the outer-directed
political activism of the sixties to turn inward, to Germany itself. In
1967, Martin Walser had written with gentle irony that "'Heimat'
is the kindest word for retardation."[7] Less than ten years later, as
progress itself had become suspect, such misgivings were forgotten.
A 1975 issue of *Kursbuch,* the literary and political journal that often
best articulates (and shapes) the latest trends, was dedicated to "the
provinces."[8] It advocated that the Left appropriate the much-

maligned concept of Heimat, which in the postwar period had mostly been used by German refugee organizations and right-wing parties. In the late seventies, political concern for the environment united with a renewed interest in the private and subjective sphere. Fear of the future also cast a new light on the past: looking backward at origins implied the hope for an orientation in the present. These distinct but secretly related hopes, fears, and interests worked together to bring about a "renaissance of feeling for 'Heimat'" by the end of the seventies.[9]

The film *Heimat* belongs to this emotionally and semantically overdetermined discourse on Heimat and regionalism; it seems like the culmination of all the positive and negative connotations associated with Heimat from the 1920s on. The film shows the hominess of a secure childhood in the country, the power of village life to create deep bonds, strenuous but unalienated manual labor, and local eccentrics. It also shows the smug narrowness of simple-minded provincials and their inhumanity which excludes everything that is not *heimisch* or "local." Nostalgic scenes lit like old Dutch genre paintings alternate with discordant scenes reminiscent of the critical Heimatfilm of the early seventies, which presented country life as a false idyll, a breeding ground for private and collective neuroses.[10] Ambivalent in its very structure, *Heimat* is a classic Heimatfilm to the extent that it adopts a stock narrative pattern and evokes sentimental pictures of regional life. Yet at the same time it runs counter to the traditional Heimatfilm because it ultimately undermines any spurious idyllic facade by its ending. But even in his polemical scenes Reitz manifests an ambivalent love for his Heimat, a nostalgic longing for identity and security that was not part of the critical Heimatfilm of the Left. Reitz knew what he was doing when he used the title *Heimat* in the 1980s: "I didn't want to film the concept of 'Heimat' as something abstract, but I tried to present a practical confrontation with everything that it triggers in people's feelings, positive and negative, in this peculiar morass of experiences and passions and fears. I was uneasy about the word, because it is burdened by our history and also by present circumstances; nowadays 'Heimat' means only something endangered, not something warm and cozy."[11]

Reitz's "practical confrontation" sought to address the contradictory multiplicity of meanings clustered around the concept of Heimat. As a result, the film itself is contradictory and ambiguous, depending on the viewer's own disposition. A cover story in *Der Spiegel,* for instance, interpreted the film as the successful result of a sustained and unrelenting attempt to rehabilitate the "longing for a 'Heimat'" that had been misused by the National Socialists,[12] but Reitz himself vehemently denied this interpretation in an interview:

> Just the opposite. I feel uncomfortable with that view. But I don't believe that the film as a whole fosters such a tendency. I would be disappointed if that would happen. The film ends with a sense of estrangement. "Heimat," closeness, childhood, security, warmth, grandmotherliness, and all these things are being destroyed and turned into memories. That happens more and more the closer we get to the present in the story . . . I would consider it a terrible corny lie if the film suggested a permanent inner world of "Heimat" which cannot exist. It can only exist as memory, as longing.[13]

The film shows both the idyll and its destruction, the reconstructed Heimat with its attributes of "security," "warmth," and so on, and the sentimental memory of Heimat. It is characteristic of the collective mood of the 1980s that most of the press reports have concentrated far more on the nostalgic than on the critical aspects of the film.

On the film's narrative level, the inherently contradictory experiential and emotional content of the German concept of Heimat corresponds to the tension between staying and leaving, between longing for distant places and homesickness. The chronicle concentrates primarily on the stories of those who stayed, willingly or unwillingly. Maria and her sister-in-law Pauline, Maria's son Ernst, whose wish to be a flier comes true for a short time during the war, and Eduard and Lucy dream of breaking out of the confines of the village. In keeping with the conventions of provincial literature, it is the women who remain at home, taking care of the house and children, occasionally venturing out to see a Zarah Leander movie and dream of escaping. The film revolves around the figure of Maria, born in 1900, who spends her whole life in the village of Schabbach. The film begins when she is nineteen and falls in love with Paul Simon; it ends when she dies, lonely and worn, at eighty-two.

Like Lene, the mother figure in Sanders-Brahms's *Germany, Pale Mother,* Maria embodies security, safety, and permanence. The film's secret message is: wherever she is, there is Heimat—another motif anticipated in many Heimat novels and much regional literature.

Sons, neighbors, and friends always return to her, occupying the same place at her wooden kitchen table. The camera emphasizes this permanence by shooting the different scenes from the same angle. *Heimat* tells Maria's story, with numerous other stories from four generations of three large families assembled around hers. She marries Paul Simon "because he is different" and has two sons with him. One day in 1928 Paul leaves the village without saying a word. He is considered missing. Maria raises her sons alone, falls in love with an engineer, and has a son with him. Suddenly, twelve years after Paul's departure, Maria receives a letter from Detroit with the return address "Simon Electrics, Inc." In 1947 Paul Simon, now a "rich American," returns to his Heimat, but he remains an outsider. He has no answer when Maria asks him why he left. In the film's narrative economy, America signifies the antithesis of Heimat; the cliché of the "great world" serves as a contrast to the scenes of provincial life.[14]

The film is filled with images of provincial life: quiet shots of landscapes, of people working, of objects and banal daily routines—long wordless passages in which the camera goes on a voyage of discovery or sequences in which people chat in an almost improvised way. Women sing at the spinning wheel, grouped in a painterly composition; the village smith stands at his anvil, pounding a wheel as sparks fly; Maria kneads dough: the film lingers over such genre scenes.

The long duration of the film's production shows that these scenes meant a great deal to Reitz. Not only did he set the action in the region of Germany in which he was born and grew up; he and his co-author, Peter Steinbach, spent more than a year doing oral history research and writing the script on location. The film was then shot over a period of a year and a half, also on location in the Hunsrück, in close contact with the local population. More than 150 amateur actors and no fewer than 4,000 extras came from the region. Whole villages seem to have played themselves. Although Schabbach, where most of the story takes place, is a fictitious place, constructed from a composite of four different Hunsrück villages, it produced such a strong impression of reality that tourists later visited the Hunsrück, looking for Schabbach.

As a result of his long presence on location, Reitz won over the local population for the project. Numerous stories and anecdotes from village inhabitants, as well as things overheard at the inn, found their way into the film. The farmers lent Reitz numerous everyday objects, which added to the film's authenticity. The language, too, strives to be authentic; the Hunsrück dialect of the amateur actors gives the film an unmistakable local color. The elaborate reconstruction of country life and work produced many scenes that contribute to the nostalgic atmosphere of the film while slowing down the narrative pace. "Take your time," Reitz told viewers of his "filmic novel," "don't make other plans while this film is showing, be sure you have a little peace and quiet, stop the hectic pace of your daily life, and enjoy the beauty in the film, a modest, simple beauty that has now become a rarity."[15] Reitz wanted the television viewer to adopt the same type of concentration as a viewer in a movie house. In the film this meditative attitude is expressed in lengthy medium shots, slow pans, and a mostly unobtrusive use of the camera that shuns dramatic effects. This descriptive chronicle style changes only in the final part of the series, as the destruction of the Heimat becomes more and more visible: the cuts become quicker and more hectic, the light harsher, the composition more cluttered.

As in the Heimat novel of the early twentieth century, Reitz divides German identity into regional identities. He feels that an authentic German identity, and a Heimat, are possible only at the periphery, far from the official centers of power—in the provinces. Germany as a nation or a state cannot be a Heimat; only the familiar landscape, the delimited and intimate scene of childhood, can serve this function.

"Heimat" in this film means first of all a place outside of history, removed from progress, caught in cyclical time, a place that seems subject only to nature and the seasons,[16] far from the Reich and its capital. Schabbach is at the center of the world: "We sit exactly between Paris and Berlin," the mayor of Schabbach says to a couple of neighbors one summer evening in 1930. "And if you draw a line from the North Pole to the South Pole, it would run straight through Schabbach, too" (129).[17] But the region did not remain self-contained for long, for the German Reich soon reached out for it. The fields were destroyed by the Autobahns that were built to transport Hitler's troops. The Reich brought war into the villages and robbed the region of its autonomy, homogenizing it through its centralized bureaucracy. The telephone and radio integrated the village into the Reich's network and connected it to the center, the metropolis of Berlin, which sent radio signals to "all of Germany." The Reich itself appears here as the destroyer of Heimat.

Reitz is concerned with Heimat in the Hunsrück region, not with Germany as a whole; for him "Heimat" and "nation" are even contradictory terms.[18] For this reason he is more conscientious than other German filmmakers about localizing his images in a particular region of Germany; more than in the films of Fassbinder or Kluge, Reitz lets us know where we are.

History of the Everyday

What is history for the elite has always been work for the masses.

HEINER MÜLLER

Since its beginnings, the filmic medium has had a natural affinity to the physical world of everyday life. The first films made by the French pioneers of early cinema, Auguste and Louis Lumière, showed documentary shots of workers leaving the factory and of a train arriving in the station. The film camera was employed as a tool to reproduce "life and its full naturalness by means of electricity," as we read in an announcement of one of the first German film showings in 1895.[19] The birth of cinema from the spirit of technology and its plebeian childhood in amusement parks and fairgrounds kept it excluded from the dominant classical-bourgeois culture for a long time (longer in Germany, with its strong tradition of the educated bourgeoisie, than elsewhere); from its inception, the cinema was a medium of and for everyday culture.[20]

No one has seen this natural connection between film and ordinary, visible reality more clearly than Siegfried Kracauer. In his *Theory of Film: The Redemption of Physical Reality,* he writes:

The small random moments which concern things common to you and me and the rest of mankind can indeed be said to constitute the dimension of everyday life, this matrix of all other modes of reality. It is a very substantial dimension. If you disregard for a moment articulate beliefs, ideological objectives, special undertakings, and the like, there still remain the sorrows and satisfactions, discords and feasts, wants and pursuits, which mark the ordinary business of living. Products of habits and microscopic interaction, they form a resilient texture which changes slowly and survives wars, epidemics, earthquakes, and revolutions. Films tend to explore this texture of everyday life, whose composition varies according to place, people, and time.[21]

This "texture of everyday life" is also the foundation of *Heimat.* Working, eating, drinking, celebrating, falling in love, marrying, raising children, worrying and rejoicing: these everyday experiences below the surface of ideology and political events are reconstructed in documentary detail in *Heimat.* Film registers ordinary physical reality more precisely and effectively than any other medium. "The cinema is materialistically minded," says Kracauer; "it proceeds from 'below' to 'above.'"[22]

In *Heimat,* the visible world is no less important than the narrated and remembered world. Places such as the street that runs through the village and the parental house are more than just film sets; they trigger and catalyze memory and become themselves objects of narration. Everyday objects are infused with emotional content through close-ups, special lighting effects, or still-life compositions. Places and things seem to have a life of their own in this film; they tell stories independent of those of the main characters. As Reitz said in 1979: "Things live longer than people, we live with them, they have their own atmosphere, a different rhythm from the human rhythm . . . I think it is proper to defend things in a society that consumes them and throws them away."[23]

Reitz also wants to preserve the scores of private untold stories that make up the fabric of history. Originally planned as a series of successive life stories in the spirit of *A Thousand and One Nights,*[24] *Heimat* takes time to pursue these private stories. As a response to the American television series *Holocaust,* Reitz wrote: "There are thousands of stories among our people worth filming, which are based on endless minutiae of experience. These stories individually rarely seem to contribute to the evaluation and explanation of history, but taken together they could compensate for this lack. We should no longer forbid ourselves to take our personal lives seriously."[25]

Reitz hopes that this anecdotal approach to history will result in stories that interlock like a jigsaw puzzle to form a larger image of German history. His approach thus corresponds to the aims of *Alltagsgeschichte,* the historiography of everyday life, a controversial recent movement that argues against traditional political history as well as against sociological and structural approaches to history.[26]

This new historiography "from below" is concerned with the stories of workers and farmers, with oral culture and native traditions not recorded in official documents. The history of everyday life not only involves "giving a voice to the nameless masses";[27] it also means discovering new, previously neglected sources of information: photograph albums, home movies, diaries, and the memories of "common people." Everyday history is the history of experience. Thus it considers historical events only insofar as they affect the private sphere; oral history records only first-hand experience. Everyday history therefore rarely acknowledges the undeniable political and economic threads which, however invisible, run through, and often determine, individual private stories.

As a logical consequence of Reitz's approach, large-scale historical events such as inflation, the political turmoil of the Weimar Republic, the currency reforms of 1924 and 1948, and the establishment of two Germanies in 1949 are not registered in *Heimat,* because they do not touch the cyclical life of the villagers in an immediate and visible way. In a certain sense, *Heimat* resists the attempt to write *one* history of Germany and thereby to reduce the multiplicity of contradictory aspects of concrete experience to a linear, causal story. For Reitz (as for Kluge, Fassbinder, and Sanders-Brahms), there is no such thing as *the* history of Germany—there is only a web of innumerable everyday stories.

The stories in *Heimat* are linked primarily through the interrelationship of three families over four generations. Since all the main characters are surrounded by their families—father, mother, siblings, children—as well as by friends, there is a multitude of possible combinations to generate stories. New constellations arise whenever new figures, usually fianceés, arrive from elsewhere (Lucy from Berlin, Martha from Hamburg, Klärchen from Silesia) and are either accepted into the interrelated and intermarried village community or, as in the case of Klärchen, excluded from it. Over a period of more than eighty years (and sixteen hours of film time) life stories unfold that are so intertwined that they cannot be separated from the tissue of the film without tearing it. The professional and amateur actors seem to be playing themselves (Reitz spent years looking for "types"); they are not subordinated to an overarching stylization as, for instance, in *The Marriage of Maria Braun,* or allegorically overdetermined as in *Germany, Pale Mother.* What is new in Reitz's film is the uneconomical plethora of characters whose plot function is often difficult to determine. This style allows him to use narrative enigmas that remain unexplained even at the end of the film. In the first sequence, for instance, the hastily concealed, naked body of an unknown woman is discovered in the woods. She is obviously the victim of a murder, but neither culprit nor motive is revealed, nor are they actively sought. The scene serves a symbolic function in that it shows a sudden invasion of the outer world into this closed, rural idyll, and the violence lurking beneath its surface. The atmospheric effect—a sense of mystery and insecurity—is more important to the film than action sequences, which in the classical narrative would inevitably lead to the discovery of the murderer. Reitz leaves the murder unsolved and thus lends a disquieting dimension to everyday reality.

The film begins with a sequence that shows an open field with a rock bearing the inscription "Made in Germany" carved in Gothic script. The association of weathered rocks that stand like ruins in the natural landscape and the antiquated script is meant to intensify the fiction of an eternal, natural presence: the inscription, and by extension Germany, will last as long as the rock does. Then the film's actual title, *Heimat,* written in capital letters and modern type, suddenly shoots out at the viewer. At the same time dark clouds, shot in time-lapse photography, move threateningly toward the viewer at an unnatural speed. Accompanied by the sound-track collage of whistling wind and harshly accented music, this sequence does not announce an idyllic mood or a nostalgic atmosphere, but rather tension and crisis, conflict and danger.

The first scene of the film proper begins with a long shot of a meadow, over which a date has been superimposed: "May 9, 1919, a Friday." Thus from the very beginning the narrative mode of a historical chronicle is established. At the same time, naming the day of the week on which the lost son comes home signals an oral narrative tradition. The rest of the superimposed text—"Paul Simon returned from the World War. He had traveled six days on foot from France to the Hunsrück"—provides the background for the story that ensues. The text informs the viewer not only that the film is consciously beginning at a certain point in time but also that it will show only a limited excerpt from a larger spatial and temporal reality; it also indicates an anonymous authorial narrator who seems to be responsible for the selection, ordering, and dating of events. Thus the very beginning of the film announces the epic and chronological narrative structure that characterizes the whole film cycle. The chronicler, who remains in the background, narrates—that is, remembers—selected stories from history, which are told as units, in closed chapters, and are given their own dates and titles (in this case, "Longing for Distant Lands").

In the first scene the camera seems to have been positioned in the open field, waiting for Paul to return from a war prison camp. When he appears on the horizon, the camera hurries toward him in an oblique tracking shot and comes to rest only when it faces him in a medium close-up. Paul stops for a moment and hesitates when he sees the familiar church tower over the hills (the camera has also stopped at this point); then he walks down into the village with a firm step, with the camera following him. The rapid convergence of camera and protagonist makes the viewer aware of the camera's presence and from the outset implies that the viewer's perceptions are dependent on what the camera captures.

After a cut to a medium close-up, Paul is seen marching through the village. When he looks up at the church tower, the camera follows in a point-of-view shot; it pans up and we see what he sees. The camera thus changes from an objective (observing) to a subjective (interpreting) perspective. Here the camera functions primarily as a narrator, first documenting the unchanged atmosphere of the village and its rural features, then briefly introducing all the figures who are important to Paul. On his way through the village he is recognized first by Maria, who later becomes his wife; we see her blurred reflection in a windowpane. The camera then shifts its attention to Maria's reaction. Thus the camera movements correspond to an epic narrative stance that highlights characters according to their narrative function within the story.

When Paul reaches his father's smithy, he looks through the window and sees his father at the anvil, engrossed in his work. The open smithy with its glowing fire and threatening blows has mythological connotations, reminiscent of the old German Nibelungen legend, that provide an "echo of the distant past" and remind one of "images of childhood."[28] The words are Adorno's, describing his reaction as he accidentally came upon a long-forgotten smithy in the Odenwald. A nostalgic glow in the style of old peasant portraits is seen in the close-up of the faces of Paul's mother and father, which Reitz intercuts as Paul enters his parents' house.

Without a word, the long-lost son begins to help his father hammer a wagon wheel. The camera captures this action in an extremely lengthy take, as if the narrator wanted to express the idea that the war had no impact on everyday work "which had to be done." Reitz's fascination with depicting manual labor in detail serves several functions in this scene. On the one hand, the scene in the smithy, in which nothing really happens, slows down the narrative flow; on the other, it deepens the emotional intensity of the son's return and intensifies the viewer's involvement and curiosity as to the further course of the story. This pleasure in containing and diverting the narrative stream determines the structure of *Heimat* and imparts to the film an epic sweep as well as a strong documentary cast.

The following scene, in which Paul sits silently at the table, brings to mind Walter Benjamin's observation that no one who came back from the First World War was able to talk about it.[29] The experiences were such that they could not be shared. As parents, siblings, and neighbors file into the kitchen to greet Paul, they all speak of the war ("I still remember, when they mobilized, we were harvesting grain" [29]), but Paul says nothing. The film allows individual characters to present themselves through typical small gestures and expressions. The camera work is relatively unsteady in this scene; pans and short tracking shots (especially around Paul) alternate with shot/countershots. But there is always intentionally more in the picture than is necessary for the plot. The often banal conversations of the assembled villagers, the partly absurd, partly horrifying news from beyond the village, which Eduard reads aloud from the newspaper,[30] and the accumulation of visual information about life in the village give rise to a dense, polyphonic text that seems to exclude nothing and—even more than Fassbinder's postwar images in *The Marriage of Maria Braun*—achieves a strongly "realistic" effect through its excessive detail.

This realism, however, is often undercut by brief incongruous and "unrealistic" scenes. At the beginning of the first episode, for instance, we are given an extreme close-up of flypaper hanging from the ceiling, with flies trapped and dying on its sticky yellow surface. This shot, with its strong visual accentuation and the emphasis it receives later in the scene—we see Paul suddenly get up on impulse and stare at the trapped flies—symbolizes the situation in which he sees the villagers and especially himself. In a later scene, the phantom of a dead fellow soldier about whom the villagers are speaking at that moment is presented as Paul's hallucination. The dead soldier who addresses Paul without the others' noticing makes the viewer skeptical about accepting the strong physical presence of everyday life in the village as the only reality. The camera in this sequence alternates constantly between its objective narrative function, when it pursues the characters or circles around Paul, and its subjective, interpretive function, for instance in the hallucination scenes, which are shot from Paul's perspective.

The most striking stylistic feature of this sequence is the intermittent use of color in the midst of black and white film. Reitz's decision to shoot most of the film in black and white underscores the film's closeness to the chronicle genre. Black and white also connotes documentary authenticity and historical truth; it imparts to the film a classical austerity which stands in dramatic contrast to the ordinary flood of color television images. The brief color sequences—sometimes only a few seconds long—in the great mass of black and white footage confused and irritated the television audience, despite the explanatory, almost apologetic, words of caution by the television announcer before each episode of *Heimat*.[31] Since no simple pattern is evident, Reitz provokes the viewer to watch carefully. The sudden switches from black and white to color let the filmic discourse forsake its purely representational function for a moment and become self-reflexive. By emphasizing its own materiality and artificiality, Reitz's film comes close to Pasolini's idea of a "cinema of poetry," in which the process of representation is not fully absorbed in what is portrayed but is itself foregrounded.[32]

The first switch from black and white to color accentuates the perspective of the returning soldier: his arrival at his father's smithy evokes such strong emotions that what he sees literally appears "colored." Paul's subjective, reality-altering gaze momentarily wins out over the documentary, distancing chronicle in black and white. The epic, discursive everyday prose of the film is interrupted again and again by short bursts of poetry. Despite its illusion of reality, this filmed version of daily life is, at a closer look, extremely artificial. It unscrupulously mixes genre styles and conventions: the documentary with the hallucinatory and the dreamlike; the chronicler's observations in black and white with the poet's reveries in color.

Reitz addresses the tension between time and place characteristic of regional narration by temporalizing space. In this way Heimat becomes tangible as a place of experience. The film shows how time intrudes into the space of Heimat and changes it. "This is the moment when time should stand still," Eduard says in 1938, "when everything that we have achieved should stay the same: the new street out there and our whole new life. And we shouldn't want anything more than that." But the new highway that Eduard admires was built by Hitler for military transports just a year before the start of World War II, and the "new life" he mentions proves to be a fleeting moment of happiness, a happiness that, moreover, is blind to the open persecution of socialist and Jewish neighbors. Starting in 1939, world history begins to interfere with the private destinies of the unworldly Schabbachers. "World history," says Hegel in his *Philosophy of History,* "is not the soil in which happiness grows. Periods of happiness are empty pages in it."[33]

Memory and Technology

The Muse of photography is not one of Memory's daughters, but Memory herself. Both the photograph and the remembered depend upon and equally oppose the passing of time.

JOHN BERGER

"The camera transforms everything it captures into something that is past. Everyone who films takes leave of the things he has in front of his lens, whether fictive, staged events or the real public or private events encountered while filming. The camera is our memory. When we edit filmed material, arrange it into new sequences of images and include sound, we enact the process of memory."[34] We can recapture the past only as memory: the initial sequence of each episode of *Heimat* (except the first) dramatizes this insight. A fictional figure, the village eccentric Glasisch-Karl, a ubiquitous presence from the beginning to the end of the film, introduces each episode by invoking our memory of previous episodes. An outsider destined to be the observer, Glasisch-Karl assumes the role of the storyteller. He sits at a table, with a stack of photographs lying before him that show snapshots from the film. The number of photographs will grow with each episode. He picks out pictures that trigger memories; he holds them under the light, scrutinizes them, and reminisces as though he were leafing through a family album. The photographs serve as the raw material for the stories that he, as chronicler and narrator, orders, assembles, and elucidates.

These introductory sequences function, at one level, as efficient and practical summaries of past episodes, maintaining narrative continuity between episodes—a traditional technique in television serials. But these sequences also play a dialectical, self-reflexive game, mediating and at the same time highlighting the tension between the photographic claim to factual authenticity and the "as if" mode of the historical fiction. Photographs typically authenticate the existence of a person or a thing; here photographs authenticate fictional characters, as if *Heimat* were dealing with real people. The photographs are largely the work of Eduard, the passionate amateur photographer, but he, after all, is also part of the fiction. To document invented characters with photographs, as images of images, sheds an ironic light on the documentary fiction of the film.

Glasisch-Karl reassembles photographs, images of memory that fix a moment of the past and now themselves belong irretrievably to that past. While the film, through its movement, simulates the immediate present (in film there is no past tense), a photograph, by its very nature, belongs to history. "All photographs are *memento mori*," said Susan Sontag in her book on photography. "To take a photograph is to participate in another person's (or thing's) mortality, vulnerability, mutability. Precisely by slicing out this moment and freezing, all photographs testify to time's relentless melt."[35] Nothing that is shown on a photograph still exists in that form; pictures freeze time. We need memory to breathe life into photographs.

Glasisch-Karl's retrospective comments about the photographs before him suggest a tension within the filmic fiction between his present moment (that is, the present moment of the observer) and the past contained in the photographs. His reminiscing corresponds to the activity of the viewer with respect to the images of the film. The introductory sequences not only thematize the film's work of memory, they also insist that the spectators look carefully at the images, wrest meanings from them, and read them in the context of their own private histories.

"Kodak—America's Storyteller": this advertising slogan from a few years ago expresses the status of visual media in the production of narratives. Photographs and films evoke memories and tell stories from the past. As technologies, they act as gigantic recording and storage systems, accumulating images from the past in a constantly growing, albeit imaginary, archive of pictures. In *Heimat* the number of pictures piled in front of Glasisch-Karl doubles from episode to episode. The viewer literally sees the increasing demands these proliferating images make on his memory. Both Glasisch-Karl and the viewers have to become increasingly selective.

"To articulate the past historically," Walter Benjamin wrote in his sixth Thesis on the Philosophy of History, "does not mean to recognize it 'the way it really was' (Ranke). It means to seize hold of a memory as it flashes up at a moment of danger."[36] Reitz adopted this concept of history based on memory for his series, which spans more than sixty years of German history. The past is not fully reconstructed, year by year, but rather selectively recollected. *Heimat* emphasizes and lingers over only those years that have a decisive impact on the characters' lives, functioning as an elliptical memory, a memory we actually see unfolding before us. By the middle of the film, characters begin more and more frequently to reminisce about their adolescence, remembering the good old days; we as viewers also remember their experiences and adventures because we have seen them ourselves in previous episodes. The series thus creates its own tradition; it becomes history to itself. Old photographs serve in this process as the most reliable witnesses.

"I wonder how people who don't film, who don't photograph, who don't use tape recorders, remember."[37] Reitz quotes this sentence from Chris Marker's experimental film *Sans soleil* in his essay on the French documentary filmmaker. Reitz's own film reflects on the relations between memory and the technical media. The constantly growing archive of pictures constitutes a collective memory that splinters into innumerable individual views, but forgets nothing. Although condensing, expanding, and above all forgetting are common when experiences are passed on in an oral tradition, experiences recorded by the technical media are stored once and for all. They become documents, forever available and retrievable at any time. Since the development of photography, Barthes says, "the past is as certain as the present, what we see on paper is as certain as what we touch."[38]

One strand in the complex narrative web of *Heimat* deals with the history of the technical media in Germany, with their social function in the modernization process and their growing impact between 1920 and 1980. In the early 1920s Paul's homemade radio can already transcend the narrow boundaries of the provinces: it connects the village to the outer world. This early passion foreshadows Paul's subsequent sudden departure from home. His son, Anton, shows an early interest in film; we see him as a child projecting 8-millimeter films for other children. During the war he joins a propaganda film company, working as a projectionist and serving as an assistant documentary cameraman. In this position he witnesses the execution of a group of captured partisans in a snowy forest somewhere in Russia. Reitz's editing shows the whirring cameras and the exploding machine guns as integral parts of a larger violence: both "shoot" at the same time.[39] The company chief checks the camera angle and the mise-en-scène—he pays attention to the smallest artistic details in filming the execution—while lecturing to his two assistants: "Not the feature film but the weekly newsreels of the war are the true art of the twentieth century. The propaganda company has already shot 2.8 million meters of film at battle scenes. That is more than ten years of studio production—more than a thousand long feature films. We manage to impress the events of the war on the souls of our audience more forcefully than if they were to see them with their own eyes" (279).

Reitz dwells on the production and effect of these filmed images, allowing us to watch as the film of the execution is developed in a Berlin laboratory. There a young technician turns away from the images of atrocity and says, "That can make one sick" (322). At the same time, another monitor shows a commercial Nazi feature film, Erich Engels's *Dr. Crippen an Bord* (*Dr. Crippen on Board*, 1942). The juxtaposition of the two films suggests parallels between the icy, calculating criminal Dr. Crippen, a fictional figure, and the unfeeling criminals of the execution squad in the documentary.

In a self-reflexive, ironic tone, a long sequence from Carl Froelich's sentimental film of 1938, *Heimat,* starring Zarah Leander, becomes part of Reitz's *Heimat.* Maria and her sister-in-law Pauline sit in the local cinema, identifying with the sad fate of a wayward daughter who, cast out by her father, returns home years later, full of remorse. The wishes, longings, fears, disappointments, hopes, and memories that Zarah Leander's screen life awakens in the two abandoned women in the movie house are directly related to their lives. Afterward, a long scene shows them in front of the mirror trying to imitate Zarah Leander's hairstyle; the scene demonstrates the importance of the movies in their everyday life.[40]

Art as a storehouse of memories and as a substitute for Heimat: Reitz explores these thoughts through the autobiographical figure of Hermann, who leaves Schabbach as a young man and returns many years later as a celebrated musician. He talks with some older members of the community who still remember him, and he tapes the song of the local nightingale. He processes this raw material and transforms it into a piece of concrete music with the help of electronic equipment that belongs to his stepfather, Paul, who has in the meantime sold his factory in Detroit and now, as a slightly senile patron, supports Hermann's artistic ambitions. The conventional, even hackneyed motif of the artist capturing the sounds of nature before they are destroyed and reshaping them as an ambitious avant-garde work of art is only partially relativized by the complete rejection this project receives from the villagers. With the exception of Glasisch-Karl, no one in Schabbach understands what the artist has done. Hermann's story suggests parallels to Reitz's *Heimat* project: here too the artist returns to his birthplace and captures on film things that are about to disappear. Heimat, as the sequence at the end tells us, can be preserved in art, on film: "We mobile inhabitants of undetermined places need new, portable pieces of evidence for our stories. Filmed images, for instance, or other pictures, that we can carry with us. Film meets these needs in a particular way. It is more comprehensive as proof, moves our entire perceptual apparatus at once, evidences the stories in image, sound and time. Film can follow us into all the various regions of the world, and can replace our lost village."[41] Film is the portable substitute for home: as exaggerated as this sounds in Reitz's metaphorical style, film and photography have indeed functioned as forms of collective memory and have provided sources of identification over the last sixty years. Films can store images and make them available for "a humanity that has left its villages."[42]

History—Made in Germany

History is an invention for which reality supplies the material. But it is not an arbitrary invention. The interest it awakens is based on the interests of those who tell it.

HANS MAGNUS ENZENSBERGER

In the Federal Republic in the autumn of 1984, *Heimat* was more than a television series. Its enormous popular success—about nine million viewers per episode—made it a media event, leading to innumerable reflections on Heimat, on national identity, and on Germany. Wolfram Schütte, for instance, wrote in the *Frankfurter Rundschau* (not in the entertainment section, but on the editorial page) that Reitz had given "images, history, stories, and spiritual contour to a word and concept that only exists in German."[43] In the *Zeit-Magazin,* an article proclaimed: "Germany's theme this fall is 'Heimat.' The television series by Edgar Reitz has provoked discussion throughout the nation. The seal of quality, 'Made in Germany,' which appears self-consciously, chiseled in stone, at the beginning of the film, has taken on new meaning."[44] At various conferences over the last few years on Heimat and the national question, Reitz's film (and its reception) has been interpreted as an emanation—and agent—of a collective longing for identity.[45] Critical voices like that of Gertrud Koch, who accused the film of falsifying historical consciousness and reverting to patterns of the old Heimat film genre, could not disrupt the rare harmony displayed by most German film critics;[46] after all, the leading British and French newspapers had also spoken out in favor of the film. Henri de Bresson wrote in *Le Monde*: "Germany has suddenly found a soul and a home. As if Edgar Reitz suddenly liberated a longing in the hearts of Germans that wants to show itself publicly . . . The immense success of 'Heimat' must be viewed together with the success of the Green Party in the Federal Republic. What do these opponents of nuclear power, these heralds of a new ecological society, really want, if not to augment the soul by confessing love of 'Heimat,' of being at home?"[47]

The warm West German approval of the film, its actors, and its director was chilled, however, by reports from New York, where critics deemed the film a dangerous whitewash of recent German history. The *Frankfurter Allgemeine Zeitung* titled its discussion of these critical voices "Irritations."[48] What had happened?

Three influential American papers, the *New York Times,* the *New York Review of Books,* and the *Village Voice,* had taken umbrage at the fact that *Heimat* had excluded important parts of the National Socialist past, or had only mentioned them in passing. For James Markham, the *New York Times* German correspondent, *Heimat,* like the popular film *The Boat,* represented an attempt to come to terms with the Nazi past by portraying Germans as "decent, normal citizens and sometimes even as victims"—an undertaking whose revisionist tendencies clearly displeased Markham.[49] According to Jim Hoberman, film critic for the *Village Voice,* the monstrous atrocities of German history should not be described in an atmosphere of the ordinary and everyday. His concluding judgment: "With *Heimat* Germany is reborn."⁵⁰ And Timothy Garton Ash wrote in a long review in the *New York Review of Books:*

> When you show the 1930s as a golden age of prosperity and excitement in the German countryside, when you are shown the Germans as victims of the war, then you inevitably find yourself asking: But what about the other side? What about Auschwitz? Where is the director's moral judgment? To which the color filters insistently reply: "Remember, remember, this is a film about what Germans remember. Some things they remember in full color. Some in sepia. Others they prefer to forget. Memory is selective. Memory is partial. Memory is amoral."
>
> With this simple trick, Reitz manages to escape from the chains that have weighed down most German artistic treatments of twentieth-century German history. "We try to avoid making judgments," he writes. Not for him the agonizing directorial evenhandedness, the earnest formulations of guilt, responsibility, or shame. Not for him the efforts to "come to terms with" or "master" the past. Not *"Vergangenheitsbewältigung."* Not Bitburg. Just memory and forgetting.⁵¹

Ash's critical perspective takes aim at *Heimat's* most vulnerable point, for it is no secret that Reitz conceived his television series as a counter-production to *Holocaust* and justified *Heimat* repeatedly in public as the German answer to the American series. *Holocaust,* which shook the whole Federal Republic in January 1979, was for Reitz a "glaring example" of an "international aesthetics of commercialism," for which the "misery produced by the Nazis in the original" is nothing but a "welcome background spectacle for a sentimental family story."⁵² Films in the style of *Holocaust,* Reitz wrote, prevent us, the Germans, from "taking narrative possession of our past, from breaking free of the world of judgments and dealing with it through art."⁵³ Reitz claims Germany's right to its own history when he demands that German filmmakers "take possession of their own history and hence the history of the population to which they belong. But often they find that their own history has been taken out of their hands. The most radical process of expropriation there is, is the expropriation of one's own history. The Americans have stolen our history through Holocaust."⁵⁴ This polemic, making the Americans responsible for "stealing" Germany's most recent history, both as subject matter for a film and as part of German identity, seems audacious; a history that unleashed a world war in the attempt to subordinate or exterminate other peoples obviously does not belong to a single nation. In the 1980s, the Germans appeared to assert vehemently their "ownership" of German history, which they had readily disavowed in the 1950s and 1960s.

For Reitz, the real scandal was "German history—Made in Hollywood." His response was a film that bore the sarcastic working title, "Made in Germany."[55] The American import was to be confronted with a German product. His film provided what Reitz perceived as lacking in the *Holocaust* television series, namely the "authentic atmosphere of individual images."[56] Reitz's project of 1979 coincided with a widespread interest in regionalism and rural life in the Federal Republic and with a new focus on everyday experience: large-scale politics were to be prismatically refracted in the limited consciousness of the "little people." Reitz's concept of "history from below" not only attacks the claim to totality made by official historiography, which radically reduces the multiplicity of stories to *one* history; it also legitimates the exclusion of all those experiences about which "simple people" either knew nothing or preferred to know nothing.

In Reitz's *Heimat,* for example, we see Hänschen Betz, a village boy, following the newly installed telegraph lines on his bicycle and coming upon a concentration camp outside the village. He sees the inmates and their armed, uniformed guards, but he tells no one in the village about his discovery, and no one else seems to know anything about the camp. It is never mentioned. In a later scene we learn that a communist labor leader, a relative of the Simon family, was picked up at dawn by the Gestapo and, we assume, taken to the nearest concentration camp—but no one asks about his fate, not even his daughter Lotti or his closest relatives. It may be the ultimate consequence of the film's origin as an answer to *Holocaust* that the annihilation of the Jews is almost completely excluded from the plot.

Reitz was well aware of the danger of rewriting history, by making the "little people" of Germany the innocent victims of an injustice committed by "Nazi criminals." When Heike Hurst, in *Nuit Blanche,* asked Reitz why he had omitted the Holocaust from *Heimat,* he answered: "The question of the Jews and National Socialism is a theme that has been explicated over and over, and as soon as I would have entered that terrain, the story would have taken a different direction."[57] The Holocaust, Reitz thus implies, would have undermined the positive attitude toward Heimat that his film conveys. Reitz in fact recognized the problem that, as Gertrud Koch put it, "in order to tell the myth of 'Heimat,' the trauma of Auschwitz had to be shut out of the story."[58] Auschwitz cannot be integrated into the continuity of German history as Reitz unfolds it.

What Koch's justified criticism does not address, however, is a central dilemma: Can Auschwitz be represented at all in a narrative form? Can a crime like the industrialized murder of millions be contained in a story without trivializing it? Can the monstrousness of Auschwitz ever be captured by aesthetic means without imposing some sort of meaning and logic? In November 1978, the French film critic Christian Zimmer wrote: "No events are incapable of being retold, but there are cases where narration betrays reality and the memory of those who lived through what they themselves called 'unspeakable.' In such cases, the only legitimate and faithful truth is the scream . . . Is not narrative an explanation and a rationalization of the unthinkable? Is it not a standardization of insanity? Does not narrative always excuse?"[59]

Cast into a narrative mold, terror loses its edge. To show the incomprehensible may require a non-narrative mixture of documentary and fiction like the one used by Claude Lanzmann in Shoah. Here the terror of the concentration camps is evoked not through familiar images but by a search for vestiges of the past in the present and by the memory traces of the survivors.[60] Conversations with witnesses and the images of faces and landscapes gain resonance because the film presents the past as an aspect of present experience. Like Lanzmann's Shoah, Eberhard Fechner's four and one-half hour film Der Prozess (The Trial), a television documentary about the Düsseldorf trial of war criminals who administered the concentration camp in Majdanek, is also almost entirely based on interviews. Fechner conducted more than seventy interviews with everyone connected with the trial—defendants, survivors, family members of victims, judges, lawyers, journalists covering the trial—and edited their statements in such a way that the trial, which lasted six years, seems completely recreated, in all its legal and emotional complexity, as a film. He often took no more than a sentence or two from one interview and juxtaposed it with another that either contradicted or confirmed it. Through this elaborate editing endeavor he could stage the whole trial again, on film, polemically confronting survivors, perpetrators, and the legal profession in ways unthinkable in the courtroom.[61] *The Trial,* shown on West German television in November 1984, only one month after *Heimat,* attempted (again like *Shoah*) to underscore the presence of the past and to record what was about to disappear: the faces and voices of those who had suffered. Despite unanimous media accolades, neither *Shoah* nor *The Trial* made a noticeable impression on the West German public.

The nearly total exclusion of the Holocaust from Reitz's *Heimat*— out of fear? or repression? or revisionism?—becomes all the more conspicuous in light of the lengthy treatment *Heimat* devotes to the Nazi period. Five of the eleven episodes (episodes 3–7) take place during the Third Reich, and the second episode includes the year 1933. Three segments deal with the years before the war (1935, 1938, 1938–39), while two concentrate on the war at home and on the front ("The Home Front," 1943, and "Soldiers' Love," 1944). Almost half of the film, a chronicle spanning sixty-three years of German history from 1919 to 1982, takes place during the twelve years of Hitler's regime; thus more narrative time is granted in *Heimat* to the exploration and visualization of the causes, progress, and consequences of German fascism than in most full-length feature films or documentaries on National Socialism. What images does Reitz find, what stories does he tell about the Germans under fascism?

As we would expect, Reitz presents stories of ordinary lives, using everyday images, which always seem to assume the spectator's retrospective awareness of this history and its consequences. Because certain events such as Hitler's rise to power are so well known, Reitz plays with them from the perspective "from below." For instance, we learn about Hitler's seizure of power from the totally apolitical perspective of Eduard, who happens to be in Berlin in January 1933. The crowd's cries of "Heil" and the glow of torchlight parades fill the shoddy room where Eduard has retreated with the prostitute Lucy, who will later become his wife. Eduard, preoccupied with Lucy, does not take notice of the momentous occasion outside on the streets. The viewer can draw various conclusions: that an apolitical person like Eduard misses even the most important milestones of political history (an attitude the film does not criticize); that the events of January 30, when Hitler seized power, were primarily an urban affair and did not concern a provincial person (a problematic interpretation, because the provinces were by no means uninvolved in Hitler's rise); or that from the perspective of everyday history, political history is literally "in the background." The fact that Eduard, at the urging of his domineering and ambitious wife, becomes a reluctant and rather ridiculous mayor in Nazi uniform shows the apolitical and undoubtedly trivializing attitude of the film toward the exercise of power under National Socialism. Accommodation with the powers that be—in the case of the Nazis, it still involved a change of costume—is portrayed in this film as comical. The preparations in Schabbach for the Führer's birthday, with a banner reading "The Führer is a Columbus" and fresh-baked Hitler rolls, likewise are presented with humor and ironic, sympathetic lightness.

Reitz also shows the upbeat mood of fundamental change characteristic of the early Hitler years. Sebastian Haffner emphasized this mood in his provocative 1978 book on Hitler, and Hans-Dieter Schäfer documented it extensively in his study on the "split consciousness" of the Germans in their daily life between 1933 and 1945.[62] "Everyone feels it," Pauline says to her husband, the watchmaker Kröber, "things are getting better every day, Robert . . . It's true, Robert, something is happening, something is coming! The customers in the store, they're all laughing, and suddenly they're all in a hurry" (147). Reitz makes note of the other side, the side of the victims, only in passing. Kröber comes to own the house he lives in because it belonged to a Jew. "Do you know," he asks his mother-in-law, "the Jew who lives above us? He owns the house, and he wants to sell it . . . The Jews don't have it so easy anymore" (148). There is no further mention of this forced sale, but the euphemistic phrase "they don't have it so easy anymore" indicates that even the people of the Hunsrück knew of the persecution of Jews, but did nothing about it; instead they, like their urban counterparts, used it as an opportunity for economic gain.[63] A few scenes later, also in 1934, the grandmother, Kat, visits family members in Bochum and sees Fritz Schirmer, a distant relative, being taken away to the nearest concentration camp "for re-education." The Nazi in charge, a friendly acquaintance of the family, reassures everyone that "at the camp they'll drive the marxist spirit out of him, and when he gets out you won't recognize him. He'll be fresh and clear-headed and he'll be glad to take part in our national reconstruction" (171). This scene, shot in an expressionist chiaroscuro with distorted camera angles, contrasts with a warmly lit scene, resembling the UFA style of the 1930s, of a Catholic Christmas mass that unites all the relatives, even Maria's younger brother Wilfried in his SS uniform. "A Christmas Like Never Before. 1934–35" is the title of this episode. It is not meant ironically.

Because the film for the most part identifies with the knowledge and consciousness of its protagonists, it often loses the distance necessary for a critical depiction of their behavior. The characters— most of whom are basically opportunistic conformists—appear to us as they appear to themselves; the linear, chronological narrative mode of *Heimat* restricts our perspective to that of the characters, so that we experience history through their eyes. The viewer is free to criticize the characters' point of view; but when a realistic narrative is so closely attuned to its characters, it is difficult to make the leap from identification to critical distance. Outsiders, who in realistic narratives are often the source of alternative, critical perspectives, remain conspicuously absent in the episodes that deal with the Hitler years. Paul and Apollonia, a young woman whom the villagers call a gypsy, both presented as outsiders in the first segment, leave Schabbach (and the narrative) well before 1933.

In the village, National Socialism appears as an agent of modernization. New communication devices like the telephone and radio reach into the farthest corners of the Reich; motorization progresses by leaps and bounds; highways cut through the landscape; the war machine organizes and mobilizes every last resource. For Ernst, Maria's son, who always wanted to be a flier, the war offers undreamed-of opportunities for pursuing his passion; after the war he seems displaced. The reactionary "blood and soil" ideology may have been advocated at mass rallies in Berlin, but in the country the "Hitler movement" took shape mainly as a dynamic process of innovation. The price for the prewar affluence (based on rearmament) had to be paid at the end of the war, even in the Hunsrück region, as the film shows. Using traditional images and a dramatic structure based on suspense that previously had not been an element of the film, *Heimat* depicts the effects of war taking their toll. Otto Wohlleben, Maria's lover and the father of her son Hermann, is killed while deactivating a bomb, and Lucy's friend is shot while fleeing. The film makes unmistakably clear how political history, which for so long had not touched the village, finally takes control over private destinies.

In 1945 the American liberators appear at the door. Eduard takes off his uniform with a sigh of relief, and his wife Lucy deliberates, in scenes that approach caricature, how she can do business with the occupying forces. It is *Stunde Null*, "zero hour," a new beginning. Kat, speaking to her husband, remembers that they have experienced two wars. "And we are all still alive . . . Mathias, isn't it strange that we're all still alive? . . . If the children are smart, they can start all over again and do it better. Better than it ever was, Mathias" (351).

Here, too, as with Fassbinder and Sanders-Brahms, we see the myth of Stunde Null combined with the illusion that "everything will be different," that Germany can begin anew as a tabula rasa. As early as 1976, Reitz dealt critically with this notion of zero hour in a film of that title.[64] *Stunde Null* seems like a preliminary study for *Heimat* in its calm narrative flow, its visual motifs of everyday life, and its simple black and white images. It portrays critically the German fascination with the United States; the young people who are enthusiastic about the "Yankees" to the point of self-surrender are unforgivingly betrayed at the end. A pervasive anti-Americanism recurs in *Heimat* as well, from the first mention of the United States as the "land of the electric chair" to the farcical cliché of showing Paul returning to the village as the "rich American" with a ten-gallon hat and a black chauffeur.

The images of the Federal Republic (seen in the last four episodes, which extend from the 1950s to the present) likewise seem by and large extremely critical. The final view of the blighted village has jet planes thundering overhead. From this perspective on high, the village, Heimat, becomes a tiny gray speck on the radar screen, a vantage point that radically undermines any potential nostalgic sentimentality. In the same vein Reitz tacks on at the end, immediately after Maria's death, a vulgar, tumultuous scene at a fairground. The older generation, united in a dream sequence like ghosts from the past, have abandoned the country to their successors, for whom the film has nothing but contempt. It is similar to the contempt displayed in Peter Handke's contemporaneous dramatic poem, *Über die Dörfer* (*Beyond the Villages*): "I would like to curse this village and its inhabitants, who only hear the bells of the automatic bowling alley. I would like to curse their mouths that are like the slits of a piggy bank, where things are put in but nothing comes out . . . I would also like to curse the descendants who already as children stand there like butchers and look about with the eyes of the slaughtered."[65]

In the concluding episodes, Reitz retracts the nostalgic attitude evoked toward Heimat, which in part extended through the Hitler era, and mercilessly documents the rapid decline of Heimat after 1945. Two images characterize this undertaking in their deliberate opposition. In the film's first sequence, the Hunsrück, seen from a glider, is presented as a wide-open green landscape where time and space are identical. In the last sequence the same landscape, now viewed from a supersonic jet, has been condensed into a few seconds of flight time, and the contemplative silence of the landscape has given way to deafening noise. Heimat as a geographic place and the locus of sensory experience has been thoroughly destroyed by modern technology.

According to the film's inner logic, this emphasis on the systematic dismantling of Heimat in the reconstruction phase of the Federal Republic makes the period prior to 1945 appear in a more conciliatory and even nostalgic light. The full weight of criticism falls on the Federal Republic, which, the film implies, has lost all traces of identity in the course of its Americanization. It has also made a military base out of the Hunsrück, where more Pershing and Cruise missiles are stationed than anywhere else in West Germany. In the last episodes of the film, nostalgic and conservative impulses unite to attack any sentimental use of the concept of Heimat in today's Federal Republic.

Nonetheless, in keeping with the general disposition of West Germans in the 1980s, the film was received as an affirmation of Germany's yearning for a sense of identity, for a feeling of Heimat. This gives reason to pause. For if it is true that fictions often evoke what a society lacks, thereby fulfilling collective wishes and compensating for deficits in the emotional life of the nation, then the public success of *Heimat* in the Federal Republic may be some indication of how strongly the West Germans, after a period of forty years, long for a relief from the burden of their past. "*Heimat*—the movie" reclaims German history for the Germans; it rewrites it from the perspective of "common people" and thus epitomizes the strong desire for a "normalization" of German history.[66]

What *Heimat* elaborates in fictional terms has in the meantime entered political discourse outside the aesthetic realm. On November 9, 1988, in a speech during a Bundestag ceremony commemorating the fiftieth anniversary of Kristallnacht, Philipp Jenninger, the

Speaker of the House of Parliament, tried to come to grips with the phenomenon of anti-Semitism and fascism by evoking an image of the Third Reich that stressed the dynamic and vigorous spirit of the early Hitler years.[67] His glowing depiction of this period sounded as if it had been taken from Edgar Reitz's *Heimat,* especially the second part, entitled "A Christmas Like Never Before: 1934–35." The resulting furor over what was seen as a glorification of the Hitler period forced Jenninger's resignation. The public's reaction to his speech took Jenninger by surprise; he did not realize that by transferring motifs from the unconstrained and "harmless" world of fiction across the border into the political realm, he was engaging in a "negotiation"[68] that was (still) seen by many as offensive. The poetic license that—in the eyes of the German film critics—allowed the filmmaker to challenge taboos and rewrite history was revoked when claimed by a politician. It seems that the desired normalization of German history will not come about without resistance.

7
EPILOGUE

History, Memory, and Film

"The most radical process of expropriation there is, is the expropriation of one's own history" (Edgar Reitz).
—Dieter Schaad in *Heimat*

I am appalled by the thought that one day the Holocaust will be measured and judged in part by the NBC TV production bearing its name.

ELIE WIESEL

"In the middle of it all is Hitler, of course."
"He was on again last night."
"He's always on. We couldn't have television without him."

DON DeLILLO

"More people relived the war than fought in it," an ABC newspaper
advertisement boasted in February 1983 when its eighteen-hour mini-
series *The Winds of War* came in close behind the 1979 blockbuster,
Roots, as one of the highest-rated programs in television history.[1]
One hundred and forty million Americans "relived" World War II
as it was restaged for television at a cost of $40 million (an additional
$25 million was spent on the promotion of the mini-series). Accord-
ing to ABC's projections, *The Winds of War* reached virtually every
American twelve years of age and older. To capture viewers not
familiar with the events of World War II, half a million copies of a
24-page color magazine (with pictures from the series) were mailed
to schools, libraries, and special-interest groups, introducing them to
the period and to the upcoming television spectacle. Although this
adaptation of Herman Wouk's novel *The Winds of War* abounds
with Hollywood clichés taken from adventure and war films, love
stories, and historical epics, and banks on the box office appeal of
such recognizable stars as Robert Mitchum and Ali McGraw, it
nevertheless maintains the illusion of providing a realistic and authentic depiction of past events. The images of this film version of
World War II went out simultaneously to 140 million people, many
of whom obtained their first impression of German history and World
War II from the series.

In much the same way, millions of Europeans have "experienced"
the Vietnam War through the lens of Francis Ford Coppola's 1979
film *Apocalypse Now* or Michael Cimino's *The Deer Hunter* (1978).
These films do not show isolated pictures of accidental, contingent
events, but rather select, narrativize, and thereby give shape to the
random material of history; they write history by "giving meaning

to what is meaningless."[2] Various narrative patterns, often taken
from literature or myth—*Apocalypse Now,* for instance, follows Joseph Conrad's *Heart of Darkness* (1899)—structure the events and
translate them into a story with a beginning, middle, and end. These
films interpret national history for the broad public and thus produce,
organize, and homogenize public memory. Along with professional
historians and schools, the mass media have become the most effective (and least acknowledged) institutional vehicles for shaping historical consciousness.[3] A film can make history come alive, can represent it, more vividly than commemorative addresses, exhibitions,
or museums. But whose history?

The Winds of War transmitted certain images of World War II to
its millions of American viewers: images of heroic and likable American soldiers and their militaristic Nazi counterparts, of battle scenes
and private sacrifices, of deserved victories and just defeats. Future
representations of World War II will be compared to the images from
these television films, just as these films use countless images from
earlier representations. Thus images of images circulate in an eternal
cycle, an endless loop. They validate and reconfirm each other,
"swiftly spreading identical memories over the earth."[4]

Since we cannot revisit the past and relive historical events like
World War II or the Hitler era, we are dependent on representations
of the past, whether documentary or reconstructed. In this century,
the emergence of film as a mass medium has come to be seen an
instrument for the faithful recording of historical persons and events;
film has also taken on the task of keeping the memory of the Third
Reich alive. However, it is a memory consisting largely of images
that have by now become so conventionalized that they determine
what is a "correct" representation of the period and what is not.
Images of Hitler or of the war have engraved themselves so indelibly
on the public consciousness that new images are hard to imagine.
Thus history films increasingly replace not only historical experience
but also historical imagination.[5] "How can the imagination survive
if our capacity for free association is constantly overpowered?" Peter
W. Jansen asks in his essay "The Cinema in Its Second Baroque,"[6]
in which he compares historical film epics like Bertolucci's *1900* or
Apocalypse Now with the encyclopedic political novel of the seven-
teenth century. He is justifiably concerned that these "political novels
of the cinema" are out to conquer and occupy the audience's historical imagination instead of stimulating and liberating it.

As early as 1946, Max Picard, in his book *Hitler in uns selbst* (*Hitler in Ourselves*), recognized how radio might well expropriate independent personal experience. He was also one of the first to reflect on how the technical media shape our perceptions of historical reality:

> The radio not only reports history, it seems to make it. The world seems to originate from the radio. People still see things and events, but they become real only after the radio has reported the event and the newspaper has run a picture of it. The radio apperceives, registers, and judges for people. Our souls are immediately connected to the radio and no longer to our own sensory organs. People no longer have an inner history, an inner continuity, the radio today is our history; it validates our existence.[7]

Anticipating subsequent reflections on the mass media and the loss of history by Günther Anders, Marshall McLuhan, and Jean Baudrillard by more than a decade,[8] Picard's misgivings about radio apply even more radically to film and television. The proliferating images that surround (and control) us everywhere constitute a second, artificial world that interposes itself between us and the world of our senses. "I remember," says Chris Marker in his film *Sans soleil*, "a January in Tokyo, or rather I remember the images I filmed in January in Tokyo. They have replaced my memories, they are my memories."[9] As a technological memory, film saves and stores the past so completely that human memory becomes superfluous.

In Wim Wenders's film *Paris, Texas* it is an old super-eight home movie that restores the memory of both the amnesiac father and his son, who was too young to remember the fullness of the recorded event. The home movie as memory's material image is the turning point in Wenders's film. Film functions here as the redemption of memory: where the two had forgotten, the film remembered. Similarly, the historical films of the New German Cinema are meant to preserve the past *and* to jog the memory of the living. They provide alternative ways of seeing with their self-reflexive narrative and visual style, their autobiographical tone and experimental form, and, above all, their refusal for the most part to recycle endlessly repeated and clichéd images of the Third Reich. Syberberg, Fassbinder, Kluge, Sanders-Brahms, and Reitz want to provide in their films a historical memory that runs counter to Hollywood notions of German history—even at the risk of appearing, or indeed becoming, revisionist.

In its beginning the New German Cinema was engaged in a critical project of providing images that polemically challenged the existing amnesia as well as the repression of the past; the filmmakers insisted on questions of responsibility, guilt, and the legacy of history for the present. This project was recast after the mid-1970s when most of their films embarked on a quest for a German identity—a quest that could entail a return to personal childhood memories or an exploration of German myths. "It's hard to teach German history in a patriotic fashion," says Gabi Teichert, the history teacher in Kluge's *The Patriot,* who desperately searches for a positive, patriotic German history. A new focus on individual life stories and the history of everyday life (rather than political history), an emphasis on subjective memory, a differently nuanced concern and empathy with the Germans as victims, and, connected with this, a characteristic shift from aggressive male protagonists to silently suffering female main characters, whose violated bodies stand as emblems of a devastated Germany—these are some of the most visible tendencies in the New German Cinema's recent attempts to reevaluate and reappropriate German history.

A memory preserved in filmed images does not vanish, but the sheer mass of historical images transmitted by today's media weakens the link between public memory and personal experience. The past is in danger of becoming a rapidly expanding collection of images, easily retrievable but isolated from time and space, available in an eternal present by pushing a button on the remote control. History thus returns forever—as film. Innumerable Westerns have made the Wild West a movie myth. As the Hitler era slowly passes from the realm of experience and personal memory into the realm of images, will it also become a mere movie myth?

Film and Videotape Sources

Selected Bibliography

Notes

Index

FILM AND VIDEOTAPE SOURCES

All the major films discussed in this book are available in German with English subtitles either on 16-millimeter film or on videotape. Fassbinder's *The Marriage of Maria Braun* is distributed as a 16-millimeter film by New Yorker Films (16 West 61st Street, New York, New York 10023) and is commercially available on videotape; Alexander Kluge's *The Patriot* and Sanders-Brahms's *Germany, Pale Mother* can be obtained in 16 millimeter through West Glen Films (1430 Broadway, New York, New York 10018), which distributes feature films for a nominal fee on behalf of the Embassy of the Federal Republic of Germany. West Glen Films also carries a complete set of (subtitled) videotapes of Edgar Reitz's 16-hour *Heimat* and Syberberg's 7-hour *Hitler, a Film from Germany*. Syberberg's film has to be ordered through Ingrid Scheib-Rothbart (Goethe House, 1014 Fifth Avenue, New York, New York 10028). Most of the other films mentioned in this book can be ordered through West Glen Films or New Yorker Films; some of them are also available on videotape through commercial video stores or such mail-order outlets as the German Language Video Center (7625 Pendleton Pike, Indianapolis, Indiana 46226) or Facets Cinémathèque (1517 West Fullerton Avenue, Chicago, Illinois 60614).

SELECTED BIBLIOGRAPHY

Postwar German Cinema

Bathrick, David, and Miriam Hansen, eds. "Special Issue on New German Cinema." *New German Critique* 24–25 (Fall/Winter 1981–82).

Bauschinger, Sigrid et al., eds. *Film und Literatur: Literarische Texte und der neue deutsche Film.* Berne/Munich: Francke, 1984.

Bechtold, Gerhard. *Sinnliche Wahrnehmung von sozialer Wirklichkeit: Die multimedialen Montage-Texte Alexander Kluges.* Tübingen: Narr, 1984.

Bliersbach, Gerhard. *So grün war die Heide: Der deutsche Nachkriegsfilm in neuer Sicht.* Weinheim/Basel: Beltz, 1985.

Bock, Hans-Michael, ed. *Cinegraph: Lexikon zum deutschsprachigen Film.* Munich: edition text + kritik, 1984–.

Böhm-Christl, Thomas, ed. *Alexander Kluge.* Frankfurt am Main: Suhrkamp, 1983.

Bronnen, Barbara, and Corinna Brocher. *Die Filmemacher: Der Neue deutsche Film nach Oberhausen.* Munich: Bertelsmann, 1973.

Byg, Barton. "The Antifascist Tradition in GDR Film." In *Purdue University Fifth Annual Conference on Film.* West Lafayette, Ind.: Purdue University Press, 1980. Pp. 81–87.

Corrigan, Timothy. *New German Film: The Displaced Image.* Austin: University of Texas Press, 1983.

Cros, Jean-Louis, and Danielle Parra. "Helma Sanders-Brahms, l'indomptable." *Revue du Cinéma/Image et son* 373 (June 1982): 65–80.

Daney, Serge, ed. *Syberberg.* Paris: Editions de l'Etoile/Cahiers du Cinéma 1980 (Hors-série 6).

Durgnat, Raymond. "From Caligari to 'Hitler.'" *Film Comment* (July/August 1980): 59–70.

Eder, Klaus, ed. *Syberbergs Hitler-Film.* Munich/Vienna: Hanser, 1980.

Elsaesser, Thomas. "Primary Identification and the Historical Subject: Fassbinder and Germany." *Ciné-tracts* 3 (Fall 1980): 43–52.

———— "Myth as the Phantasmagoria of History: H. J. Syberberg, Cinema, and Representation." *New German Critique* 24/25 (Fall/Winter 1981–82): 108–154.

———— "*Lili Marleen:* Fascism and the Film Industry." *October* 21 (Summer 1982): 115–140.

Fassbinder, Rainer Werner. *Filme befreien den Kopf: Essays und Arbeitsnotizen,* ed. Michael Töteberg. Frankfurt am Main: Fischer, 1984.

———— *Die Anarchie der Phantasie: Gespräche und Interviews,* ed. Michael Töteberg. Frankfurt am Main: Fischer, 1986.

———— *The Marriage of Maria Braun,* ed. Joyce Rheuban. New Brunswick, N.J.: Rutgers University Press, 1986.

Feinstein, Howard. "BRD 1-2-3: Fassbinder's Postwar Trilogy and the Spectacle." *Cinema Journal* 23 (Fall 1983): 44–56.

Fischer, Robert, and Joe Hembus. *Der Neue Deutsche Film 1960–1980.* Munich: Goldmann, 1981.

Fischli, Bruno. "Rekonstruktion, Retro-Scenario, Trauerarbeit, Aufarbeitung—oder was? Neue Filme über den deutschen Faschismus." *Jahrbuch Film* (1979–80): 63–75.

Franklin, James. *New German Cinema: From Oberhausen to Hamburg.* Boston: Twayne, 1983.

Friedländer, Saul. *Reflections of Nazism: An Essay on Kitsch and Death.* New York: Harper and Row, 1984.

Geisler, Michael E. "'Heimat' and the German Left." *New German Critique* 36 (Fall 1985): 25–66.

Hansen, Miriam. "Alexander Kluge, Cinema, and the Public Sphere: The Construction Site of Counter-History." *Discourse* 6 (Fall 1983): 53–74.

———— "Dossier on *Heimat.*" *New German Critique* 36 (Fall 1985): 3–24.

Hayman, Ronald. *Fassbinder Filmmaker.* London: Weidenfeld and Nicolson, 1984.

Helt, Richard C., and Marie E. Helt. *West German Cinema since 1945: A Reference Handbook.* Metuchen, N.J.: Scarecrow Press, 1987.

Hembus, Joe. *Der deutsche Film kann gar nicht besser sein.* Munich: Rogner & Bernhard, 1981.

Höfig, Willi. *Der deutsche Heimatfilm 1947–1960.* Stuttgart: Ehnke, 1973.

Insdorf, Annette. *Indelible Shadows: Film and the Holocaust.* New York: Random House, 1983.

Jacobs, Diane. "Hitler's Ungrateful Grandchildren: Today's German Filmmakers." *American Film* (May 1980): 34–40.

Jaeger, Klaus, and Helmut Regel, eds. *Deutschland in Trümmern: Filmdokumente der Jahre 1945–1949.* Oberhausen: K. M. Laufen, 1976.

Jaehne, Karen. "Old Nazis in New Films: The German Cinema Today." *Cineaste* 9 (Fall 1978): 32–35.

Jameson, Fredric. "'In the Destructive Element Immerse': Hans Jürgen Syberberg and Cultural Revolution." *October* 17 (Summer 1981): 99–118.

Jansen, Peter W. "Zwanzig Jahre danach: Oberhausen und die Folgen." *Jahrbuch Film* (1982–83): 26–36.

——— and Wolfram Schütte, eds. *Herzog/Kluge/Straub.* Munich: Hanser, 1976 (Reihe Film 9).

——— *Rainer Werner Fassbinder,* 5th ed. Munich: Hanser, 1985 (Reihe Film 2).

Kaes, Anton. "Distanced Observers: Perspectives on the New German Cinema." *Quarterly Review of Film Studies* 10 (Summer 1985): 238–245.

——— "Über den nomadischen Umgang mit der Geschichte: Aspekte zu Alexander Kluges Film 'Die Patriotin.'" *Text + Kritik* 85 (January 1985): 132–144.

——— "History, Fiction, Memory: Fassbinder's *The Marriage of Maria Braun.*" In *German Film and Literature* ed. Eric Rentschler. New York: Methuen, 1986. Pp. 276–288

Kiderlen, Elisabeth, ed. *Deutsch-jüdische Normalität . . . Fassbinders Sprengsätze.* Frankfurt am Main: Pflasterstrand, 1985.

Kluge, Alexander. *Die Patriotin: Texte/Bilder 1–6.* Frankfurt am Main: Zweitausendeins, 1979.

——— ed. *Bestandsaufnahme: Utopie Film.* Frankfurt am Main: Zweitausendeins, 1983.

——— *Die Macht der Gefühle.* Frankfurt am Main: Zweitausendeins, 1984.

——— *Der Angriff der Gegenwart auf die übrige Zeit.* Frankfurt am Main: Syndikat, 1985.

——— "The Political as Intensity of Everyday Feelings." *Cultural Critique* 4 (Fall 1986): 119–128.

——— *Theoretical Writings, Stories, and an Interview,* ed. Stuart Liebman. *October* 46 (special issue, Fall 1986).

——— and Klaus Eder. *Ulmer Dramaturgien: Reibungsverluste.* Munich: Hanser, 1980.

——— and Oskar Negt. *Geschichte und Eigensinn.* Frankfurt: Zweitausendeins, 1981.

Knilli, Friedrich. "Die Judendarstellung in den deutschen Medien." In *Antisemitismus nach dem Holocaust,* ed. Alphons Silbermann and Julius H. Schoeps. Cologne: Verlag Wissenschaft und Politik, 1986. Pp. 115–132.

———— and Siegfried Zielinski, eds. *Holocaust zur Unterhaltung: Anatomie eines internationalen Bestsellers.* Berlin: Elefanten Press, 1982.

Koch, Gertrud. "How Much Naivité Can We Afford? The New *Heimat* Feeling," *New German Critique* 36 (Fall 1985): 13–16.

———— "Torments of the Flesh, Coldness of the Spirit: Jewish Figures in the Films of Rainer Werner Fassbinder," *New German Critique* 38 (Spring/Summer 1986): 28–38.

Koch, Krischan. *Die Bedeutung des "Oberhausener Manifestes" für die Filmentwicklung in der BRD.* Frankfurt am Main: Lang, 1985.

Kracauer, Siegfried. *From Caligari to Hitler: A Psychological History of the German Film.* Princeton, N.J.: Princeton University Press, 1947.

Kreimeier, Klaus. *Kino und Filmindustrie in der BRD: Ideologieproduktion und Klassenwirklichkeit nach 1945.* Kronberg: Scriptor, 1973.

———— "Der westdeutsche Film in den fünfziger Jahren." In *Die fünfziger Jahre: Beiträge zu Politik und Kultur,* ed. Dieter Bänsch. Tübingen: Narr, 1985. Pp. 283–305.

Kurowski, Ulrich. "Was ist ein deutscher Film?" *Film-Korrespondenz* 11 (November 1973): 8–12.

Kötz, Michael, and Petra Höhne. *Die Sinnlichkeit des Zusammenhangs: Zur Filmarbeit von Alexander Kluge.* Cologne: Prometh, 1981.

Lewandowski, Rainer. *Die Filme von Alexander Kluge.* Hildesheim/New York: Olms Presse, 1980.

———— *Die Filme von Volker Schlöndorff.* Hildesheim/New York: Olms Presse, 1981.

———— *Die Oberhausener: Rekonstruktion einer Gruppe 1962–1982.* Diekholzen: Regie-Verlag für Bühne und Film, 1982.

Lichtenstein, Heiner, ed. *Die Fassbinder-Kontroverse oder das Ende der Schonzeit.* Königstein: Athenäum, 1985.

Limmer, Wolfgang. *Rainer Werner Fassbinder, Filmemacher.* Reinbek: Rowohlt, 1981.

McCormick, Ruth, ed. *Fassbinder.* New York: Tanam, 1981.

Möhrmann, Renate. *Die Frau mit der Kamera. Filmemacherinnen in der Bundesrepublik Deutschland. Situation, Perspektiven. Zehn exemplarische Lebensläufe.* Munich/Vienna: Hanser, 1980.

Monaco, Paul. *Ribbons in Time: Movies and Society since 1945.* Bloomington: Indiana University Press, 1987.

Pflaum, Hans Günther. *Deutschland im Film. Themenschwerpunkte des Spielfilms in der Bundesrepublik Deutschland. Materialien zur Landeskunde.* Munich: Hueber, 1985.

———— and Hans Helmut Prinzler. *Cinema in the Federal Republic of Germany. The New German Film. Origins and Present Situation. A Handbook.* Bonn: Inter Nationes, 1983.

Phillips, Klaus, ed. *New German Filmmakers from Oberhausen through the 1970s*. New York: Ungar, 1984.

Pleyer, Peter. *Deutscher Nachkriegsfilm 1946–1948*. Münster: Fahle, 1965.

Rayns, Tony, ed. *Fassbinder*, 2nd ed. London: British Film Institute, 1976.

Reimer, Robert, and Carol Reimer. "Nazi-retro Filmography." *Journal of Popular Film and Television* 14 (Summer 1986): 81–92.

Reitz, Edgar. "Inquiry on *Holocaust*." *Framework* 12 (1980): 10–11.

—— *Liebe zum Kino: Utopien und Gedanken zum Autorenfilm 1962–1983*. Cologne: Verlag KÖLN 78, 1984.

—— and Peter Steinbach. *Heimat: Eine deutsche Chronik*. Nördlingen: Greno, 1985.

Rentschler, Eric, ed. "West German Film in the 1970s." *Quarterly Review of Film Studies* 5 (special issue, Spring 1980).

—— *West German Film in the Course of Time*. Bedford Hills, N.Y.: Redgrave, 1984.

—— "How American Is It: The U.S. as Image and Imaginary in German Film." *German Quarterly* 57 (Fall 1984): 603–620.

—— "The Use and Abuse of Memory: New German Film and the Discourse of Bitburg." *New German Critique* 36 (Fall 1985): 67–90.

—— ed. *German Film and Literature: Adaptations and Transformations*. New York/London: Methuen, 1986.

—— "Germany: The Past That Would Not Go Away." In *World Cinema since 1945*, ed. William Luhr. New York: Ungar, 1987. Pp. 213–219.

—— ed. *West German Filmmakers on Film: Visions and Voices*. New York/London: Holmes and Meier, 1988.

Rosenbaum, Jonathan, ed. *The Cinema of Jean-Marie Straub and Danièle Huillet*. New York: Film at the Public, 1982.

Rosenfeld, Alvin. *Imagining Hitler*. Bloomington: Indiana University Press, 1985.

Roth, Wilhelm. *Der Dokumentarfilm seit 1960*. Munich/Lucerne: Bucher, 1982.

Roud, Richard. *Straub*. London: Secker and Warburg, 1971.

Sanders-Brahms, Helma. *Deutschland, bleiche Mutter: Film-Erzählung*. Reinbek: Rowohlt, 1980.

Sandford, John. *The New German Cinema*. New York: Da Capo Press, 1980.

Sauvaget, Daniel: "Syberberg: dramaturge antinaturaliste et Germanitude." *La Revue du cinéma/Image et son* 335 (January 1979): 94–102.

Seidl, Claudius. *Der deutsche Film der fünfziger Jahre*. Munich: Heyne, 1987.

Syberberg, Hans Jürgen. "Form is Morality." *Framework* 12 (1980): 11–15.

────── *Die freudlose Gesellschaft.* Munich/Vienna: Hanser, 1981.

────── *Hitler, A Film from Germany,* trans. Joachim Neugroschel. New York: Farrar, Straus and Giroux, 1982.

────── *Der Wald steht schwarz und schweiget.* Zurich: Diogenes, 1984.

────── "The Abode of the Gods." *Sight and Sound* 54 (Spring 1985): 125.

────── "Seeing the Light." *The New Republic,* 3 October 1988, pp. 32–36.

Wenders, Wim. *Emotion Pictures: Essays und Filmkritiken.* Frankfurt am Main: Verlag der Autoren, 1986.

Wetzel, Kraft. "New German Cinema: Economics without Miracle." *Semiotext(e)* ("The German Issue") 4 (1982): 220–229.

────── "Die Krise des Neuen deutschen Films." *Media Perspektiven* 2 (1987): 90–99.

Zielinski, Siegfried. "Faschismusbewältigung im frühen deutschen Nachkriegsfilm." *Sammlung* 2 (1979): 124–133.

────── "History as Entertainment and Provocation: The TV Series 'Holocaust.'" *New German Critique* 19 (Winter 1980): 81–96.

────── "Aspekte des Faschismus als Kino- und Fernseh-Sujet: Tendenzen zu Beginn der achtziger Jahre." *Sammlung* 4 (1981): 47–56.

Film and History

Allio, René, and Michel Foucault. "La retour de Pierre Rivière." *La Revue du cinéma/Image et son* ("Cinéma et histoire") 312 (December 1976): 29–51.

Arcand, Denys. "The Historical Film: Actual and Virtual." *Cultures* 2 (1974): 13–26.

Aumont, Jacques. "Comment on écrit l'histoire." *Cahiers du Cinéma* 238/39 (May/June 1972): 64–71.

Avisar, Ilan. *Screening the Holocaust: Cinema's Images of the Unimaginable.* Bloomington: Indiana University Press, 1988.

Baldizzone, José, and Pierre Guibbert, eds. "Cinéma et Histoire, Histoire du Cinéma." *Les Cahiers de la Cinémathèque* (numéro spécial) 35/36 (1983).

Baudrillard, Jean. "L'histoire: un scénario rétro." *Ça cinéma* 1976: 16–19.

────── *Simulations,* trans. Paul Foss et al. New York: Semiotext(e), 1983.

Bawden, Liz-Anne. "Film and the Historian." *University Vision* 2 (1968): 32–36.

Benson, Susan Porter, Stephen Brier, and Roy Rosenzweig. *Presenting the Past: Essays on History and the Public.* Philadelphia: Temple University Press, 1986.

Berger, John, and Jean Mohr. *Another Way of Telling.* New York: Pantheon, 1982.

Bertub-Maghit, Jean-Pierre, and Alain Marty, eds. "Nouvelle histoire, cinéma, nouvelle critique." *La Revue du cinéma* 352 (July/August 1980): 88–117.

Bordwell, David. *Narration in the Fiction Film.* Madison: The University of Wisconsin Press, 1985.

Boyers, Robert. "Politics and History: Pathways in European Film." *Salmagundi* (Summer/Fall 1977): 50–79.

Certeau, Michel de, and Jean Chesneaux. "Le film historique et ses problèmes." *Ça cinéma* 10/11 (1976): 3–15.

"Cinéma et Histoire" (numéro spécial). *Ça cinéma* 10/11 (1973).

Comolli, Jean-Louis. "Historical Fiction—A Body Too Much." *Screen* 19 (Summer 1978): 41–54.

Ernst, Wolfgang. "DIStory: Cinema and Historical Discourse." *Journal of Contemporary History* 18 (1983): 397–409.

Ferro, Marc. "1917: History and Cinema." *Journal of Contemporary History* 3 (October 1968): 45–61.

———— *Analyse de film, analyse de sociétés: Une source nouvelle pour l'histoire.* Paris: Hachette, 1975.

————"Film as an Agent, Product and Source of History." *Journal of Contemporary History* 18 (July 1983): 357–364.

———— *Cinema and History,* trans. Naomi Greene. Detroit: Wayne State University Press, 1988.

Fledelius, Karsten. "Zur Semiotik der Geschichte: Abriss einer semiotischen Methodologie der Geschichte, mit besonderer Rücksicht auf filmische Aufzeichnungen als historisches Quellenmaterial." In *Semiotik und Massenmedien,* ed. Günter Bentele. Munich: Ölschläger, 1981. Pp. 362–370.

———— et al., eds. *History and the Audio-visual Media.* Kopenhagen: Eventus, 1979.

Foucault, Michel. "Interview." *Edinburgh Magazine* 2 (1977): 20–25.

Fürstenau, Theo. "The Nature of Historical Films." *Cultures* 2 (1974): 27–42.

Harcourt, Peter, "The Cinema, Memory, and the Photographic Trace." *Ciné-Tracts* 17 (Summer/Fall 1982): 33–38.

Heath, Stephen. "Contexts." *Edinburgh Magazine* 2 (1977): 37–43.

———— "Questions of Property: Film and Nationhood." *Ciné-Tracts* 1 (Spring 1977): 2–11.

———— "Screen Images, Film Memory." *Ciné-Tracts* 1 (Spring 1977): 27–36.

Hernadi, Paul. "Re-presenting the Past: A Note on Narrative Historiography and Historical Drama." *History and Theory* 15 (1976): 45–51.

Hess, Klaus-Peter. "Film und Geschichte: Kritische Einführung and Literaturüberblick." *Film Theory. Bibliographic Information and Newsletter* 13 (December 1986): 196–226.

Jackson, Martin A. "Films as a Source Material: Some Preliminary Notes toward a Methodology." *Journal of Interdisciplinary History* 4 (Summer 1973): 73–80.

Kahlenberg, Friedrich P. "Spielfilm als historische Quelle?" In *Aus der Arbeit des Bundesarchivs: Beiträge zum Archivwesen, zur Quellenkunde und Zeitgeschichte,* ed. Heinz Boberach and Hans Booms. Boppard: Boldt, 1977. Pp. 511–532.

Kracauer, Siegfried. *Theory of Film.* Oxford: Oxford University Press, 1960.

—— *History: The Last Things before the Last.* Oxford: Oxford University Press, 1973.

Lanzmann, Claude. "From the Holocaust to *Holocaust.*" *Telos* 42 (Winter 1979/80): 137–143.

Metz, Christian. "Story/Discourse: Notes on Two Kinds of Voyeurism." In *Movies and Methods,* vol. 2, ed. Bill Nichols. Berkeley: University of California Press, 1985. Pp. 543–549.

Moltmann, Günther, and Karl-Friedrich Reimers. *Zeitgeschichte im Film und Tondokument.* Frankfurt am Main: Musterschmidt, 1970.

Muth, Heinrich. "Der historische Film: Historische und filmische Grundprobleme." *Geschichte in Wissenschaft und Unterricht* 6 (1955): 670–682.

Neale, Steve, and Mark Nash. "Film: History/Production/Memory." *Screen* 18 (Autumn 1977): 77–91.

O'Connor, John E. *Teaching History with Film and Television.* Washington, D.C.: American Historical Association, 1987.

Raak, R. C. "Historiography as Cinematography: A Prolegomenon to Film Work for Historians." *Journal of Contemporary History* 18 (July 1983): 411–438.

Rosenfeld, Alvin. *Imagining Hitler.* Bloomington: Indiana University Press, 1985.

Schanze, Helmut. "Literarisches Erinnern—filmisches Erinnern." In *Kontroversen, alte und neue,* ed. Albrecht Schöne. Tübingen: Niemeyer, 1986. Vol. 10, pp. 302–308.

Schmid, Georg. *Die Figuren des Kaleidoskops: Über Geschichte(n) im Film.* Salzburg: Wolfgang Neugebauer Verlag, 1983.

—— ed. *Die Zeichen der Historie: Beiträge zu einer semiologischen Geschichtswissenschaft.* Vienna/Cologne: Böhlau, 1986.

Short, K. R. M. *Feature Films as History.* London: Croom Helm, 1981.

—— and Karsten Fledelius, eds. *History and Film: Methodology, Research, Education,* Proceedings of the Eighth International Conference on History and the Audio-Visual Media. Kopenhagen: Eventus, 1980.

Smith, Paul. *The Historian and Film.* Cambridge: Cambridge University Press, 1976.

Sorlin, Pierre. "Un chantier à ouvrir: Le cinéma d'Histoire." *La Revue de Cinéma/Image et son* 312 (December 1976): 84–92.

—— *The Film in History: Restaging the Past.* Oxford: Blackwell, 1980.

Tribe, Keith. "History and the Production of Memories." *Screen* 18 (Winter 1977–78): 9–22.

Virilio, Paul. *Guerre et cinéma.* Paris: Editions de l'Ecole, 1984.

Zielinski, Siegfried. "History as Entertainment and Provocation: The TV Series 'Holocaust.'" *New German Critique* 19 (Winter 1980): 81–96.

Zöllner, Walter. "Der Film als Quelle der Geschichtsforschung." *Zeitschrift für Geschichtswissenschaft* 13 (1965): 638–647.

German History and Identity

Augstein, Rudolf, et al. *"Historikerstreit": Die Dokumentation der Kontroverse um die Einzigartigkeit der nationalsozialistischen Judenvernichtung.* Munich/Zurich: Piper, 1987.

Baier, Lothar. *Gleichheitszeichen: Streitschriften über Abweichung und Identität.* Berlin: Wagenbach, 1985.

Barkin, Kenneth D. "Modern Germany: A Twisted Vision." *Dissent* (Spring 1987): 252–255.

Bergmann, Rudij, ed. *Nachrichten vom Zustand des Landes.* Frankfurt am Main: Fischer, 1981.

Blackbourn, David, and Geoff Eley. *Mythen deutscher Geschichtsschreibung.* Berlin: Ullstein, 1980.

Bredow, Wilfried v. *Deutschland—ein Provisorium.* Berlin: Siedler, 1985.

Broszat, Martin. "Plädoyer für eine Historisierung des Nationalsozialismus." *Merkur* 435 (May 1985): 373–385.

Brückner, Peter. *Versuch, uns und anderen die Bundesrepublik zu erklären.* Berlin: Wagenbach 1978.

Buch, Hans Christian, ed. *Thema: Deutschland. Das Kind mit den zwei Köpfen.* Berlin: Wagenbach, 1978.

Calleo, D. P. *Legende und Wirklichkeit der deutschen Gefahr.* Bonn: Keil, 1980.

Craig, Gordon A. *The Germans.* New York: New American Library, 1982.

Diner, Dan, ed. *Ist der Nationalsozialismus Geschichte? Zu Historisierung und Historikerstreit.* Frankfurt am Main: Fischer, 1987.

Epstein, Helen. *Die Kinder des Holocaust: Gespräche mit Söhnen und Töchtern von Überlebenden.* Munich: Beck, 1987.

Estermann, Alfred, et al., eds. *Unsere Republik: Politische Statements westdeutscher Autoren.* Wiesbaden: Akademische Verlagsanstalt, 1980.

Evans, Richard J. "The New Nationalism and the Old History: Perspectives on the West German *Historikerstreit.*" *Journal of Modern History 59* (December 1987): 761–797.

Friedländer, Saul. "Some Reflections on the Historisation of National Socialism." *Tel Aviver Jahrbuch für deutsche Geschichte* 16 (1987): 310–324.

—— and Martin Broszat. "A Controversy about the Historicization of National Socialism." *New German Critique* 44 (Spring/Summer 1988): 85–126.

Gaus, Günther. *Wo Deutschland liegt: Eine Ortsbestimmung.* Hamburg: Hoffman & Campe, 1983.

—— *Die Welt der Westdeutschen: Kritische Betrachtungen.* Cologne: Kiepenheuer & Witsch, 1986.

Goss, A. J. *Deutschlandbilder im Fernsehen: Eine vergleichende Analyse politischer Informationssendungen in der Bundesrepublik Deutschland und der DDR.* Cologne: Verlag Wissenschaft und Politik, 1980.

Grass, Günter. *Kopfgeburten oder die Deutschen sterben aus.* Darmstadt/Neuwied: Luchterhand. 1980.

Greiffenhagen, Martin, and Silvia Greiffenhagen. *Ein schwieriges Vaterland: Zur politischen Kultur Deutschlands.* Munich: List, 1979.

Habermas, Jürgen, ed. *Observations on 'The Spiritual Situation of the Age':* *Contemporary German Perspectives,* trans. Andrew Buchwalter. Cambridge, Mass.: MIT Press, 1984.

—— *Eine Art Schadensabwicklung.* Frankfurt am Main: Suhrkamp, 1987.

Haffner, Sebastian. *The Meaning of Hitler,* trans. Ewald Osers. Cambridge, Mass.: Harvard University Press, 1983.

Hartman, Geoffrey, ed. *Bitburg in Moral and Political Perspective.* Bloomington: Indiana University Press, 1986.

Haug, Wolfgang Fritz. "Vergangenheit, die Zukunft werden soll. Über den Historiker-Streit." *Das Argument* 29 (January/February 1987): 9–23.

Heinrich, Hans-Jürgen, ed. *Abschiedsbriefe aus Deutschland.* Frankfurt am Main/Paris: Qumran, 1984.

Hennig, Eike. *Zum Historikerstreit: Was heisst und zu welchem Ende studiert man Faschismus?* Frankfurt am Main: Athenäum, 1988.

Hillgruber, Andreas. *Zweierlei Untergang: Die Zerschlagung des Deutschen Reiches und das Ende des europäischen Judentums.* Berlin: Siedler, 1985.

Janssen-Jurreit, Marieluise, ed. *Lieben Sie Deutschland? Gefühle zur Lage der Nation.* Munich: Piper, 1985.

Jung, Jochen, ed. *Deutschland, Deutschland: 47 Schriftsteller aus der BRD und der DDR schreiben über ihr Land.* Salzburg: Residenz Verlag, 1979.

Kaltenbrunner, G. K., ed. *Was ist deutsch? Die Unvermeidlichkeit, eine Nation zu sein.* Freiburg: Herder, 1980.

Kipphardt, Heinar, ed. *Vom deutschen Herbst zum bleichen deutschen Winter: Ein Lesebuch zum Modell Deutschland.* Königstein/Taunus: Athenäum, 1981.

Kolb, Ulrike, ed. *Die Versuchung des Normalen.* Frankfurt am Main: Tende, 1987.

Levkov, Ilya, ed. *Bitburg and Beyond: Encounters in American, German and Jewish History.* New York: Shapolsky Publishers, 1987.

Lübbe, Hermann. "Politischer Historismus: Zur Philosophie des Regionalismus." *Merkur* 5 (1979): 415–424.

———— "Der Nationalsozialismus im politischen Bewusstsein der Gegenwart." In *Deutschlands Weg in die Diktatur,* ed. Martin Broszat et al. Berlin: Siedler, 1983. Pp. 329–349.

Maier, Charles S. *The Unmasterable Past: History, Holocaust, and German National Identity.* Cambridge, Mass.: Harvard University Press, 1988.

Markovits, Andrei S. "Regarding the Historikerstreit." *German Politics and Society* 13 (February 1988): 38–45.

Miller, Judith. "Erasing the Past: Europe's Amnesia about the Holocaust." *New York Times Magazine,* 14 November 1986, pp. 109–116.

Mohler, Arnim, ed. *Die deutsche Neurose: Über die beschädigte Identität der Deutschen.* Frankfurt am Main/Berlin: Ullstein, 1980.

Noelle-Neumann, Elisabeth, and Renate Köcher. *Die verletzte Nation: Über den Versuch der Deutschen, ihren Charakter zu ändern.* Frankfurt am Main: Deutsche Verlagsanstalt, 1987.

Plack, Arno. *Wie oft wird Hitler noch besiegt?* Düsseldorf: Erb-Verlag, 1982.

Pohrt, Wolfgang. *Endstation. Über die Wiedergeburt der Nation. Pamphlete und Essays.* Berlin: Rotbuch, 1982.

———— "One Nation, One Reich, One Peace." *Telos* 56 (Summer 1983): 180–183.

Pollak, Wolfgang, and Derek Rutter. *German Identity—Forty Years after Zero.* St. Augustin: Liberal Verlag, 1986.

Pross, Harry. "Randbemerkung zu neuesten Geschichtsbildern." *Merkur* 435 (May 1985): 439–444.

Pross, Helge. *Was ist heute deutsch?* Reinbek: Rowohlt, 1982.

Rabinbach, Anson. "German Historians Debate the Nazi Past." *Dissent* (Spring 1988): 192–200.

———— "The Jewish Question in the German Question." *New German Critique* 44 (Spring/Summer 1988): 159–192.

———— and Jack Zipes, eds. *Germans and Jews since the Holocaust: The Changing Situation in West Germany.* New York/London: Holmes & Meier, 1986.

Reden über das eigene Land: Deutschland, vols. 1 ff. Munich: Bertelsmann, 1983–.

Rudolph, Hagen. *Die verpassten Chancen: Die vergessene Geschichte der Bundsrepublik.* Munich: Goldmann, 1979.

Ruppert, Wolfgang, ed. *Erinnerungsarbeit: Geschichte und demokratische Identität in Deutschland.* Opladen: Leske, 1982.

Schäfer, Hans-Dieter. *Das gespaltene Bewusstsein: Über deutsche Kultur und Lebenswirklichkeit 1933–1945.* Munich/Vienna: Hanser, 1981.

Schulze, Hagen. *Wir sind, was wir geworden sind: Vom Nutzen der Geschichte für die deutsche Gegenwart.* Munich: Piper, 1987.

Schweigler, Gebhard L. "Anti-Americanism in Germany." *The Washington Quarterly* (Winter 1986): 67–84.

Seitz, Norbert, ed. *Die Unfähigkeit zu feiern: Der 8. Mai.* Frankfurt am Main: Verlag Neue Kritik, 1985.

Sichrovsky, Peter. *Born Guilty: Children of Nazi Families,* trans. Jean Steinberg. New York: Basic Books, 1988.

Stackelberg, Roderick. "1986 vs. 1968: The Turn to the Right in German Historiography." *Radical History Review* 40 (January 1988): 50–63.

Wagenbach, Klaus, et al. *Vaterland, Muttersprache: Deutsche Schriftsteller und ihr Staat seit 1945.* Berlin: Wagenbach, 1979.

Wandrey, Uwe, ed. *Kein schöner Land? Deutschsprachige Autoren zur Lage der Nation.* Reinbek: Rowohlt, 1979.

Walser, Martin. *Über Deutschland reden.* Frankfurt am Main: Suhrkamp, 1988.

Wehler, Hans-Ulrich. *Entsorgung der deutschen Vergangenheit? Ein polemischer Essay zum "Historikerstreit."* Munich: Beck, 1988.

Weidenfeld, Werner, ed. *Die Identität der Deutschen.* Munich/Vienna: Hanser, 1983.

Weizsäcker, Richard von. *A Voice from Germany: Speeches by Richard von Weizsäcker,* trans. Karin von Abrams. New York: Weidenfeld and Nicolson, 1986.

NOTES

1. Images of History

1. For a description of the production history and the political background of *Kolberg,* see Veit Harlan's autobiography, *Im Schatten meiner Filme* (Gütersloh: Sigbert Mohn Verlag, 1966), pp. 180ff. According to his account, the film was eight times more expensive than the average film of the time, costing eight and a half million marks. "Goebbels wanted to see huge battles," Harlan wrote. "He wanted to make 'the biggest film of all time,' one that would overshadow the cast-of-thousands films of the Americans" (p. 184). On *Kolberg,* see also Hermann Hinkel, *Zur Funktion des Bildes im deutschen Faschismus* (Steinbach/Giessen: Anabas, 1975), pp. 114–117. On Harlan, see Siegfried Zielinski, *Veit Harlan: Analysen und Materialien zur Auseinandersetzung mit einem Film-Regisseur des deutschen Faschismus* (Frankfurt am Main: R. G. Fischer, 1981).

2. Paul Virilio, *Guerre et cinéma* (Paris: Éditions de l'École, 1984), p. 100. All translations of quotations are mine unless a published English source is given.

3. Quoted in Erwin Leiser, *Nazi Cinema,* trans. Gertrud Mander and David Wilson (New York: Macmillan, 1975), p. 132. Saul Friedländer uses this quotation as a motto for his study *Reflections of Nazism: An Essay on Kitsch and Death,* trans. Thomas Weyr (New York: Harper & Row, 1984).

4. Leiser, *Nazi Cinema,* p. 124. Goebbels also said, in a speech given on February 27, 1942, "Optimism is simply part of waging a war. You do not win battles by hanging your head or discussing philosophical theories. For that reason it is necessary to keep our people in a good mood and to strengthen the power of moral resistance in the broad masses." Quoted in Gerd Albrecht, *Nationalsozialistische Filmpolitik* (Stuttgart: Enke, 1969), p. 58.

5. Karsten Witte, "Visual Pleasure Inhibited: Aspects of the German Revue Film," *New German Critique* 24/25 (Fall/Winter 1981–82): 261.

6. On the aesthetics of Riefenstahl's films, see Siegfried Kracauer, *From Caligari to Hitler: A Psychological History of the German Film* (Princeton, N.J.: Princeton University Press, 1947), pp. 300ff; Richard Barsam, *Triumph of the Will* (Bloomington: University of Indiana Press, 1975); Glenn B. Infield, *Leni*

Riefenstahl: The Fallen Goddess (New York: Crowell, 1976); David B. Hinton, *The Films of Leni Riefenstahl* (Metuchen, N.J.: Scarecrow Press, 1978); Renata Berg-Pan, *Leni Riefenstahl* (Boston: Twayne, 1980); Peter Nowotny, *Leni Riefenstahls Triumph des Willens: Zur Kritik dokumentarischer Filmarbeit im NS-Faschismus* (Lollar: Prolit, 1981); Martin Loiperdinger, *Rituale der Mobilmachung: Der Parteitagsfilm 'Triumph des Willens' von Leni Riefenstahl* (Opladen: Leske and Budrich, 1987).

7. Wim Wenders, "That's Entertainment: Hitler," in *West German Filmmakers on Film: Visions and Voices,* ed. Eric Rentschler (New York/London: Holmes & Meier, 1988), p. 128. (Wenders's review first appeared under the same sarcastic English title in *Die Zeit,* 5 August 1977; it is reprinted in his recent collection of essays, *Emotion Pictures: Essays und Filmkritiken* (Frankfurt am Main: Verlag der Autoren, 1986).

8. *Hitler: A Career* had its premiere at the Berlin Film Festival in February 1977. It ran with great success in movie theaters across West Germany and was rated "besonders wertvoll" (especially valuable). On January 4, 1987, the film was shown on prime-time television with the following disclaimer, meant to preempt criticism: "When this film ran in 1977, it provoked much controversy. It does not try to portray the history of the Third Reich. Instead, it deals with the relationship of Adolf Hitler to the German people: the circumstances that shaped him and made possible his rise to power, and the following he had until the catastrophic end. The terrible crimes of the regime have caused a whole generation to disclaim this experience: No one rejoiced, no one knew, no one participated. But how did Hitler find the resolve to commit unprecedented crimes if not from the feeling of accord with his people? Who is served by denying that the majority of Germany agreed with him? Recognized itself in him? Was happy with him for a long time? This film will show by what means and to what purpose this fatal happiness was produced. How much delusion it contained. The price it exacted is well known."

9. See Albert Speer, *Inside the Third Reich: Memoirs,* trans. Richard Winston and Clara Winston (New York: Macmillan, 1970). On the renewed interest in Hitler, see Claus Heinrich Meyer, "Warum wird Hitler wieder ausgegraben? Analyse einer Nostalgie," *Süddeutsche Zeitung,* 18/19 August 1973; and "Hitler-Veredlung: Wie in den siebziger Jahren das Führerbild restauriert wurde," *Süddeutsche Zeitung,* 17/18 May 1980. The numerous portrayals of Hitler in current popular novels and theater are discussed by Alvin Rosenfeld in *Imagining Hitler* (Bloomington: Indiana University Press, 1985).

10. Joachim Fest, "Revision des Hitler-Bildes?" *Frankfurter Allgemeine Zeitung,* 29 July 1977.

11. Wenders, "That's Entertainment," p. 127.

12. The visual documentary material is also selected and arranged largely from Hitler's perspective. For instance, when anti-Semitism is being discussed, we see close-ups of long-bearded Hassidic Jews from Vienna of 1900, followed by a sketch of a revenging angel drawn by the young Hitler, who aspired to become an artist. On the criticism of Fest's film on Hitler, see Jörg Berlin et al., *Was verschweigt Fest? Analysen und Dokumente zum Hitler-Film* (Cologne: Pahl-

Rugenstein, 1978); Karen Jaehne, "Old Nazis in New Films: The German Cinema Today," *Cinéaste* 9 (Fall 1978): 32–35.

13. Wenders, "That's Entertainment," p. 128. See also Wenders's obituary for Fritz Lang, "Death is No Solution: The German Film Director Fritz Lang," in *West German Filmmakers on Film*, pp. 101–104.

14. Wenders, "That's Entertainment," pp. 127–128.

15. See Hans Günther Pflaum and Hans Helmut Prinzler, *Cinema in the Federal Republic of Germany. The New German Film. Origins and Present Situation. A Handbook* (Bonn: Inter Nationes, 1983), p. 5. See also Rainer Lewandowski, *Die Oberhausener: Rekonstruktion einer Gruppe 1962–1982* (Diekholzen: Regie-Verlag für Bühne und Film, 1982); Krischan Koch, *Die Bedeutung des "Oberhausener Manifestes" für die Filmentwicklung in der BRD* (Frankfurt am Main: Lang, 1985); Peter W. Jansen, "Zwanzig Jahre danach: Oberhausen und die Folgen," *Jahrbuch Film* (1982/83): 26–36. On the development of the New German Film, see Robert Fischer and Joe Hembus, *Der Neue Deutsche Film 1960–1980* (Munich: Goldmann, 1981); John Sandford, *The New German Cinema* (New York: Da Capo Press, 1980); James Franklin, *New German Cinema: From Oberhausen to Hamburg* (Boston: Twayne, 1983); Timothy Corrigan, *New German Film: The Displaced Image* (Austin: University of Texas Press, 1983); *New German Filmmakers from Oberhausen through the 1970s*, ed. Klaus Phillips (New York: Ungar, 1984); Eric Rentschler, *West German Film in the Course of Time: Reflections on the Twenty Years since Oberhausen* (Bedford Hills, N.Y.: Redgrave, 1984). See also my collective review, "Distanced Observers: Perspectives on the New German Cinema," *Quarterly Review of Film Studies* 10 (Summer 1985): 238–245.

16. After a meeting between the authors of the Gruppe 47 and the Oberhausen filmmakers the differences became clear, as Alexander Kluge recalls, and from then on each group went its own way. See Lewandowski, *Die Oberhausener*, p. 89.

17. For an interpretation of *Young Törless* with respect to Schlöndorff's treatment of the National Socialist past, see Eric Rentschler, "Specularity and Spectacle in Schlöndorff's Young Törless," in *German Film and Literature: Adaptations and Transformations*, ed. Eric Rentschler (New York/London: Methuen, 1986), pp. 176–192. On Schlöndorff in general, see Rainer Lewandowski, *Die Filme von Volker Schlöndorff* (Hildesheim/New York: Olms, 1981).

18. Consider, for instance, the way in which scholars of German studies reflected on their National Socialist involvement at the Munich Conference of Germanists in 1966. See *Germanistik: Eine deutsche Wissenschaft*, ed. Eberhard Lämmert (Frankfurt am Main: Suhrkamp, 1967).

19. Of the 108 films that were in distribution in the period 1945–1956, 104 came from England, France, or the United States, a ratio that did not change materially in the succeeding years. See Siegfried Zielinski, "Faschismusbewältigung im frühen deutschen Nachkriegsfilm," *Sammlung: Jahrbuch für antifaschistische Literatur und Kunst* 2 (1979): 124–133.

20. Anniversary pamphlet of the DEFA (1951), quoted in Zielinski, "Faschismusbewältigung," p. 130. See also *Film- und Fernsehkunst der DDR: Traditi-*

onen, Beispiele, Tendenzen, ed. Käthe Rülicke-Weiler (Berlin/GDR: Henschel-verlag, 1979), especially pp. 94ff; *Film in der DDR,* ed. Peter W. Jansen and Wolfram Schütte (Munich/Vienna: Hanser, 1977); and Barton Byg, "The Anti-faschist Tradition in GDR Film," *Purdue University Fifth Annual Conference on Film* (West Lafayette, Ind.: Purdue University Press, 1980), pp. 81–87.

21. From today's perspective it is striking how strongly the film emphasizes male heroes. Women seem to have no history of their own; they are only projections of male fantasies. Not until the late 1970s was the female perspective of history addressed. See Helma Sanders-Brahms's representation of women in her 1980 film *Deutschland, bleiche Mutter (Germany, Pale Mother).*

22. On the "Trümmerfilm" see Peter Pleyer, *Deutscher Nachkriegsfilm 1946–1948* (Münster: Fahle, 1965) and *Deutschland in Trümmern: Filmdokumente der Jahre 1945–1949,* ed. Klaus Jaeger and Helmut Regel (Oberhausen: K. M. Laufen, 1976).

23. Sven Papcke, "Schade um den Neubeginn 1945: Anmerkungen zur un-bewältigten Gegenwart," in *Vernunft und Chaos: Essays zur sozialen Ideenge-schichte* (Frankfurt am Main: Fischer, 1985), p. 231.

24. See Lutz Niethammer, *Die Mitläuferfabrik: Die Entnazifizierung am Bei-spiel Bayerns* (Berlin: Dietz, 1982). According to Niethammer, in 1948 only 14 percent of the population believed in the necessity of denazification.

25. See my article "Literatur und nationale Identität: Kontroversen um Goethe 1945–49," in *Kontroversen, alte und neue: Akten des VII. Internationalen Germanisten-Kongresses* 10, ed. Albrecht Schöne (Tübingen: Niemeyer, 1986), pp. 199–206.

26. Papcke, "Schade um den Neubeginn," p. 233.

27. See Willi Höfig, *Der deutsche Heimatfilm 1947–1960* (Stuttgart: Ehnke, 1973); Klaus Kreimeier, "Der westdeutsche Film in den fünfziger Jahren," in *Die fünfziger Jahre: Beiträge zu Politik und Kultur,* ed. Dieter Bänsch (Tübingen: Narr, 1985), pp. 283–305; Heide Schlüpmann, "'Wir Wunderkinder': Tradition und Regression im bundesdeutschen Film der Fünfziger Jahre," *Frauen und Film* 35 (October 1983): 4–11; Joe Hembus, *Der deutsche Film kann gar nicht besser sein* (Munich: Rogner & Bernhard, 1981); Gerhard Bliersbach, *So grün war die Heide: Der deutsche Nachkriegsfilm in neuer Sicht* (Weinheim/Basel: Beltz, 1985); Claudius Seidl, *Der deutsche Film der fünfziger Jahre* (Munich: Heyne, 1987); Eric Rentschler, "Germany: The Past That Would Not Go Away," in *World Cinema since 1945,* ed. William Luhr (New York: Ungar, 1987), pp. 213–219.

28. Hans Deppe (1897–1969) made about half of his approximately seventy films between 1934 and 1945. There were many who, along with Deppe, stood behind the camera again soon after the denazification and continued the tradi-tional UFA style, purged of obvious Nazism and anti-Semitism. Goebbels's UFA had been dissolved as a company, but its staff, its style, and its spirit lived on through the entire 1950s.

29. On the critical Heimatfilm, see Eric Rentschler, "Calamity Prevails over the Country: Young German Filmmakers Revisit the Homeland," in Rentschler, *West German Film,* pp. 103–128.

30. See in this context the discussion about *Das Boot* in *Die Zeit*, 8, 15, and 29 March 1985. The articles deal with the six-hour, three-part television broadcast of 1985, not with the shorter film version of 1981. This film about the submarine war of 1944 was Germany's most expensive film up to that date (1982), and especially in the United States it is probably the most commercially successful German film ever made, repeatedly shown on cable television and readily available in video rental outlets. The West German television broadcast, which reached a record 60 percent of all households (that is, 24 million viewers), engendered a short but intense controversy. The film, as is often the case with historical subjects, provided the impetus for debates about larger issues. See the telling titles of the published reviews, "Are Soldiers Criminals?" and "Culprits Are Also Victims."

31. See Wolfgang Staudte's critique, "Der Heldentod füllt immer noch die Kinokassen," in *Der Film: Manifeste, Gespräche, Dokumente, 1945 bis heute,* ed. Theodor Kotulla (Munich: Piper, 1964), pp. 193–195. See also Klaus Kreimeier, *Kino und Filmindustrie in der BRD: Ideologieproduktion und Klassenwirklichkeit nach 1945* (Kronberg: Scriptor, 1973), especially pp. 108–129.

32. Konrad Adenauer, "Verständigung, Frieden und Freiheit: Ansprache in der Frankfurter Universität am 30. Juni 1952," in *Konrad Adenauer: Reden 1917–1967: Eine Auswahl,* ed. Hans-Peter Schwarz (Stuttgart: Deutsche Verlags-Anstalt, 1975), p. 255.

33. See, for instance, the influential speech "The 8th of May 1945—Forty Years After" by the President of the Federal Republic, Richard von Weizsäcker, published in *A Voice from Germany: Speeches by Richard von Weizsäcker,* trans. Karin von Abrams (New York: Weidenfeld and Nicolson, 1986), pp. 43–60.

34. The most important of these are Wolfgang Staudte's social-critical films *Rosen für den Staatsanwalt (Roses for the Prosecutor,* 1959) and *Kirmes (Fairground,* 1960), Herbert Vesely's experimental films *nicht mehr fliehen (Stop Running,* 1955) and *Das Brot der frühen Jahre (The Bread of the Early Years,* 1962), Ottomar Domnick's debut feature film, the neo-expressionistic *Jonas* (1957) with texts by Hans Magnus Enzensberger, and Kurt Hoffmann's satire on the continuities between the Third Reich and the Adenauer era, *Wir Wunderkinder (Aren't We Wonderful?,* 1958).

35. The West German film also had no Günther Grass, no Wolfgang Koeppen, no Siegfried Lenz. On the thematization of the "unmastered past" in German literature, see Hamida Bosmajian, *Metaphors of Evil: Contemporary German Literature and the Shadow of Nazism* (Iowa City: University of Iowa Press, 1979); Felicia Letsch, *Auseinandersetzung mit der Vergangenheit als Moment der Gegenwartskritik* (Cologne: Pahl-Rugenstein, 1982); Judith Ryan, *The Uncompleted Past: Postwar German Novels and the Third Reich* (Detroit: Wayne State University Press, 1983); Donna Reed, *The Novel and the Nazi Past* (New York: Peter Lang, 1985).

36. Quoted in Peter Nau, "Die Kunst des Filmesehens," *Filmkritik* 23 (June 1979): 264. On Straub and Huillet, see also *The Cinema of Jean-Marie Straub and Danièle Huillet,* ed. Jonathan Rosenbaum (New York: Film at the Public,

1982); *Herzog/Kluge/Straub,* ed. Peter W. Jansen and Wolfram Schütte (Munich/ Vienna: Hanser, 1976); Richard Roud, *Straub* (London: Secker and Warburg, 1971). For an analysis of *Machorka-Muff,* see Eric Rentschler, "The Use and Abuse of Memory: New German Film and the Discourse of Bitburg," *New German Critique* 36 (Fall 1985): 67–90, especially pp. 74ff.

37. Kraft Wetzel, "New German Cinema: Economics without Miracle," *Semiotext(e)* 4, "The German Issue" (1982): 221. See also his updated survey, "Die Krise des Neuen deutschen Films," *Media Perspektiven* 2 (1987): 90–99. On the economic dimension of New German Cinema, see also Thomas Elsaesser, "The Postwar German Cinema," in *Fassbinder,* ed. Tony Rayns, 2nd ed. (London: British Film Institute, 1979), pp. 1–16; *Förderung essen Filme auf: Positionen—Situation—Materialien,* ed. Louis Saul (Munich: Ölschläger, 1984).

38. See, for instance, the German Press Agency article, "Goethe-Institut betont Bedeutung der Filmarbeit," *Süddeutsche Zeitung,* 9 July 1986: "The Goethe Institute believes that film as a medium of international cultural exchange is becoming increasingly important for German foreign cultural policy." According to this source, in the 146 Goethe Institutes in 66 countries, "30 to 35 events are organized around films" every day. See also the report, "Fassbinder-Zyklus lockt Zuschauer: Bundesdeutsche Kulturarbeit in Osteuropa," *Das Parlament,* 22/29 December 1984. The article claims that the Cultural Institute of the Federal Republic in Bucharest has shown 150 German films in two years. See also Elmar Brandt, "Medien und Medienprojekte zur Förderung der internationalen kulturellen Zusammenarbeit," *Zeitschrift für Kulturaustausch* 32 (1982): 67–70. And see the thematic study by Hans Günther Pflaum, *Deutschland im Film: Themenschwerpunkte des Spielfilms in der Bundesrepublik Deutschland: Materialien zur Landeskunde* (Munich: Hueber, 1985).

39. There were, for instance, "problems" in 1983 with a statement added on to the ending of Paul Verhoeven's *Die weisse Rose* (*The White Rose*), a film about the organized resistance to Hitler. The statement claimed that, in the view of the Federal Constitutional Court of West Germany, resistance groups like the "Weisse Rose" had objectively violated the laws of that time. The statement goes on to demand that all judgments passed by Hitler's People's Court ("Volksgerichtshof") must today be annulled by law. The Goethe Institute intended to present the film in this form at a West German film week in Budapest, but the showing was forbidden because the text was considered to be politically offensive. The German Parliament even made an inquiry into the matter at its 31st session, October 27, 1983.

40. See Robert Reimer and Carol Reimer, "Nazi-retro Filmography," *Journal of Popular Film and Television* 14 (Summer 1986): 82. The authors also present an annotated list of more than sixty feature films. See also *30 Jahre danach: Dokumentation zur Auseinandersetzung mit dem Nationalsozialismus im Film 1945 bis 1975,* ed. Heiko R. Blum (Cologne: Horst May Verlag, 1975). A brief summary of films set in the Third Reich can be found in Paul Monaco, "The Bitburg Syndrome," in *Ribbons in Time: Movies and Society since 1945* (Bloomington: Indiana University Press, 1987), pp. 62–92. Annette Insdorf, in her study *Indelible Shadows: Film and the Holocaust* (New York: Random House, 1983),

discusses more than eighty films from various countries that deal with the annihilation of the Jews. See also Judith E. Doneson, *The Holocaust in American Film* (Philadelphia/New York/Jerusalem: The Jewish Publication Society, 1987); Ilan Avisar, *Screening the Holocaust: Cinema Images of the Unimaginable* (Bloomington: Indiana University Press, 1988).

41. In 1974 these films, representing "la mode rétro," provoked an intensive discussion in the *Cahiers du Cinéma* about film, popular memory, and the rewriting of history. The discussion also emphasized the inherent conservativism of historical films that show fascism as a fate that both fascinates and paralyzes. See the interview with Michel Foucault in "Film and Popular Memory—Cahiers du Cinéma/Extracts," *Edinburgh Magazine* 2 (1977): 20–25, originally published in *Cahiers du Cinéma* 251 (1974), in which he argues that a battle for collective memory, the "mémoire populaire," has begun. Foucault believes that whoever controls the memory of people controls their experience and knowledge of the past as well. He claims that there are no more films about the resistance because someone wants the resistance to be forgotten. The defeatist films about fascism which aim to prove that *no one* was immune to fascism (implying that nothing can be done about fascism) unwittingly play, according to Foucault, into the hands of the dominant powers. See also the contributions by Colin MacCabe, Stephen Heath, Jacques Rancière, and Jean Narboni in the issue of *Edinburgh Magazine* 2 (1977) which is entitled "History/Production/Memory."

42. Karsten Witte, "Weinte sonst niemand? Hitler, Höss & Co.," *Medium* 7/8 (August 1977): 28. See also the critique by Siegfried Zielinski, "Aspekte des Faschismus als Kino- und Fernseh-Sujet: Tendenzen zu Beginn der achtziger Jahre," *Sammlung* 4 (1981): 47–56.

43. See Karl Heinz Bohrer, "Hitler, der Held der siebziger Jahre?" *Frankfurter Allgemeine Zeitung*, 29 June 1977; Marion Gräfin Dönhoff, "Was bedeutet die Hitlerwelle?" *Die Zeit*, 26 September 1977. At the same time, surveys showed that young students knew grotesquely little about Hitler. See Dieter Bossman, *Was ich über Adolf Hitler gehört habe* (Frankfurt am Main: Fischer, 1977). Some students thought, for instance, that Hitler was an Italian or that he belonged to the Christian Democratic Union.

44. Norbert Elias, "Gedanken über die Bundesrepublik, Herbst 1977," *Merkur* 439/40 (September-October 1985): 734. (The essay was written between 1977 and March 1978 but not published until 1985.)

45. Ibid., p. 744f.

46. Jillian Becker, *Hitler's Children: The Story of the Baader-Meinhof Gang* (New York: J. B. Lippincott, 1978). In the German translation a question mark was added to the title: *Hitlers Kinder? Der Baader-Meinhof-Terrorismus* (Frankfurt am Main: Fischer, 1978).

47. Alexander Kluge, *Die Patriotin* (Frankfurt am Main: Zweitausendeins, 1979), p. 28 (emphasis mine).

48. Alexander Kluge et al., "Germany in Autumn: What Is the Film's Bias?" in *West German Filmmakers on Film*, pp. 132–133.

49. Ibid., p. 132. On *Germany in Autumn*, see Miriam Hansen, "Cooperative Auteur Cinema and Oppositional Public Sphere: Alexander Kluge's Contribution

to 'Germany in Autumn,'" *New German Critique* 24/25 (1981–82): 36–56. In 1969 a plan was proposed to deal with the German present and past in about 100 documentary films under the overall title "On Germany"; the project never materialized. See Fischer and Hembus, *Der Neue Deutsche Film*, p. 277. *Germany in Autumn* was followed by two additional cooperative films: *Der Kandidat* (*The Candidate*, 1980) and *Krieg und Frieden* (*War and Peace*, 1982–83).

50. This means that every other American watched at least one episode of this television series. See Sabina Lietzmann, "Die Judenvernichtung als Seifenoper: *Holocaust*—eine Serie im amerikanischen Fernsehen," *Frankfurter Allgemeine Zeitung*, 20 April 1978; Thomas Kielinger, "Wie das amerikanische Fernsehen deutsche Vergangenheit bewältigt," *Die Welt*, 22 April 1978; "Fernsehen: Gaskammern à la Hollywood?" *Der Spiegel*, 15 May 1978, pp. 228–231; Rainer Paul and Hans Hoyng, "Massenmord gemischt mit Deo-Spray," *Stern*, 27 April 1978, pp. 202–207.

51. Elie Wiesel, "Trivializing the Holocaust: Semi-Fact and Semi-Fiction," *The New York Times,* 16 April 1978. On the ambivalent fictional status of the televised *Holocaust,* see Christian Zimmer, *Le retour de la fiction* (Paris: Les Éditions du Cerf, 1984), pp. 75–76. See also Claude Lanzmann, "From the Holocaust to *Holocaust*," *Telos* 42 (Winter 1979–80): 137–143.

52. See Georg Lukács, *The Historical Novel,* trans. Hannah Mitchell and Stanley Mitchell (Boston: Beacon, 1963); Wolfgang Iser, "Fiction—The Filter of History: A Study of Sir Walter Scott's *Waverly*," in *New Perspectives in German Literary Criticism,* trans. D. H. Wilson et al., ed. Richard E. Amacher and Victor Lange (Princeton, N.J.: Princeton University Press, 1979), pp. 86–104.

53. Quoted in Cecil Smith, "Docudrama: Fact or Forum," *Los Angeles Times,* 17 April 1978. Although he is aware of the "inherent dangers" of the "docudrama," Gerald Green here legitimates the process of mixing fact and fiction: "The technique, of course, is as old as literature itself. Tolstoy created all those Rostovs and Volkonskys and others—they didn't exist in history. Then he placed them among the Napoleons, the actual generals and the real events of *War and Peace* . . . I think what's important is that even though in a dramatic structure you can't get every nuance 100% historically correct, you can get the thrust and the essence of history, probably more effectively than any other way. I think there's more truthful, documented history in *Holocaust* than in anything I have ever seen about the Nazi destruction of the Jews."

54. See *Holocaust zur Unterhaltung: Anatomie eines internationalen Bestsellers,* ed. Friedrich Knilli and Siegfried Zielinski (Berlin: Elefanten-Press, 1982), pp. 13–14 and 44.

55. Sabina Lietzmann, in her *Frankfurter Allgemeine Zeitung* article of 20 April 1978, explains it as follows: "'Holocaust' is the burnt sacrifice of ancient Israel, where not only animals but also human beings were offered. God had demanded a burnt offering of Abraham, who was ready to slaughter his son Isaac. In America, 'Holocaust' has come to mean the mass slaughter of the Jews in the Third Reich. And 'Holocaust' is the title of a television series that is running every evening this week on American television sets." The word "Holocaust" was elected "Word of the Year" by the Bibliographic Institute in 1979.

56. See the many empirical studies on the reception and effect of *Holocaust* in the Federal Republic: Dieter Prokop, *Medienwirkungen* (Frankfurt am Main: Suhrkamp, 1981), pp. 98–187; Yizhak Ahren et al., *Das Lehrstück Holocaust: Zur Wirkungspsychologie eines Medienereignisses* (Opladen: Westdeutscher Verlag, 1982); *Betrifft 'Holocaust': Zuschauer schreiben an den WDR,* ed. Friedrich Knilli and Siegfried Zielinski (Berlin: Volker Spiess, 1983); Joachim Siedler, *Holocaust: Die Fernsehserie in der deutschen Presse: Eine Inhalts- und Verlaufsanalyse* (Münster: Lit Verlag, 1984). The periodical *Medium* dealt in especially great detail with the effects of the "media event" *Holocaust.* See the discussion in 1979, especially in no. 1, "Die 'Endlösung' als Medienereignis" ("The 'Final Solution' as a Media Event") and in no. 3, "Deutsches Weissmachen." ("German White-washing" is an allusion to the protagonist's name, Weiss.) The selected bibliography of the volume *Holocaust zur Unterhaltung* (1982) contains over 150 titles of essays on *Holocaust* in German-language periodicals. The discussion carried on in the West German daily press is beyond calculation. For articles on the German reception of *Holocaust* in English, see Barton Byg, "Holocaust and West German 'Restoration,'" *Telos* 42 (Winter 1979/80): 143–149; Mark E. Cory, "Some Reflections on NBC's Film *Holocaust,*" *German Quarterly* 53 (November 1980): 444–451; the special issue of *New German Critique* 19 (Winter 1980); also *German and Jews since the Holocaust: The Changing Situation in West Germany,* ed. Anson Rabinbach and Jack Zipes (New York/London: Holmes & Meier, 1986), especially pp. 185–283; Doneson, *The Holocaust in American Film,* pp. 141–196 ("Television and the Effects of *Holocaust*"); Avisar, *Screening the Holocaust,* p. 130.

57. Heinz Höhne, "Schwarzer Freitag für die Historiker: Holocaust: Fiktion oder Wirklichkeit?" *Spiegel,* 29 January 1979, p. 22.

58. Günter Rohrbach, "Ende der Von-oben-nach-unten Kultur? Erkenntnisse und Folgerungen für die Arbeit in den Fernsehanstalten," *Frankfurter Allgemeine Zeitung,* 1 February 1979.

59. Ibid.

60. On the long tradition of different attitudes toward mass culture in Germany and America, see my article "Mass Culture and Modernity: Notes toward a Social History of Early American and German Cinema," in *America and the Germans: An Assessment of a Three-Hundred Year History,* ed. Frank Trommler and Joseph McVeigh, vol. 2 (Philadelphia: University of Pennsylvania Press, 1985), pp. 317–333.

61. Marion Gräfin Dönhoff, "Eine deutsche Geschichtsstunde: *Holocaust*-Erschrecken nach dreissig Jahren," *Die Zeit,* 2 February 1979. See also Wolfram Schütte's apt critique of Dönhoff's rigid dichotomy between morality and aesthetics, "Wie einige Intellektuelle den Kopf verlieren und den anderer fordern: *Holocaust* und erste Folgen einer 'Revision unseres Kulturbegriffs,'" *Frankfurter Rundschau,* 5 February 1979: "That questions of aesthetics are also (or even: necessarily) questions of morality as well; and that the critics of *Holocaust* expressed their aesthetic reservations for moral reasons; further, that an aesthetic process can or even must also be one of reflection and of learning: —the possibility of such considerations and of such a self-critical treatment of reality

and of its aesthetic appropriation, shaping, and reproduction is no longer permitted by the existential dismay that *Holocaust* caused, and not only in Mrs. Dönhoff. Such a differentiated attitude was dismissed with scorn as elitist intellectual arrogance in an article by Günter Rohrbach in the *Frankfurter Allgemeine Zeitung,* as he pointed triumphantly to audience figures, market shares, and the degree of public arousal . . . Under the pretense of populism: the newest form of iconoclasm and contempt for art?"

62. Sabina Lietzmann, "Kritische Fragen," *Frankfurter Allgemeine Zeitung,* 28 September 1978.

63. Mary McGrory, "The Holocaust: Indisputable, Unbearable. On TV, 'Docu' Outdoes 'Drama,' but It Probably Won't Cure Anti-Semitism," *Los Angeles Times,* 20 April 1978. On the American perspective, see also *Germans and Jews since the Holocaust,* ed. Rabinbach and Zipes.

64. Günter Rohrbach, "Holocaust im WDR," quoted in *Im Kreuzfeuer: Der Fernsehfilm 'Holocaust': Eine Nation ist betroffen* (Frankfurt am Main: Fischer, 1979), p. 45.

65. Heinz Werner Hübner, "Kein Lehrstück, sondern Lernstück," *Süddeutsche Zeitung,* 22 September 1978.

66. Günther Rühle, "Wenn Holocaust kommt," quoted in *Im Kreuzfeuer,* p. 59.

67. Peter Schulz-Rohr, "Keine Frage von rechts oder links," *Die Zeit,* 23 June 1978.

68. Edgar Reitz, "Unabhängiger Film nach Holocaust?" in *Liebe zum Kino: Utopien und Gedanken zum Autorenfilm 1962–1983* (Cologne: KÖLN 78, 1984), p. 102.

69. On Sunday, May 5, 1985, President Reagan and Chancellor Kohl visited the military cemetery at Bitburg—a highly symbolic act that sparked a long and bitter controversy because the cemetery also included the graves of SS soldiers. "Bitburg" was seen, especially in the United States, as a bold attempt to blur the lines between culprits and victims in the name of reconciliation. All the major American newspapers and periodicals dealt in detail with the far-reaching moral and political questions posed by Reagan's Bitburg visit. See the anthology of critical essays, *Bitburg in Moral and Political Perspective,* ed. Geoffrey Hartman (Bloomington: Indiana University Press, 1986) and the exhaustive documentation *Bitburg and Beyond: Encounters in American, German and Jewish History,* ed. Ilya Levkov (New York: Shapolsky Publishers, 1987). See also Eric Rentschler, "The Use and Abuse of Memory: New German Film and the Discourse of Bitburg," *New German Critique* 36 (Fall 1985): 67–90. And see "Reagan at Bitburg: Spectacle and Memory" (with statements from Hans Jürgen Syberberg and Jean-Marie Straub, among others) in *On Film* 14 (1985): 36–40; also *Die Unfähigkeit zu feiern: Der 8. Mai,* ed. Norbert Seitz (Frankfurt am Main: Verlag Neue Kritik, 1985).

70. The "Historians' Debate" began with an article by Jürgen Habermas ("Eine Art Schadensabwicklung") in *Die Zeit* of 1 July 1986. The article attacked the "apologist tendencies in German contemporary historiography," especially the question of whether one can compare Hitler's "final solution" with Stalin's crimes. The article, which was followed by a surprisingly widespread and acri-

monious discussion that included all media, was a response especially to Andreas Hillgruber's controversial study, *Zweierlei Untergang: Die Zerschlagung des Deutschen Reiches und das Ende des europäischen Judentums* (Berlin: Siedler, 1986), in which he compares the defeat of the German army with the annihilation of the Jews, and to the position taken by Ernst Nolte in his article "Vergangenheit, die nicht vergehen will," *Frankfurter Allgemeine Zeitung*, 6 June 1986, with its thesis that the Gulag Archipelago predated Auschwitz. Nolte's main thesis had in fact already been published in English a year earlier: "Between Myth and Revisionism? The Third Reich in the Perspective of the 1980s," in *Aspects of the Third Reich*, ed. H. W. Koch (New York: Macmillan, 1985), pp. 17–38. There has been a staggering amount of subsequent literature on this topic. The fifty-five most cogent and influential essays are compiled in two anthologies: Rudolf Augstein et al., *"Historikerstreit." Die Dokumentation der Kontroverse um die Einzigartigkeit der nationalsozialistischen Judenvernichtung* (Munich/Zurich: Piper, 1987) and *Ist der Nationalsozialismus Geschichte? Zu Historisierung und Historikerstreit*, ed. Dan Diner (Frankfurt am Main: Fischer, 1987). For a contentious summary of the debate, see also Hans-Ulrich Wehler, *Entsorgung der deutschen Vergangenheit? Ein polemischer Essay zum "Historikerstreit"* (Munich: Beck, 1988). The debate has also been widely discussed in the United States. See James Markham, "German Book Sets Off New Holocaust Debate," *New York Times*, 6 September 1986; Judith Miller, "Erasing the Past: Europe's Amnesia about the Holocaust," *New York Times Magazine*, 14 November 1986; Gordon A. Craig, "The War of the German Historians," *New York Review of Books*, 15 January 1987; Richard J. Evans: "The New Nationalism and the Old History: Perspectives on the West German *Historikerstreit*," *The Journal of Modern History* 59 (December 1987): 761–797; Anson Rabinbach, "German Historians Debate the Nazi Past. A Dress Rehearsal for a New German Nationalism?" *Dissent* (Spring 1988): 192–200; Roderick Stackelberg, "1986 vs. 1968: The Turn to the Right in German Historiography," *Radical History Review* 40 (January 1988); *German Politics and Society* 13 (February 1988), special issue on the *Historikerstreit*; *New German Critique* 44 (Spring/Summer 1988), special issue on the *Historikerstreit*; Charles S. Maier, *The Unmasterable Past: History, Holocaust, and German National Identity* (Cambridge, Mass.: Harvard University Press, 1988).

71. Apart from that: "You see, it is thoroughly impractical if the emotional shock of German families, which would have meant something important for the victims of Auschwitz in 1942, is made up for in 1979; for today it is an essentially useless, that is, timeless form of shock." The words are Alexander Kluge's in his essay, "The Political as Intensity of Everyday Feelings," *Cultural Critique* 4 (Fall 1986): 126. The article, Kluge's acceptance speech on the occasion of the award of the Fontane Prize for literature, first appeared in 1979.

2. Germany as Myth

1. The page numbers in parentheses refer to the filmscript, Hans Jürgen Syberberg, *Hitler, a Film from Germany*, trans. Joachim Neugroschel (New York: Farrar, Straus and Giroux, 1982). This is a translation from the German

edition, *Hitler, ein Film aus Deutschland* (Reinbek: Rowohlt, 1978). The English version contains numerous still photographs from the film, an eight-page glossary of names and references, and the first three sections of Syberberg's lengthy introductory essay to the German edition under the title, "Art as Salvation from the German Misery." This edition also includes a preface by Susan Sontag.

2. "The story of my film is the story of its reception," Syberberg wrote in his aphoristic diary *Die freudlose Gesellschaft: Notizen aus dem letzten Jahr* (Munich/Vienna: Hanser, 1981), p. 53. On the history of the reception of his Hitler film, see especially the chapter "Letzte Reisen mit dem Hitler-Film," pp. 107–199. "After three years of the Hitler film's existence, there is not even a 'No' in Germany to this film based on reasoned, clear argument after careful examination, honest and forthright and liberal and dialectical or educational. What a flop" (p. 179).

3. Susan Sontag, "Eye of the Storm," *The New York Review of Books,* 21 February 1980; reprinted under the title "Syberberg's Hitler" in *Under the Sign of Saturn* (New York: Farrar, Straus and Giroux, 1980), pp. 137–165. See Syberberg's comments on Sontag's review in *Freudlose Gesellschaft,* pp. 60ff. He was truly touched by Sontag's enthusiastic and informed response, a response he has not to this day received from his German critics, who in general seem to find it difficult to "read," understand, and describe a complex, postmodernist (as well as political) film like Syberberg's on its own terms *before* judging and dismissing it on ideological grounds.

4. Hans Jürgen Syberberg, *Syberbergs Filmbuch* (Frankfurt am Main: Fischer, 1979), p. 11.

5. Ibid.

6. Ibid., pp. 12–13.

7. The 8-millimeter documentary films are collected in his 1970 compilation film called *Nach meinem letzten Umzug (After My Last Move).* In his book *Freudlose Gesellschaft,* Syberberg says: "Everything I am doing today is based on these early experiments" (p. 306).

8. Even in his most recent films with the actress Edith Clever, Syberberg is clearly oriented toward the theater. See especially the dramatic monologue *Die Nacht (The Night,* 1985) and the scenic reading *Fräulein Else (Miss Else,* 1987); in *Parsifal* (1982) he combined theater, opera, performance art, and film. See Manfred Schneider, "Der ungeheure Blick des Kinos auf die Welt: Die Wissensmächte Musik und Film in Wagner/Syberbergs *Parsifal,*" *Merkur* 430 (December 1984): 882–892.

9. On the affinity between Expressionist theater and film, see my article "The Expressionist Vision in Theater and Cinema," in *Expressionism Reconsidered,* ed. G. B. Pickar and K. E. Webb (Munich: Fink, 1979), pp. 90–98.

10. Ulrich Kurowski, "Was ist ein deutscher Film?" *Film-Korrespondenz* 10/11 (November 1973): 8–12.

11. See *Syberbergs Filmbuch,* p. 14: "The mathematical principles of construction that are expressed in musical terms like requiem, chamber music, chorus, aria, sonata, passion, rhapsody, recitative, leitmotif, development, stretto, variation, solo, fugue, counterpoint, vertical blending, dialinear system of equilib-

rium, linear interweaving, repetition, and rhythm, help in understanding how the motifs and signals of a film blend in their necessary simultaneity and sequence, how they resonate across and through the film and correspond between above and below, beginning and end in the labyrinthine mathematics of the optical-acoustical web of emotion and intellect."

12. See Syberberg's contribution to the Zurich exhibition catalogue, *Gesamtkunstwerk: Europäische Utopien seit 1800* (Aarau: Sauerländer, 1983), pp. 434–436; see also Bazon Brock's essay, "Der Hang zum Gesamtkunstwerk," ibid., especially pp. 30–34, which places the Hitler film in this tradition. On Syberberg's relation to Wagner, see Hans Rudolf Vaget, "Syberberg's *Our Hitler*: Wagnerianism and Alienation," *The Massachusetts Review* 23 (1982): 593–612.

13. See also Friedrich A. Kittler, "Weltatem. Über Wagners Medientechnologie," *Diskursanalysen* 1 (1987): 94–107. See further Syberberg's remark in his second volume of cultural criticism, entitled *Der Wald steht schwarz und schweiget: Neue Notizen aus Deutschland* (Zurich: Diogenes, 1984), p. 92: "Richard Wagner . . . stood at the threshold of film, not as a film composer: the music of the future was the film."

14. At the end of his book *From Caligari to Hitler: A Psychological History of the German Film* (Princeton, N.J.: Princeton University Press, 1947), Kracauer writes: "Irretrievably sunk into retrogression, the bulk of the German people could not help submitting to Hitler. Since Germany thus carried out what had been anticipated by her cinema from its very beginning, conspicuous screen characters now came true in life itself. Personified daydreams of minds to whom freedom meant a fatal shock, and adolescence a permanent temptation, these figures filled the arena of Nazi Germany. Homunculus walked about in the flesh. Self-appointed Caligaris hypnotized innumerable Cesares into murder. Raving Mabuses committed fantastic crimes with impunity, and mad Ivans devised unheard-of tortures. Along with this unholy procession, many motifs known from the screen turned into actual events . . . It all was as it had been on the screen" (p. 272).

15. Hans Jürgen Syberberg, "Alpträume akzeptieren," *Frankfurter Allgemeine Zeitung*, 3 May 1979.

16. See Walter Benjamin, "Theses on the Philosophy of History," in *Illuminations*, trans. Harry Zohn, ed. Hannah Arendt (New York: Schocken, 1969), p. 257.

17. I am following Hannes Böhringer's terminology in "Die Ruine in der Posthistoire," *Merkur* 406 (April 1982): 367–375, where he designates *posthistoire* as "the epoch of postmodernism" (p. 371).

18. See the 25-page bibliography on postmodernism in Linda Hutcheon, *A Poetics of Postmodernism: History, Theory, Fiction* (New York/London: Routledge, 1988); see also *Postmoderne: Zeichen eines kulturellen Wandels*, ed. Andreas Huyssen and Klaus R. Scherpe (Reinbek: Rowohlt, 1986); *The Anti-Aesthetic: Essays on Postmodern Culture*, ed. Hal Foster (Port Townsend, Wash.: Bay Press, 1983); *New German Critique* 33 (Fall 1984), special issue on "Modernity and Postmodernity."

19. See Arnold Gehlen, "Einblicke," in *Gesamtausgabe*, vol. 7 (Frankfurt am

Main: Klostermann, 1978), pp. 19 and 140; Hendrik de Man, *Vermassung und Kulturverfall. Eine Diagnose unserer Zeit* (Berne: Francke, 1951), pp. 135–136. See also Norbert Bolz, "Die Zeit des Weltspiels," *Ästhetik und Kommunikation* 17 (1986): 113–120.

20. Arnold Gehlen, "Über kulturelle Kristallisation," in *Studien zur Anthropologie und Soziologie* (Darmstadt/Neuwied: Luchterhand, 1963), p. 323.

21. See Klaus Scherpe, "Dramatisierung und Entdramatisierung des Untergangs—Zum ästhetischen Bewusstsein von Moderne und Postmoderne," in *Postmoderne*, pp. 270–301.

22. Syberberg, *Freudlose Gesellschaft*, p. 83.

23. Quoted in Eva-Suzanne Bayer, "Hitler in uns: H. J. Syberberg dreht den 3. Teil der deutschen Trilogie," *Stuttgarter Zeitung*, 15 April 1977.

24. Ibid.

25. Max Picard, *Hitler in uns selbst* (Erlenbach-Zurich: Eugen Rentsch-Verlag, 1949), pp. 207ff.

26. See Susan Sontag's essay about Leni Riefenstahl, "Fascinating Fascism," in *Under the Sign of Saturn*, pp. 73–105; and Klaus Theweleit, *Male Fantasies*. vol. 1, trans. Stephen Conway (Minneapolis: University of Minnesota Press, 1987). See also the exhibition catalogue *Inszenierung der Macht: Ästhetische Faszination im Faschismus* (Berlin: Nishen, 1987).

27. Erika Fischer-Lichte, "Jenseits der Interpretation: Anmerkungen zum Text von Robert Wilson/Heiner Müllers 'CIVIL warS,'" in *Kontroversen, alte und neue*, ed. Albrecht Schöne, vol. 6 (Tübingen: Niemeyer, 1986), pp. 191–201; on Heiner Müller see also Hans-Thies Lehmann, "Raum-Zeit: Das Entgleiten der Geschichte in der Dramatik Heiner Müllers und im französischen Poststrukturalismus," *Text + Kritik* 73 (January 1982): 71–81; Arlene Teraoka, *The Silence of Entropy or Universal Discourse: The Postmodernist Poetics of Heiner Müller* (New York: Lang, 1985). On the postmodern theater see also Andrzej Wirth, "Vom Dialog zum Diskurs: Versuch einer Synthese der nachbrechtschen Theaterkonzepte," *Theater heute* (January 1980): 16–19.

28. Hans-Thies Lehmann, "Robert Wilson, Szenograph," *Merkur* 437 (July 1985): 554.

29. Syberberg, *Freudlose Gesellschaft*, p. 103.

30. Ibid. (emphasis mine).

31. Roland Barthes, *The Pleasure of the Text*, trans. Richard Miller (New York: Hill and Wang, 1975), p. 53.

32. "Les quatre cavaliers de l'Apocalypse et les vermisseaux quotidiens. Entretien avec Michel Foucault," *Cahiers du Cinéma* (February 1980): 95f. Hannah Arendt's account of the Eichmann trial, *Eichmann in Jerusalem* (New York: Viking, 1963) carries the subtitle: "A Report on the Banality of Evil." See also Alice Yaeger Kaplan, "Fascism and Banality," in *Reproductions of Banality: Fascism, Literature and French Intellectual Life* (Minnesota: University of Minnesota Press, 1986), pp. 41–58.

33. Theodor Kotulla's film *Aus einem deutschen Leben* (*Death Is My Trade*, 1977) concentrates on this aspect. It shows the "career" of the commandant of Auschwitz, Rudolf Hoess, from childhood to execution in images that emphasize

the prosaic life of a man who murdered millions from his desk. The banality of his life makes his deeds all the more horrendous.

34. Sontag, "Syberberg's Hitler," p. 154.

35. The father of postmodernist architecture, Robert Venturi, called himself a "combiner of significant old clichés" in *Complexity and Contradiction in Architecture* (1966; New York: The Museum of Modern Art, 1977), p. 44. In his manifesto "Nonstraightforward Architecture: A Gentle Manifesto" he states his program as follows: "I like elements which are hybrid rather than 'pure,' compromising rather than 'clean,' distorted rather than 'straightforward,' ambiguous rather than 'articulated,' perverse as well as impersonal, boring as well as 'interesting,' conventional rather than 'designed,' accommodating rather than excluding, redundant rather than simple, vestigial as well as innovating, inconsistent and equivocal rather than direct and clear. I am for messy vitality over obvious unity. I include the non-sequitur and proclaim the duality. I am for richness of meaning rather than clarity of meaning" (p. 16). Venturi's plea for an architecture full of references and his interest in ambiguity, contradiction, and ironic polyvalence correspond precisely to Syberberg's film aesthetics.

36. Syberberg, *Freudlose Gesellschaft*, p. 60.

37. See Fritz J. Raddatz, "Die Aufklärung entlässt ihre Kinder: Vernunft, Geschichte, Fortschritt werden verabschiedet: Mythos ist der neue Wert," *Die Zeit*, 29 June and 6 July 1984; Raimundo Panikkar, *Rückkehr zum Mythos* (Frankfurt am Main: Insel, 1985); Claude Lévi-Strauss, *Myth and Meaning* (Toronto/Buffalo: University of Toronto Press, 1978); *Faszination des Mythos*, ed. Renate Schlesinger (Basel/Frankfurt am Main: Stroemfeld/Roter Stern, 1985); Thomas Nipperdey, "Neue Sehnsucht," *Süddeutsche Zeitung*, 21–22 March 1987.

38. Manfred Frank, *Der kommende Gott: Vorlesungen über die Neue Mythologie* (Frankfurt am Main: Suhrkamp, 1982), p. 9.

39. *Mythos und Moderne: Begriff und Bild einer Rekonstruktion*, ed. Karl Heinz Bohrer (Frankfurt am Main: Suhrkamp, 1983).

40. See Wolfgang Max Faust, "Deutsche Kunst, hier heute," *Kunstforum International* (December 1981-January 1982): 25–40; Mark Rosenthal, *Anselm Kiefer* (Chicago/Philadelphia: Prestel, 1987), especially pp. 32–75 ("On Being German and an Artist: 1974–1980").

41. See, for instance, Peter Handke, *Slow Homecoming*, trans. Ralph Manheim (New York: Farrar, Straus and Giroux, 1985; orig. 1979); Botho Strauss, *Der Park: Schauspiel* (Munich: Hanser, 1983); Michael Ende, *Momo*, trans. J. Maxwell Brownjohn (New York: Doubleday, 1985; orig. 1973).

42. See Karl Heinz Bohrer, "The Three Cultures," in *Observations on "The Spiritual Situation of the Age": Contemporary German Perspectives*, ed. Jürgen Habermas (Cambridge, Mass.: MIT Press), pp. 125–155, especially the subsection "The Return of Myth in West German Auteur film" (pp. 142–145). Bohrer discusses Herzog, Wenders, and Syberberg. On Herzog, see Timothy Corrigan, ed., *Werner Herzog: Between Mirage and History* (New York/London: Methuen, 1986); Hans-Thies Lehmann, *"Die Raumfabrik—Mythos im Kino und Kinomythos,"* in *Mythos und Moderne*, pp. 572–609.

43. In this context, see also the new interpretations of medieval myths by Robert Bresson (*Lancelot du Lac*), Eric Rohmer (*Perceval le Gallois*), and John Boormann (*Excalibur*).

44. Hans Jürgen Syberberg, "Ludwig: Requiem für einen jungfräulichen König (1972)," in *Syberbergs Filmbuch*, p. 15.

45. Ibid., p. 39.

46. Ibid., p. 38.

47. See Ernst Bloch's essays (for instance, "Die Silberbüchse Winnetous") in *Erbschaft dieser Zeit*, expanded edition, *Gesamtausgabe der Werke*, vol. 4 (Frankfurt am Main: Suhrkamp, 1962).

48. The trilogy is augmented by two additional films, works that supplement and complement it. *Theodor Hirneis oder: Wie man ehem. Hofkoch wird (Ludwig's Cook,* 1972) looks at Ludwig II through the eyes of his cook Hirneis, a demystifying, materialistic look from below at a "great figure" of history that prefigures the valet scene in the Hitler film. In 1975 there followed a five-hour documentary, *Winifred Wagner und die Geschichte des Hauses Wahnfried 1914– 1975 (The Confessions of Winifred Wagner)*, which deals mainly with the private friendship of Wagner's daughter with Hitler. The interviews with Winifred Wagner show Syberberg's interest in Hitler as a failed artist, for whom Winifred Wagner's family became a kind of substitute home. See also Marcia Landy, "Politics, Aesthetics, and Patriarchy in the *Confessions of Winifred Wagner*," *New German Critique* 18 (Fall 1979): 151–166. On the Hitler trilogy as a whole, see Thomas Elsaesser, "Myth as the Phantasmagoria of History: H. J. Syberberg, Cinema and Representation," *New German Critique* 24/25 (Fall/ Winter 1981–82): 108–154.

49. Roland Barthes, *Mythologies*, trans. Annette Lavers (New York: Hill and Wang, 1975), p. 129; see also p. 151: "Myth deprives the object of which it speaks of all History. In it, history evaporates."

50. Ernst Bloch, *The Principle of Hope*, trans. Neville Plaice et al., vol. 2 (Cambridge, Mass.: MIT Press, 1986), p. 756.

51. Syberberg, *Der Wald steht schwarz*, p. 96.

52. Michel Delaye and Jacques Rivette, "Entretien avec Claude Lévi-Strauss," *Cahiers du Cinéma* 156 (June 1964): 29.

53. See Ernst Cassirer, *The Myth of the State* (New Haven, Conn.: Yale University Press, 1946); see also Hans Blumenberg, *Work on Myth*, trans. Robert M. Wallace (Cambridge, Mass.: MIT Press, 1985).

54. Syberberg, *Freudlose Gesellschaft*, p. 100.

55. See, for instance, *Visions of Apocalypse: End or Rebirth?* ed. Saul Friedländer et al. (New York/London: Holmes & Meier, 1985); *Das Spiel mit der Apokalypse: Über die letzten Tage der Menschheit*, ed. Leonhard Reinisch (Freiburg/Basel/Vienna: Herder, 1984); *Weltuntergänge*, ed. Heiner Boencke et al. (Reinbek: Rowohlt, 1984); Hans-Jürgen Heinrichs, *Die katastrophale Moderne* (Frankfurt am Main/Paris: Qumran, 1984); Anton Andreas Guha, *Ende: Tagebuch aus dem 3. Weltkrieg* (Königstein: Athenäum, 1983); Jacques Derrida, *D'un ton apocalyptique adopté naguère en philosophie* (Paris: Éditions Galilé, 1986); for literary references to this "newest mood of the West" in German

literature, see Scherpe, "Dramatisierung und Entdramatisierung des Untergangs," in *Postmoderne*, pp. 270–301. For a polemical discussion of "catastrophism" and the "apocalyptic discourse," see Michael Schneider, "Apokalypse, Politik als Psychose und die Lebemänner des Untergangs," in *Nur tote Fische schwimmen mit dem Strom: Essays, Aphorismen und Polemiken* (Cologne: Kiepenheuer & Witsch, 1984), pp. 34–75; and "Die Intellektuellen und der Katastrophismus: Krise oder Wende der deutschen Aufklärer?" ibid., pp. 76–133.

56. Max Weber, "Science as a Vocation," in *From Max Weber: Essays in Sociology*, trans. and ed. H. H. Gerth and C. Wright Mills (New York: Oxford University Press, 1958), p. 139.

57. See Ulrich Linse, *Barfüssige Propheten: Erlöser in den zwanziger Jahren* (Berlin: Siedler, 1983).

58. See Ernst Bloch, "Amusement Co., Grauen, Drittes Reich" (first published in September 1930), in *Erbschaft dieser Zeit*, p. 65: "It is not the 'theory' of National Socialism that is serious but its energy, the fanatic-religious component that comes only from despair and ignorance—the rarely awakened power of belief."

59. Syberberg himself refers repeatedly to his origins, since he believes they allow him to judge more freely. "I lived outside the Nazi society," he writes in *Freudlose Gesellschaft*, "and today I can move about undamaged by its consequences, immunized, without having had to set myself apart from my parents through protest and without being raised with thoughts of revenge on the former persecutors" (p. 146).

60. *Syberbergs Filmbuch*, p. 306.

61. See Wolfram Schlenker, *Das "kulturelle Erbe" in der DDR: Gesellschaftliche Entwicklung und Kulturpolitik 1945–1965* (Stuttgart: Metzler, 1977).

62. See the chapter "Konservative Revolution und die Idee der deutschen Sendung," in *Weimarer Republik. Texte und Dokumente zur deutschen Literatur 1918–1933*, ed. Anton Kaes (Stuttgart: Metzler, 1983), pp. 485–513.

63. See Syberberg, *Freudlose Gesellschaft*, pp. 21ff.

64. Ibid.

65. Syberberg considers Hitler a "cinéaste" who allegedly watched two feature movies every evening between 1933 and 1939; he is also convinced that Hitler "staged" and "directed" World War II as a film. See "Hans Jürgen Syberberg— A Cycle Concluded," *The Filmex Society Newsletter* 7 (June 1979): 3: "I played with the idea that Hitler created war only for the newsreels. To see his own epic Hollywood movie. The war became the biggest home movie ever made."

66. Alexander Mitscherlich and Margarete Mitscherlich, *The Inability to Mourn: Principles of Collective Behavior*, trans. Beverly R. Placzek (New York: Grove, 1975; orig.: *Die Unfähigkeit zu trauern*, 1958). See also Ivo Frenzel, "Müssen wir trauern? Wiedergelesen: 'Die Unfähigkeit zu trauern' von A. und M. Mitscherlich," *Frankfurter Allgemeine Zeitung*, 7 June 1978.

67. Margarete Mitscherlich-Nielsen, "Rede über das eigene Land," in *Reden über das eigene Land: Deutschland* (Munich: Bertelsmann, 1985), pp. 60–61.

68. Ibid., p. 62.

69. Saul Friedländer, *Reflections of Nazism*, p. 21.

70. *Cahiers du Cinéma* dedicated a special issue to Syberberg in February 1980, 100 pages long and lavishly illustrated. Extensive interviews with him appeared in many publications, including *Le Monde,* 8 December 1977; *Télerama,* 19 July 1978; *Cinématographe* 39 (June 1978): 29–32; *Écran,* July 1978; *Cahiers du Cinéma* 292 (September 1978): 8–14. The same issue of *Cahiers du Cinéma* carried long analytical articles about the Hitler film by Yann Lardeau, Serge Daney, Jean-Louis Comolli, and François Géré. See further Daniel Sauvaget, "Syberberg: Dramaturgie antinaturaliste et Germanitude," *La Revue du Cinéma/Image et son* 335 (January 1979): 94–102; *Revue Belge du Cinéma* no. 3 (Spring 1983) also published a Syberberg issue. Other articles by French authors (Jean-Pierre Faye, Christian Zimmer, Jean-Pierre Oudart, and Michel Foucault) appeared in German translation in *Syberbergs Hitler-Film,* ed. Klaus Eder (Munich: Hanser, 1980). An analysis of Syberberg's reception in France, which cannot be undertaken here, could provide information about the French perception and evaluation of the Hitler era, as well as France's own relationship to the legacy of fascism.

71. Michel Tournier's novel shares with Syberberg's project a highly ambiguous attitude toward fascism. The French title refers to the mythological figure Erl-King taken from the poem "Erlkönig" by Goethe. For Saul Friedländer (in *Reflections of Nazism*), *The Ogre* belongs to the "new discourse" on Nazism. See also Winifred Woodhull, "Fascist Bonding and Euphoria in Michel Tournier's *The Ogre,*" *New German Critique* 42 (Fall 1987): 79–112.

72. Jean-Pierre Faye, "Le troisième Faust," *Le Monde,* 22 July 1978.

73. Christian Zimmer, "Our Hitler," *Telos* 42 (Winter 1979/80): 156. (First published in *Les Temps Modernes,* October-November 1978).

74. Sontag, "Syberberg's Hitler" (see note 3 above).

75. Numerous examples of Syberberg's boundless love-hate relationship to Germany are found in his two autobiographical books, *Freudlose Gesellschaft* (1981) and *Der Wald steht schwarz und schweiget* (1984).

76. Hans Jürgen Syberberg, "The Abode of the Gods," *Sight and Sound* 54 (Spring 1985): 125.

3. The Presence of the Past

1. The epithet is from Wolfram Schütte's obituary, "Das Herz: Die künstlerische Physiognomie Rainer Werner Fassbinders im Augenblick seines Verlustes," *Frankfurter Rundschau,* 19 June 1982.

2. See "Auskunft über Deutschland: Ausländische Reaktionen auf den Tod von Rainer Werner Fassbinder," *Frankfurter Allgemeine Zeitung,* 12 June 1982.

3. Ibid.

4. Ibid.

5. See Ernst Burkel, "Responding to What You Experience: An Interview with the Film Directors Douglas Sirk and Rainer Werner Fassbinder," in *Rainer Werner Fassbinder, The Marriage of Maria Braun,* ed. Joyce Rheuban (New Brunswick, N.J.: Rutgers University Press, 1986), pp. 193–196, where Fassbinder speaks of Douglas Sirk: "After I had made ten films which were very

personal, the time came when we said, we have to find a way to make films for the public—and then came my encounter with his films, and then with Douglas Sirk himself. That was tremendously important for me. And then—to come back to this supposed father-son relationship—it was, and is not the same thing, because most father-son relations are usually relations of conflict. I found a person who makes art in a way, as I've said, that was bound to change something in me. I'm making something—and maybe he sees this—that takes what he made the next step" (p. 195).

6. On Sirk's aesthetics and the function of the melodrama, see Thomas Elsaesser, "Tales of Sound and Fury: Observations on the Family Melodrama," *Monogram* 3 (1972): 2–15; Laura Mulvey, "Notes on Sirk and Melodrama," *Movie* 25 (1977–78): 53–56.

7. See Fassbinder's 1971 analysis of Sirk films, in which he speaks directly about his own stylistic intentions: "Six Films by Douglas Sirk," in *Fassbinder, Maria Braun*, pp. 197–207.

8. This will be discussed in greater detail later in the chapter, in the section "History as Trauma."

9. Rainer Werner Fassbinder, "Die dritte Generation," in *Rainer Werner Fassbinder: Filme befreien den Kopf, Essays und Arbeitsnotizen,* ed. Michael Töteberg (Frankfurt am Main: Fischer, 1984), p. 73. This sentence recurs almost verbatim in Edgar Reitz's *Heimat.*

10. See the article by Bernd Neumann, "'Als ob das Zeitgenössische leer wäre . . .': Über die Anwesenheit der fünfziger Jahre in der Gegenwartsliteratur," *Zeitschrift für Literaturwissenschaft und Linguistik* 35 (1979): 82–95.

11. Helma Sanders-Brahms's film *Germany, Pale Mother* and Jutta Brückner's *Hungerjahre (Years of Hunger)* present a similarly critical, although more autobiographical, view of the fifties from the perspective of the present. Edgar Reitz devotes a two-hour episode of his film cycle *Heimat* to the fifties. Here, too, despite the strong presence of nostalgic and autobiographical elements, what is called into question is the smug, repressive German society during the time of the economic miracle.

12. See Walter Benjamin, "Theses on the Philosophy of History," in *Illuminations,* ed. Hannah Arendt, trans. Harry Zohn (New York: Schocken, 1969), p. 255.

13. See the analysis of the Fassbinder sequence in Eric Rentschler, *West German Film in the Course of Time* (Bedford Hills, N.Y.: Redgrave, 1984), especially pp. 191–202.

14. The dialogue is reprinted in *Rainer Werner Fassbinder: Die Anarchie der Phantasie, Gespräche und Interviews,* ed. Michael Töteberg, pp. 214–218 (Frankfurt am Main: Fischer, 1986); here p. 215.

15. Fassbinder, "Ich habe mich mit meinen Filmfiguren verändert," in *Die Anarchie der Phantasie,* p. 128 (first published April 1978). See also his view on the social function of the cooperative film *Germany in Autumn:* "When we met then, one of the reasons we said that we had to make the film was to fight fear. So that people, who had no means of production and were perhaps even more frightened than we, shouldn't be intimidated by the feeling that was

prevalent in Germany at the time, that criticism in any form was unwelcome and must be suppressed. To avoid that we wanted to say clearly, because we had the means of production at our disposal, 'You can and must keep talking, no matter what happens'" (ibid., p. 98).

16. See the conversation with Peter Märthesheimer, "Ein Drehbuch ist eben keine eigene Kunstform," *ARD Fernsehspiel* (January-March 1985), pp. 46–51.

17. Gerhard Zwerenz, *Die Ehe der Maria Braun* (Munich: Goldmann, 1979). The novel reduces the film to the protagonist's love story; the political dimension, so important in Fassbinder's film, is completely missing. For a comparison between the film and its novelization, see Hans-Bernhard Moeller, "Fassbinders and Zwerenz' im deutschen Aufstieg verlorene *Ehe der Maria Braun*: Interpretation, vergleichende Kritik und neuer filmisch-literarischer Adaptionskontext," in *Film und Literatur: Literarische Texte und der neue deutsche Film*, ed. Sigrid Bauschinger et al. (Berne/Munich: Francke, 1984), pp. 105–123.

18. "Geschichtsergänzung: Gespräch mit Rainer Werner Fassbinder," *ARD Fernsehspiel* (January-March 1985), p. 60. What Fassbinder says here about *Veronika Voss* is also true of *Maria Braun* and *Lola*. See also his evaluation of the fifties in "Frauen haben in dieser Gesellschaft mehr Freiheiten," *Film-Korrespondenz*, 16 March 1982, p. 6: "The more I work with the 1950s, the more I realize that the Third Reich was not some accident of history; it must have been inherent in the form of German society or in the way Germans live with capitalism."

19. See Félix Guattari, "Towards a Micro-Politics of Desire," in *Molecular Revolution: Psychiatry and Politics*, trans. Rosemary Sheed (Harmondsworth: Penguin, 1984), pp. 82–107. In "Le divan du pauvre," *Communications* 23 (1975): 96, Guattari writes: "The cinema has become a gigantic machine to shape the social libido."

20. Rainer Werner Fassbinder, "Ich bin ein romantischer Anarchist," in *Die Anarchie der Phantasie*, p. 186.

21. On the relationship between postwar German history and Maria Braun's history, see Thomas Elsaesser, "Primary Identification and the Historical Subject: Fassbinder and Germany," in *Fassbinder: The Marriage of Maria Braun*, pp. 248–264; Howard Feinstein: "BRD 1-2-3: Fassbinder's Postwar Trilogy and the Spectacle," *Cinema Journal* 23 (Autumn 1983): 44–56.

22. The page numbers in parentheses refer subsequently to the production script, so far published only in English: *The Marriage of Maria Braun*, ed. Joyce Rheuban (New Brunswick, N.J.: Rutgers University Press, 1986). The book also contains essays by and about Fassbinder and a bibliography. The West German publishing house of Schirmer and Mosel has announced the publication of the script for *Die Ehe der Maria Braun* in the sixth volume of its series *Fassbinder: Die Kinofilme* (1987–   ).

23. Hannah Arendt, "Besuch in Deutschland 1950," in *Zur Zeit: Politische Essays* (Berlin: Rotbuch, 1986), p. 44.

24. Jean-François Lyotard: *Instructions païennes* (Paris: Galilee, 1977), p. 39.

25. Karlheinz Stierle, "Geschehen, Geschichte, Text der Geschichte," in *Geschichte: Ereignis und Erzählung*, ed. Reinhart Koselleck und Wolf-Dieter Stempel

(Munich: Fink, 1973), p. 532. See also Hayden White, "The Historical Text as Literary Artifact," in *Tropics of Discourse: Essays in Cultural Criticism* (Baltimore: The Johns Hopkins University Press, 1978), pp. 81–100; Reinhart Koselleck, *Futures Past: On the Semantics of Historical Time,* trans. Keith Tribe (Cambridge, Mass.: MIT Press, 1985).

26. Fassbinder himself plays one of these, in a cameo appearance. He wants to sell an edition of Heinrich von Kleist's works to Maria Braun, but she has become "realistic" through her experience of history, that is, the book burnings of 1933, and answers: "Books burn so quickly. And they don't give heat."

27. See, for instance, Bertolt Brecht's *Trommeln in der Nacht* (*Drums in the Night,* 1922), Ernst Toller's *Hinkemann* (1923), or Wolfgang Borchert's *Draussen vor der Tür* (*The Man Outside,* 1947).

28. Significantly, we learn the least about Hermann Braun. Fassbinder consciously leaves it to the viewer to construct Hermann's story, because essentially Hermann lives only in Maria's imagination, as the idealized object of her desire.

29. Hans-Dieter Seidel, "Stationen einer Deutschen," *Stuttgarter Zeitung,* 22 February 1979.

30. Speaking in 1983 at the "International Conference on the National Socialist Seizure of Power," held in the rebuilt Reichstag in Berlin, Herman Lübbe argued that to shape an identity in the period of reconstruction the Federal Republic *had* to repress the past as a matter of existential necessity. He defends the "restraint" and "discretion" of the Germans in treating their own past; only from the perspective of what he calls "theorists of repression" and "national therapists" is this "discretion" the symptom of a failure to come to terms with the past. See Lübbe, "Der Nationalsozialismus im politischen Bewusstsein der Gegenwart," in *Deutschlands Weg in die Diktatur,* ed. Martin Broszat et al. (Berlin: Siedler, 1983), pp. 329–349. See also the critical discussion that followed his paper (ibid., pp. 350–378) and the essay by Helmut Dubiel and Günther Frankenberg, "Entsorgung der Vergangenheit: Widerspruch gegen eine neokonservative Legende," *Die Zeit,* 18 March 1983.

31. This dual status can be seen most clearly in the criticism commonly leveled at historical films, that, for instance, the uniforms or the haircuts are not "historically accurate," which is the same as saying that the filmmaker did not do enough research or did not consult enough eyewitnesses of the period.

32. M. M. Bakhtin, "Discourse in the Novel," in *The Dialogic Imagination,* ed. Michael Holquist (Austin: University of Texas Press, 1982) p. 411.

33. By speaking about the "Germans" on the one hand and the "Jews" on the other, exclusion through language is perpetuated. See Henry Pachter, "On Germans and Jews: Reply to Dennis Klein," *New German Critique* 21 (Fall 1980): 143: "One does not read books or essays entitled 'Blacks and Americans,' 'Mormons and Americans' or 'Jews and Americans.'" *New German Critique* published three special issues in 1980 (nos. 19–21) entitled "Germans and Jews." In his polemical essay "Der deutsch-jüdische Verbrüderungskitsch," *tageszeitung* (Berlin), 8 April 1986, Wolfgang Pohrt writes about this linguistic division, claiming we cannot "compare apples and fruit." On this question, see especially Max Horkheimer, "Nachwort zu Porträts deutsch-jüdischer Geistesgeschichte,"

in *Gesammelte Schriften,* vol. 8, ed. Alfred Schmidt and G. S. Noerr (Frankfurt am Main: Fischer, 1985), pp. 192–193: "By the way, 'Jews' and 'Germans' seem to me to be terms on different conceptual levels . . . there are Jewish Germans just as there are Protestant, Catholic, and atheist Germans. The Jews are as little deficient as the Christians in their patriotism, that is, in their good will toward the state . . . The terminological opposition German and Jew sounds all too current in this world that has become increasingly marked, and not to its advantage, by nationalisms and other collectivisms and in which individuals and groups that deviate from the majority have an increasingly difficult time living peacefully in the same state. It would be better to talk about Jews and Christians, the more so since in times of totalitarian barbarism, which by no means belong exclusively to the past, true Christians—note, true Christians—are threatened by the same horrors that have long been part of the Jewish fate."

34. Gerhard Zwerenz, *Die Erde ist so unbewohnbar wie der Mond* (Frankfurt am Main: März, 1973). In 1986 the novel was reprinted together with the script for the planned film. See also Gerhard Zwerenz, "Linker Antisemitismus ist unmöglich," *Die Zeit,* 9 April 1976, and "Politik mit Vorurteilen," *Vorwärts,* 22 February 1986, where he says, "No, Fassbinder's play is not anti-Semitic, but it is politically naive, easily misunderstood, and incomplete."

35. Rainer Werner Fassbinder, *Garbage, the City and Death,* in *Rainer Werner Fassbinder: Plays,* trans. and ed. Denis Calandra (New York: PAJ Publications, 1985), p. 186.

36. Theodor W. Adorno, "Zur Bekämpfung des Antisemitismus heute," *Das Argument* 29 (May 1964): 94.

37. A sociological study by Alphons Silbermann, *Sind wir Antisemiten? Ausmass und Wirkung eines sozialen Vorurteils in der Bundesrepublik Deutschland* (Cologne: Verlag Wissenschaft und Politik, 1982), comes to the conclusion "that between 15 and 20% of the population have strong anti-Semitic prejudices and another 30% are more or less latently anti-Semitic" (pp. 124–125). On this problem, see also the essays in *Antisemitismus nach dem Holocaust: Bestandsaufnahme und Erscheinungsformen in deutschsprachigen Ländern,* ed. Alphons Silbermann and Julius H. Schoeps (Cologne: Verlag Wissenschaft und Politik, 1986).

38. Henryk M. Broder, *Der ewige Antisemit: Über Sinn und Funktion eines beständigen Gefühls* (Frankfurt am Main: Fischer, 1986), p. 10.

39 The text appeared as vol. 803 (*Stücke 3*) of the series "edition suhrkamp" in the spring of 1976, but it was almost immediately withdrawn and shredded. In 1981 the play was published by a different publisher, the Verlag der Autoren; in 1986 it appeared in a second, revised edition. The English translation, *Garbage, the City and Death,* is based on the first edition; it was published by Performing Arts Journal Publications, New York, in 1985.

40. Joachim Fest, "Reicher Jude von links," *Frankfurter Allgemeine Zeitung,* 19 March 1976. Wolfram Schütte responded to Fest's accusations in the *Frankfurter Rundschau* of 26 March 1976.

41. Siegfried Unseld, "In dieser Form nie mehr," *Die Zeit,* 9 April 1976. Despite the fully justified fear of misinterpretation that had been voiced in 1976,

Günther Rühle, the new director of the Frankfurt Playhouse, included the play in his plans for the 1985 season. Unmoved by violent press attacks, petitions, and public protest by the Jewish community and the Catholic and Protestant churches, he refused to cancel the premiere of the play scheduled for October 31, 1985. But the premiere was prevented by opponents of the play who seized the stage; further performances were canceled. The objections to the play, apart from its weak quality focused on the stereotypical presentation of the figure of a Jewish real estate speculator. The debates unleashed by the play in 1976 and again 1985–1986 involve significant issues: censorship and the autonomy of art, fictional representation and intentionality, the relationship between Jewish and non-Jewish Germans after Auschwitz, Jewish identity and memory, and German history and its terrible legacy. The controversy is extensively documented in *Die Fassbinder-Kontroverse oder das Ende der Schonzeit*, ed. Heiner Lichtenstein (Königstein: Athenäum, 1985). See also *Deutsch-jüdische Normalität . . . Fassbinders Sprengsätze*, ed. Elisabeth Kiderlen (Frankfurt am Main: Pflasterstrand, 1985), and the heated debate in *Ästhetik und Kommunikation* 51, 52, 53/54 (1982–83), entitled "Deutsche, Linke und Juden." See also the special issue of *New German Critique* 38 (Spring/Summer 1986) on the "German-Jewish Controversy," which contains contributions by Andrei S. Markowits, Seyla Benhabib, and Moishe Postone to a symposium at Harvard University on Fassbinder's *Garbage, the City and Death*.

42. See the documentation in *Film-Korrespondenz* 1 (16 March 1977): 12–15; see also Wolfram Schütte, "Da stimmt doch was nicht," *Frankfurter Rundschau*, 12 March 1977. The text was published by Suhrkamp Verlag, ostensibly without the author's knowledge (as Fassbinder claimed in a 1977 television interview, printed in the Berlin *tageszeitung* of 21 July 1986).

43. Rainer Werner Fassbinder, "Gehabtes Sollen—gesolltes Haben: Über Gustav Freytags Roman 'Soll und Haben' und die verhinderte Fernsehverfilmung," in *Filme befreien den Kopf*, pp. 36–37 (first published March 1977).

44. Ibid., p. 37.

45. Quoted in Schütte, "Da stimmt doch was nicht:" "In any case it is worth considering that in our country the recent critical preoccupation with the complex of bourgeois society and anti-Semitism immediately raised the suspicion that it would result in anti-Semitism. . . so it is considered suspect and banned by those very conservatives who never said a word against the unscrupulous exploitation of the stock of Nazi films by television."

46. See the report on this in the *Frankfurter Allgemeine Zeitung*, 9 April 1977.

47. Rainer Werner Fassbinder, "Probleme nicht verdrängen, sondern sie bewusst machen," in *Die Anarchie der Phantasie*, p.88 (first published June 1977).

48. See Joachim Fest, "Linke Schwierigkeiten mit 'links': Ein Nachwort zu R. W. Fassbinder," *Frankfurter Allgemeine Zeitung*, 10 April 1976.

49. Fassbinder, "Probleme nicht verdrängen," p. 88. This was the direction of his "Public Statement Regarding *Garbage, the City and Death*," *Frankfurter Rundschau*, 31 March 1976, trans. and reprinted in *West German Filmmakers on Film*, p. 155: "There are also anti-Semites in this play; they do not only exist in the play, though, but also for instance in Frankfurt. It goes without saying

that these figures—I find it truly superfluous to repeat this—do not represent the opinion of the author, whose own stance toward minorities should have become clear enough in his previous work. Particularly some of the cheap shots in the discussion make me all the more concerned about a 'new fascism,' which was one of the reasons I wrote this play."

50. Fassbinder, "Gehabtes Sollen—gesolltes Haben," p. 39.

51. Ibid., p. 38.

52 Ibid.

53. Bertolt Brecht, *Arbeitsjournal,* vol. 1 (Frankfurt am Main: Suhrkamp, 1973), p. 294. The entry is dated August 1941.

54. On *Schatten der Engel,* see the telling judgment of the Working Committee for Voluntary Self-Control of the Film Industry (FSK), which considers the film "not anti-Semitic and hence not racially inflammatory in its thematic conception and its overall form," but noted the fear that certain dialogue passages "promote clichés of the Jew as a cynical, scrupulous maker of deals and confirm anti-Semitic attitudes because the film always refers to the Jewish real estate speculator as the 'rich Jew,' without a name, in a way that could lead to generalization, and because the dialogue passages in question are spoken by a man who is part of our contemporary society and does not appear, say, as an incorrigible Nazi." Quoted in Helmut Schmitz, "'So denkt es in mir': Zum Antisemitismus-Vorwurf gegen Daniel Schmids Fassbinder-Verfilmung *Schatten der Engel,*" *Frankfurter Rundschau,* 11 October 1976.

55. See Anni Goldmann, "Un nouveau 'Juif Süss': *Lili Marleen,*" *Le Monde,* 18 May 1981. See also Thomas Elsaesser, *"Lili Marleen:* Fascism and the Film Industry," *October* 21 (Summer 1982): 115–140. In Saul Friedländer's study, *Reflections of Nazism,* Fassbinder's *Lili Marleen* serves as a prime example for the "new discourse with respect to the Third Reich," which tries to reevoke the Nazi period in all its false and dangerous glamour. On *Lili Marleen,* see especially pp. 47–53.

56. Gertrud Koch, "Torments of the Flesh, Coldness of the Spirit: Jewish Figures in the Films of Rainer Werner Fassbinder," *New German Critique* 38 (Spring/Summer 1986): 37.

57. Ibid., p. 38.

58. Fassbinder, *Garbage, the City and Death,* p. 180. My translation follows here the original German version: "Schuld hat der Jud, weil er uns schuldig macht, denn er ist da."

59. See Benjamin Henrich's interview with Fassbinder, "Philosemiten sind Antisemiten," *Die Zeit,* 16 April 1976:

Fassbinder: I think that the constant practice of making Jews taboo, which has existed since 1945 in Germany, can lead to an antipathy toward Jews, especially with young people who have no direct experience with Jews. As a child, whenever I met a Jew, someone whispered to me, that's a Jew, act polite, be friendly. And that continued with certain variations until I was 28 and wrote the play. I was never able to think that that was a correct attitude.

Henrichs: So you are afraid that philo-Semitism, to which we have almost all been raised, which is a kind of rule of the game in the Federal Republic, could promote a new anti-Semitism?
Fassbinder: Absolutely. Robert Neumann said, philo-Semites are anti-Semites who love Jews. . . I cannot say I am not unaffected about what happened to the Jews in the Third Reich. But I am absolutely more unaffected than those who are attacking me.

60. A small underground group, "Thieves' Theater," premiered the play (newly translated as *Trash, the City, and Death*) in New York's Lower East Side on April 16, 1987, with hardly any local publicity. There was no public outcry or protest in the United States. See Rainer Weber, "Der reiche Jude in Manhattan," *Spiegel* 15 (1987): 218–220.

61. See the essay by Dan Diner, "Negative Symbiose: Deutsche und Juden nach Auschwitz," *Babylon* 1 (1987): 9–21.

62. See Friedrich Knilli, "Die Judendarstellung in den deutschen Medien," in *Antisemitismus nach dem Holocaust,* ed. Silbermann and Scheops, pp. 115–132; Ruth K. Angress, "Gibt es ein 'Judenproblem' in der deutschen Nachkriegsliteratur?" *Neue Sammlung* 26 (January-March 1986): 22–40, especially pp. 32–40 on Schlöndorff and Fassbinder. See also Heidy M. Müller, *Die Judendarstellung in der deutschsprachigen Erzählprosa (1945–1981)* (Königstein: Forum Academicum/Hain, 1984).

63. Quoted in Diner, "Negative Symbiose," p. 11.

64. There were comical and grotesque filmic presentations of the Third Reich and the persecution of the Jews before Achternbusch: Charlie Chaplin's *The Great Dictator,* Ernst Lubitsch's *To Be or Not To Be,* and Lina Wertmüller's *Seven Beauties,* for instance. On this issue see Uwe Naumann, *Zwischen Tränen und Gelächter: Satirische Faschismuskritik 1933 bis 1945* (Cologne: Pahl-Rugenstein, 1983).

65. Herbert Achternbusch, *Das Haus am Nil* (Frankfurt am Main: Suhrkamp, 1981), p. 153. Achternbusch continues to deal with the Third Reich in his film *Heilt Hitler* (1986) and his play *Linz* (1987).

66. Wolfram Schütte, "CDU-Politiker fragt Bundesregierung, 'Warum geht Fassbinder?' . . . und Versuch einer Antwort an jemand hinterm Mond," *Frankfurter Rundschau,* 13 August 1977. The press release quoted by Schütte reads further: "In an interview with an American news magazine, Fassbinder said that the only films the Federal Republic supports are those that confirm the present situation of democracy 'with all its mediocrity.'"

67. Rainer Werner Fassbinder, "Egal, was ich mache, die Leute regen sich auf," in *Die Anarchie der Phantasie,* p. 169.

68. See Marc Ferro, "Film: A Counter-analysis of Society," in *Cinema and History,* trans. Naomi Greene (Detroit: Wayne State University Press, 1988).

69. Jean de Baroncelli, "Procès d'un miracle," *Le Monde,* 19 January 1980.

70. Rainer Werner Fassbinder, "Nur so entstehen bei uns Filme: Indem man sie ohne Rücksicht auf Verluste macht. Ein Gespräch mit Wolfram Schütte," in *Die Anarchie der Phantasie,* p. 138 (first published February 1979).

71. Hans Magnus Enzensberger, "Klare Entscheidungen und trübe Aussichten," in *Über Hans Magnus Enzensberger,* ed. Joachim Schickel (Frankfurt am Main: Suhrkamp, 1970), p. 229.

72. Ibid.

73. Ibid., p. 231.

74. Rainer Werner Fassbinder, "Ich bin ein romantischer Anarchist," in *Die Anarchie der Phantasie,* p. 194.

75. Rainer Werner Fassbinder, "Ich habe mich mit meinen Filmfiguren verändert," ibid., p. 113.

76. In the credit sequence, we read: "A comedy in six parts about social games full of tension, excitement, and logic, horror and madness, like the fairy tales we tell to children to help them bear their life until they die." Fassbinder's settling of accounts with terrorism as a "social game" was filmed at his own expense (with Fassbinder himself as cameraman).

77. Jürgen Habermas, "Die Krise des Wohlfahrtsstaates und die Erschöpfung utopischer Energien," in *Die neue Unübersichtlichkeit: Kleine politische Schriften 5,* ed. Jürgen Habermas (Frankfurt am Main: Suhrkamp, 1985), p. 143. In the course of his argument, Habermas criticizes this discourse about the end of utopia: "It is not that utopian energies are retreating from the historical consciousness. Rather a specific utopia has come to an end, one that in the past crystallized around the potential of the working society" (pp. 145–146).

78. Fassbinder, "Ich habe mich mit meinen Filmfiguren verändert," in *Die Anarchie der Phantasie,* p. 115.

79. Ibid., pp. 115–116.

4. In Search of Germany

1. Alexander Kluge, "The Political as Intensity of Everyday Feelings," *Cultural Critique* 4 (Fall 1986): 127. The translation has been slightly modified in accordance with the German original, "Das Politische als Intensität alltäglicher Gefühle," in *Alexander Kluge,* ed. Thomas Böhm-Christl (Frankfurt am Main: Suhrkamp, 1983), p. 318.

2. At the premiere of the film at the Hamburg Film Festival in September 1979, a shortened version was shown. In December 1979, a two-hour version of *The Patriot* premiered. On the comparison of the two versions, see Wolfram Schütte, "Kälte- & Wärmestrom: Alexander Kluges 'Ur- und Kino-'Patriotin,'" *Frankfurter Rundschau,* 9 January 1981. My analysis is based on the second, final version.

3. Kluge's original plan to use the events of Autumn 1977 as the impetus for a six-hour film about German history proved unworkable. It did, however, create an "excess of motivation" to pursue the project that eventually resulted in *The Patriot.* See "Alexander Kluge: Die Patriotin," *Filmkritik* 11 (1979): 503–504; "Eine Baustelle ist vorteilhafter als ganze Häuser: Ein Gespräch mit Alexander Kluge," *Spuren* 1 (1980): 16; Miriam Hansen, "Alexander Kluge, Cinema, and the Public Sphere: The Construction Site of Counter-History," *Discourse* 6 (1983): 53–74. *The Patriot* was originally planned as a collective

production in the style of *Germany in Autumn*. But only Margarethe von Trotta made a contribution, which was incorporated into the film: a fictional scene in which a television set is delivered to an army mess hall.

4. See the classic passage in Robert Musil, *The Man Without Qualities,* trans. Eithne Wilkins and Ernst Kaiser, vol. 2 (New York: Coward-McCann, 1954), p. 436: "What puts our minds at rest is the simple sequence, the overwhelming variegation of life now represented in, as a mathematician would say, an undimensional order: the stringing upon one thread of all that has happened in space and time, in short, that notorious 'narrative thread' . . . In their basic relation to themselves most people are narrators . . . What they like is the orderly sequence of facts, because it has the look of a necessity, and by means of the impression that their life has a 'course' they manage to feel somehow sheltered in the midst of chaos. And now Ulrich observed that he seemed to have lost this elementary narrative element to which private life still holds fast, although in public life everything has now become non-narrative, no longer following a 'thread,' but spreading out as an infinitely interwoven surface." It is possible that Kluge's concept of the "narrative surface" derives from this passage. See also Jean-François Lyotard, who speaks of the decline of the "grand narratives" in *The Postmodern Condition: A Report on Knowledge,* trans. Geoff Bennington and Brian Massumi (Minneapolis: University of Minnesota Press, 1984).

5. Characters such as chroniclers, archivists, and history professors frequently appear in historical novels. Gabi Teichert is reminiscent of the reporter and biographer in Bertolt Brecht's unfinished novel *Die Geschäfte des Herrn Julius Caesar* (*The Business Affairs of Mr. Julius Caesar,* 1937–39), who also searches for sources and interviews his contemporaries in a futile attempt to write a historically "objective" account of Julius Caesar's life.

6. Kluge's character teaches history in the state of Hesse for good reasons. In 1977 the Hessian Cultural Ministry decreed that history should be abolished as a subject in the high schools; history was to be merged with geography and social studies in the subject "social science." This made for a situation full of contradictions. On the one hand, a poll in 1977 had shown enormous deficits in students' historical knowledge; on the other hand, the Ministry of Culture seriously contemplated doing away with history as an independent discipline. From this perspective, Kluge's *The Patriot* is not only an indirect and ironic reflection on how history can be mediated through the institution of the school; it is also an intervention in the debate about cultural policy in Hesse.

7. Alexander Kluge, "On Film and the Public Sphere," *New German Critique* 24/25 (1981–82): 206.

8. The current chancellor of the Federal Republic, Helmut Kohl, was born in 1930 and hence also belongs to this generation. On a state visit to Israel in 1984 he claimed the "blessing of having been born late" for himself and his generation. This expression has since become a proverbial cliché. Gert Heidenreich, for instance, titled his collection of stories after it: *Die Gnade der späten Geburt* (Munich/Zurich: Piper, 1986).

9. See Kluge's narrative montage, "Der Luftangriff auf Halberstadt am 8. April 1945," in Alexander Kluge, *Neue Geschichten, No. 1–18, 'Unheimlichkeit*

der Zeit' (Frankfurt am Main: Suhrkamp, 1977), pp. 33–107. See also the exhaustive analysis of that piece in David Roberts, "Alexander Kluge und die deutsche Zeitgeschichte: Der Luftangriff auf Halberstadt am 8.4.1945," in *Kluge,* ed. Böhm-Christl, pp. 77–116.

10. On Kluge's *Abschied von gestern* (*Yesterday Girl*), see Enno Patalas and Frieda Grafe, "Tribüne des Jungen Deutschen Films. II. Alexander Kluge," *Filmkritik* 9 (1966): 487–491; see also the extensive analysis by Miriam Hansen, "Space of History, Language of Time: Kluge's *Yesterday Girl*," in *German Film and Literature: Adaptations and Transformations,* ed. Eric Rentschler (New York/London: Methuen, 1986), pp. 193–216.

11. The numbers in parentheses following quotations in this chapter refer to pages in Alexander Kluge's book *Die Patriotin* (Frankfurt am Main: Zweitausendeins, 1979), which contains the complete text of the film as well as many additional pictures and theoretical and documentary material.

12. In a conversation with editors of the periodical *Filmkritik* 11 (1979), Kluge characterized the relationship between "ice" and "history" as the "core" of *Yesterday Girl* and *The Patriot.*

13. Walter Benjamin, *Das Passagen-Werk,* vol. 2 (Frankfurt am Main: Suhrkamp, 1983), p. 1058.

14. See Hannes Böhringer, "Die Ruine in der Posthistoire," *Merkur* 406 (April 1982): 367–375.

15. Kluge, "Die Patriotin," p. 504.

16. See Hans V. Geppert, *Der 'andere' historische Roman: Theorie und Strukturen einer diskontinuierlichen Gattung* (Tübingen: Niemeyer, 1976). Geppert assumes a "hiatus between fiction and history" (p. 34). While historical novels typically tend to cover up this hiatus, the "other" historical novel accentuates it. "It is not so much a matter of the fictional presentation of history as of the 'fictions of history'" (p. 135).

17. Benjamin, *Das Passagen-Werk,* p. 595.

18. Walter Benjamin, "Theses on the Philosophy of History," in *Illuminations,* ed. Hannah Arendt, trans. Harry Zohn (New York: Schocken, 1969), p. 255.

19. See "Gespräch mit Alexander Kluge," *Filmkritik* 11 (1979): 518. "I developed the knee of Corporal Wieland from this Morgenstern poem. You never see it except in the gap between the shots . . . And that is the point: the main things in the film are between the shots."

20. Alexander Kluge, "Die Utopie Film," *Merkur* 18 (1964): 1142 (emphasis mine).

21. Quoted in Alexander Kluge, "Gespräch über Film," in Klaus Eder and Alexander Kluge, *Ulmer Dramaturgien: Reibungsverluste* (Munich/Vienna: Hanser, 1980), p. 48.

22. "Die Macht der Gefühle: Geschichte, Gespräche und Materialien von und über Alexander Kluge," *Ästhetik und Kommunikation* 53/54 (December 1983): 184: "As a filmmaker I know that an uncanny number of images must be destroyed before some effect is achieved. I have to be able to produce the sun at midnight so that it can begin to shine again. I have to destroy a whole series of images so that something moves again in the human being."

23. Bertolt Brecht, "The Literarization of the Theatre (Notes to the *Three-penny Opera*)," in *Brecht on Theatre*, ed. and trans. John Willett (New York: Hill and Wang, 1966), pp. 43–44.

24. Feminist critics have noted that the female protagonist does not speak for herself but is portrayed and subtly satirized by the invisible male commentator. See Claudia Lenssen, "kein dunkel hat seinesgleichen: zu Alexander Kluges Film *Die Patriotin*," *frauen und film* 23 (April 1980): 6–8; B. Ruby Rich, "She Says, He Says: The Power of the Narrator in Modernist Film Politics," *Discourse* 6 (Autumn 1983): 31–47.

25. Alexander Kluge, "On Film and the Public Sphere," pp. 218–219. On Kluge's use of montage see also Klaus Kreimeier, "Film-Montage und Montage-Film," *Spuren* 3 (1980): 28–30; David Roberts, "Die Formenwelt des Zusammenhangs: Zur Theorie und Funktion der Montage bei Alexander Kluge," *Zeitschrift für Literaturwissenschaft und Linguistik* 12 (1982): 104–119.

26. Theodor W. Adorno, *Aesthetic Theory*, ed. Gretel Adorno and Rolf Tiedemann, trans. C. Lenhardt (London/New York: Routledge & Kegan Paul, 1984), p. 222. (Translation modified.)

27. Kluge, "On Film and the Public Sphere," p. 206.

28. For an exposition of the emergence of traditional Hollywood film aesthetics, see David Bordwell, Janet Staiger, and Kristin Thompson, *The Classical Hollywood Cinema: Film Style and Mode of Production to 1960* (New York: Columbia University Press, 1985).

29. See Christian Metz's elaboration of Emile Benveniste's distinction between *énoncé* and *énonciation* and between *histoire* and *discours* in *The Imaginary Signifier: Psychoanalysis and the Cinema* (Bloomington: Indiana University Press, 1982), p. 97. See also Miriam Hansen, "The Stubborn Discourse: History and Story-Telling in the Films of Alexander Kluge," *Persistence of Vision* 2 (Fall 1985): 19–29.

30. Ernst Bloch, *Erbschaft dieser Zeit* (Frankfurt am Main: Suhrkamp, 1977), p. 221. Also, compare the passage from Brecht that Kluge likes to quote: "The situation is complicated by the fact that less than ever does a simple 'reproduction of reality' tell us anything about reality. A photograph of the Krupp factory or of the AEG reveals practically nothing about these institutions. The genuine reality has slipped into the functional . . . Hence something has to be 'constructed,' something 'artificial,' something not given but 'put together.'" Quoted in Kluge, "On Film and the Public Sphere," p. 218 n4.

31. Kluge and Negt, *Geschichte und Eigensinn*, p. 154. See also *Bestandsaufnahme: Utopie Film. Zwanzig Jahre neuer deutscher Film*, ed. Alexander Kluge (Frankfurt am Main: Zweitausendeins, 1983), p. 427: "We need an enterprising, investigating type of collector, a kind of detective."

32. Alexander Kluge, "Anmerkungen zu Jutta Brückner," *Ästhetik und Kommunikation* 53/54 (December 1983): 233.

33. Kluge, "The Political as Intensity of Everyday Feelings," p. 123. (Translation modified.)

34. Alexander Kluge, "Zu einer Stein-Konstruktion," in Udo Klückmann, Klaus Heinrich, et al., *Foto-Assemblagen* (Berlin: Medusa, 1979), p. 29.

35. See Kluge's afterword to his *Schlachtbeschreibung* (Frankfurt am Main: Suhrkamp, 1978), p. 368: "All those in Stalingrad who saw something, wrote official documents, transmitted news, and created sources, had to rely on what they could see with their own two eyes. A disaster that strikes a mass of 300,000 men cannot be grasped by these means (quite apart from the fact that the disaster itself blurs the vision)."

36. The expression comes from Claude Lévi-Strauss, *The Savage Mind* (Chicago: University of Chicago Press, 1966), pp. 16ff. See Kluge's reference in Kluge and Negt, *Geschichte und Eigensinn*, p. 222: "In our book we use a procedure that treats living relations and conditions as if they were things, that places them side by side, takes them apart, gathers them, pursues them in their dispersion, tests them out. Lévi-Strauss called this way of working 'bricolage.'"

37. Viktor Shklovsky, "Art as Technique," in *Russian Formalist Criticism: Four Essays,* trans. Lee T. Lemon and Marion J. Reis (Lincoln: University of Nebraska Press, 1965), p. 7.

38. Kluge, "On Film and the Public Sphere," p. 206.

39. See Alexander Kluge, "Interview," in Rainer Lewandowski, *Die Filme von Alexander Kluge* (Hildesheim/New York: Olms, 1980), p. 39: "Everyone is constantly producing a film, whether he is sitting in a movie house or not; that is the film of his experiences and it is basically associative. If I remember something . . . when I dream in German, then I am working on a film according to the same rules of montage, epiphany, third-person perception, polyvocality, countermovement, fantasy activity and so forth that the filmmaker uses, and it plays just like a film provided that the film does not dominate."

40. Benjamin, *Das Passagen-Werk,* p. 272.

41. Ibid., p. 993.

42. Kluge, "Cinéma pure, cinéma impure," *Filmfaust* 26 (1982): 64.

43. Ibid., p. 62. See also the close analysis of this scene in Gerhard Bechtold, "Die Sinne entspannen: Zur Multimedialität in Alexander Kluges Texten," in *Kluge,* ed. Böhm-Christl, pp. 220–227.

44. Kluge, *Die Macht der Gefühle,* p. 195.

45. Kluge, "Cinéma pure," p. 43.

46. Alexander Kluge, "Der Phantasie-Betrieb," in *Die Filmemacher: Zur neuen deutschen Produktion nach Oberhausen,* ed. Barbara Bronnen and Corinna Brocher (Munich: Bertelsmann, 1973), p. 235. On the function of fantasy see also Kluge and Oskar Negt, *Öffentlichkeit und Erfahrung: Zur Organisationsanalyse von bürgerlicher und proletarischer Öffentlichkeit* (Frankfurt am Main: Suhrkamp, 1972), pp. 69ff, where fantasy is interpreted as a kind of relay station between present, past, and future.

47. Kluge, "On Film and the Public Sphere," p. 215.

48. See Reiner Frey and Alexandra Kluge, "'Eine realistische Haltung müsste der Zuschauer haben, müsste ich haben, müsste der Film haben': Gespräch mit Alexander Kluge," *Filmfaust* 20 (November 1980): 22. On the viewer in Kluge's film, see Gerhard Bechtold, *Sinnliche Wahrnehmung von sozialer Wirklichkeit: Die multimedialen Montage-Texte Alexander Kluges* (Tübingen: Narr, 1983); Michael Kötz and Petra Höhne, *Die Sinnlichkeit des Zusammenhangs: Zur*

Filmarbeit von Alexander Kluge (Cologne: Prometh, 1981); Michael Kötz, *Der Traum, die Sehnsucht und das Kino: Film und Wirklichkeit des Imaginären* (Frankfurt am Main: Syndikat, 1986), especially pp. 51–57.

49. Kluge, "Eine Baustelle ist vorteilhafter als ganze Häuser," p. 17.

50. Ibid.

51. Ibid. See also Kluge, "On Film and the Public Sphere," p. 211: "Understanding a film completely is conceptual imperialism which colonizes its objects. If I have understood everything then something has been emptied out. We must make films that thoroughly oppose such imperialism of consciousness. I encounter something in film which still surprises me and which I can perceive without devouring it. I cannot understand a puddle on which the rain is falling—I can only see it; to say that I understand the puddle is meaningless. Relaxation means that I myself become alive for a moment, allowing my senses to run wild: for once not to be on guard with the police-like intention of letting nothing escape me."

52. Kluge, *Die Macht der Gefühle,* p. 195.

53. Kluge, *Neue Geschichten,* p. 9.

54. See *Briefe zur Verteidigung der Republik,* ed. Freimut Duve, Heinrich Böll, and Klaus Staeck (Reinbek: Rowohlt, 1977); Walter Laqueur, *The Age of Terrorism* (Boston: Little, Brown, 1987); Stefan Aust, *The Baader-Meinhof Group: The Inside Story of a Phenomenon,* trans. Anthea Bell (London: Bodley Head, 1987).

55. See, for instance, Martin Walser's essay, "Händedruck mit Gespenstern," in *Stichworte zur geistigen Situation der Zeit,* ed. Jürgen Habermas, vol. 1, *Nation und Republik* (Frankfurt am Main: Suhrkamp, 1979), pp. 39–50. No less "patriotic" are the essays in the same volume by Horst Ehmke, "Was ist des Deutschen Vaterland?", Dieter Wellershoff, "Deutschland—ein Schwebezustand," and Iring Fetscher, "Die Suche nach der nationalen Identität." The chapter is entitled: "The National Question, Reconsidered." See also Willy Brandt, "Deutscher Patriotismus," *Spiegel,* 1 February 1982.

56. Lothar Baier, "Bewegte BRD," in *Gleichheitszeichen: Streitschriften über Abweichung und Identität* (Berlin: Wagenbach, 1985), p. 37. Originally printed in *Abschiedsbriefe aus Deutschland,* ed. Hans-Jürgen Heinrichs (Frankfurt am Main/Paris: Qumran, 1984).

57. Peter Schneider, *Lenz: Eine Erzählung* (Berlin: Rotbuch, 1973), p. 90.

58. See, for example, Peter Brückner, *Versuch, uns und anderen die Bundesrepublik zu erklären* (Berlin: Wagenbach, 1978); Martin Greiffenhagen and Silvia Greiffenhagen, *Ein schwieriges Vaterland: Zur politischen Kultur Deutschlands* (Munich: List, 1979); *Die deutsche Neurose: Über die beschädigte Identität der Deutschen,* ed. Armin Mohler (Frankfurt am Main/Berlin: Ullstein, 1980); *Die Identität der Deutschen,* ed. Werner Weidenfeld (Munich/Vienna: Hanser, 1983); *Reden über das eigene Land: Deutschland,* vols. 1 ff. (Munich: Bertelsmann, 1983–). See also the coffee-table book by René Burri, *Die Deutschen: Mit Texten von Hans Magnus Enzensberger* (Munich: Schirmer/Mosel, 1986).

59. See Rudolf Walter Leonhardt, "Von der Last, Deutscher zu sein: Die

244 NOTES TO PAGES 129–132

unbeantwortete Frage nach der nationalen Identität," *Die Zeit,* 9 September 1983; Günther Kunert, "Unsere Angst hat es uns gelehrt: Warum die Deutschen so sind wie sie sind," *Frankfurter Allgemeine Zeitung,* 8 December 1979; François Bondy, "Warum wollen die Deutschen geliebt werden? Mutmassungen über ein 'schwieriges Vaterland,'" *Süddeutsche Zeitung,* 30 December 1979. On the other hand, writers like Lea Fleischmann have published books with titles like *Dies ist nicht mein Land: Eine Jüdin verlässt die Bundesrepublik* (Hamburg: Hoffmann und Campe, 1980). Lothar Baier had to make explicit that his move to Paris was not emigration ("Bewegte BRD," p. 35).

60. "Gespräch mit Volker Schlöndorff: Was ist deutsch an meinen Filmen?", *Deutsche Zeitung/Christ und Welt,* 28 September 1979. There we read, for instance: "What is German about me? What is German identity to begin with? I looked for the answers in literature. Of course, I started out searching back in history. Because I couldn't identify with the most recent German past, the Nazi era, the barbarism; I didn't want to be that kind of German. Like all Germans I tried again and again to negate everything German, tried to speak a foreign language so perfectly that I would not be recognized as a German. Until I noticed: that's not getting me anywhere, I have to go back to Germany, have to try to find a place to begin."

61. See (as a selection) the collections *Thema: Deutschland: Das Kind mit den zwei Köpfen,* ed. Hans Christoph Buch (Berlin: Wagenbach, 1978); *Vaterland, Muttersprache: Deutsche Schriftsteller und ihr Staat seit 1945,* ed. Klaus Wagenbach et al. (Berlin: Wagenbach, 1979); *Vom deutschen Herbst zum bleichen deutschen Winter: Ein Lesebuch zum Modell Deutschland,* ed. Heinar Kipphardt (Königstein: Athenäum, 1981); *Lieben Sie Deutschland? Gefühle zur Lage der Nation,* ed. Marielouise Janssen-Jurreit (Munich: Piper, 1985).

62. See my article "Tucholsky und die Deutschen: Anmerkungen zu 'Deutschland, Deutschland über alles,'" *Text + Kritik* 29 (June 1985): 12–23.

63. See the conversation with Kluge about *The Patriot* in *Filmkritik* 11 (1979): 505, where he speaks about the relationship between "ice" and "history." Regarding the poem quoted in the text, he says: "That reminded me very strongly of what I associate with German history."

64. Ibid., p. 507.

65. See, above all, the revisionist positions of Ernst Nolte, Andreas Hillgruber, and Joachim Fest in the current "Historikerstreit," the debate among West German historians about the origin and legacy of Auschwitz. Hillgruber's book *Zweierlei Untergang: Die Zerschlagung des Deutschen Reiches und das Ende des europäischen Judentums* (Berlin: Siedler, 1986) links in its title the fate of the Jews with the fate of the German army on the Eastern front in 1944–45. Habermas called this interpretation symptomatic for the "apologetic tendencies in contemporary German historiography." See Jürgen Habermas, "Eine Art Schadensabwicklung: Die apologetischen Tendenzen in der deutschen Zeitgeschichtsschreibung," *Die Zeit,* 11 July 1986; reprinted in *Historikerstreit,* ed. Rudolf Augstein et al. (Munich/Zurich: Piper, 1987), pp. 62–76. Although Kluge has nothing in common with the revisionist goals of Hillgruber and others, *The Patriot* does share the discourse of the New Patriotism. The film has a political

subtext that resonates, in the light of this new discourse, in a different way than it would have a decade ago. None of the German critics, by the way, have pointed out that in *The Patriot* Stalingrad is part of the tragic history of Germany, whereas Auschwitz is not.

66. Kluge is concerned with the *principle* of war. World War II is only one in a series of wars. World War III, the voice-over tells us toward the end of the film, will start in "thirteen years and six weeks or two years and eleven months" (168).

67. Kluge focuses not on victims and wrongdoers, not on guilt and atonement; he is concerned with finding identity. This point was made explicit in a conversation with Bernhard Sinkel on the occasion of the premiere of Sinkel's television mini-series *Väter und Söhne* (*The Sins of the Fathers*) in 1986, published in Bernhard Sinkel, *Väter und Söhne: Eine deutsche Tragödie* (Frankfurt am Main: Athenäum, 1986), pp. 414–415:

> *Kluge:* Why is it that American dramaturgy always asks about guilt and atonement while we tend increasingly to put those values aside as uninteresting and ask about something completely different: where do I come from, what can I know, what can I become?
> *Sinkel:* I think that is because Americans only know the dramaturgy of good and evil. Their heroes are either good or evil, good guy or bad guy, and that is why they are necessarily in a moral straitjacket when the showdown comes.
> *Kluge:* That is difficult to do in German history.

68. Alexander Kluge, "Rede über das eigene Land: Deutschland," in Stefan Heym et al., *Reden über das eigene Land* (Munich: Bertelsmann, 1983), p. 80. And yet: ". . . something must have disappeared; that would explain the energy the Germans put into repressing all of German history after 1945, the failure to do *Trauerarbeit,* to mourn. Losses have occurred in terms of the emotions that were directed at an emphatic concept of Germany at least in the 1930s, also in terms of the vehement emotions that arose in opposition to the dictate of Versailles after 1918 (and that could not have been only a matter of persuasion from above), and in terms of the basic relationship to tradition for more than a thousand years" (ibid).

69. See Cornelius Castoriadis, "Die imaginären gesellschaftlichen Bedeutungen," *Merkur* 406 (April 1982): 332–333: "Everyone defines himself in relation to a 'we' and is also so defined by others. But who is the 'we,' this group, this collective, this society, what is that? At first a symbol: the insignia with which each tribe, every city, and every people has always guaranteed its own existence. Primarily, of course, a name. But is this conventional and arbitrary name really so conventional and arbitrary? Such a signifier points to *two* signifieds, which it conflates inseparably: it refers to the collective, but not only in an extensional sense. The word also refers to the content of the collective as something with a quality or individual nature . . . We (or the others) call ourselves Germans, Franks, Teutons, Slavs. If this name were a symbol with merely rational functions, it would be a pure sign that simply referred to everyone belonging to a

certain collective that is in turn characterized by clear external features . . . For the communities of the past, their name not only *denoted* but also *connoted* them, and these connotations refer to a signified that is neither real nor rational, nor can it be—it is imaginary, whatever the content and the peculiar nature of the imagining . . . Two World Wars and continuing nationalism have . . . shown that this imaginary element of the nation is more enduring than any reality."

70. Kluge, "Rede über das eigene Land," p. 81.

71. Ibid., p. 84. See also Kluge and Negt, *Geschichte und Eigensinn*, pp. 361–769, for an extensive discussion of the problem.

72. Kluge and Negt, *Geschichte und Eigensinn*, p. 390.

73. Ibid., p. 393.

74. Ibid., p. 391. Kluge and Negt find it worthwhile to mention that working with the "Germany identity material" was like wading through a river of mud (pp. 389ff).

75. Ibid., p. 392.

76. Kluge, "Rede über das eigene Land," p. 91. The final part of the talk is reprinted as "Mangel an Deutschland," *Merkur* 38 (January 1984): 423.

5. Our Childhoods, Ourselves

1. See the seminal article by Helmut Kreuzer, "Neue Subjektivität: Zur Literatur der siebziger Jahre in der Bundesrepublik Deutschland," in *Deutsche Gegenwartsliteratur*, ed. Manfred Durzak (Stuttgart: Reclam, 1981) pp. 77–106; see also Hinrich C. Seeba, "Zur Autorenpoetik der siebziger Jahre," *Monatshefte* 73 (1981): 140–154; David Roberts, "Tendenzwenden: Die sechziger und siebziger Jahre in literaturhistorischer Perspektive," *Deutsche Vierteljahresschrift* 56 (1982): 290–313; Karen Ruoff, "Rückblick auf die Wende zur 'Neuen Subjektivität,'" *Das Argument* 142 (1983): 802–820; Leslie Adelson, "Subjectivity Reconsidered: Botho Strauss and Contemporary German Prose," *New German Critique* 30 (Fall 1983): 3–59; Richard McCormick, "The Politics of the Personal: West German Literature and Cinema in the Wake of the Student Movement," Ph.D. diss., University of California, Berkeley, 1986.

2. Christa Wolf, *Patterns of Childhood*, trans. Ursule Molinaro and Hedwig Rappolt (New York: Farrar, Straus and Giroux, 1980), p. 209.

3. There was a general reawakened interest in questions of childhood in the late 1970s. See, for instance, Peter Handke, *Kindergeschichte* (Frankfurt am Main: Suhrkamp, 1981).

4. See Sigmund Freud, "Remembering, Repeating and Working-through," *The Complete Psychological Works*, trans. and ed. James Strachey, vol. 12 (London: Hogarth Press and the Institute of Psychoanalysis, 1966), pp. 147–166.

5. See Michael Schneider, "Fathers and Sons, Retrospectively: The Damaged Relationship between Two Generations," *New German Critique* 31 (Winter 1984): 3–51. *Die Versuchung des Normalen*, ed. Ulrike Kolb (Frankfurt am Main: Tende, 1986); Peter Sichrovsky, *Born Guilty: Children of Nazi Families*, trans. Jean Steinberg (New York: Basic Books, 1988); Helen Epstein, *Die Kinder*

des Holocaust: Gespräche mit Söhnen und Töchtern von Überlebenden (Munich: Beck, 1987).

6. Precursors of this "literature about fathers" are Elisabeth Plessen's *Such Sad Tidings,* trans. Ruth Hein (New York: Viking, 1979; originally *Mitteilung an den Adel,* 1976) and Bernward Vesper's posthumously published book, *Die Reise: Romanessay* (Frankfurt am Main: Zweitausendeins, 1977), which deals with his father, the writer Will Vesper, a prominent Nazi poet. Examples of the so-called *Väterliteratur* include Paul Kersten, *Der alltägliche Tod meines Vaters. Erzählung* (Cologne: Kiepenheuer und Witsch, 1978); Ruth Rehmann, *Der Mann auf der Kanzel. Fragen an einen Vater* (Munich/Vienna: Hanser, 1979); Sigfrid Gauch, *Vaterspuren. Eine Erzählung* (Königstein: Athenäum, 1979); Heinrich Wiesner, *Der Riese am Tisch* (Basel: Lenos, 1979); Peter Härtling, *Nachgetragene Liebe* (Darmstadt: Luchterhand, 1980); Christoph Meckel, *Suchbild: Über meinen Vater* (1980); Jutta Schutting, *Der Vater* (Salzburg: Residenzverlag, 1980); Brigitte Schwaiger, *Lange Abwesenheit* (Vienna/Hamburg: Zsolnay, 1983); and Ludwig Harig, *Ordnung ist das ganze Leben: Roman meines Vaters* (Munich/Vienna: Hanser, 1985). A late addition to this subgenre of father-son books is Peter Schneider's story *Vati* (Darmstadt: Luchterhand, 1987), in which the relationship between the infamous concentration camp doctor Mengele and his son is told in the first person, from the son's viewpoint. The son undertakes a journey to find his father in a South American hideout; he comes away emotionally bewildered about his love-hate relationship with his father, who is not shown as monstrous but, on the contrary, as vulnerable.

7. Thomas Harlan's *Der Wundkanal* (*The Wound Passage*) was shown in 1985 at the Berlin Film Festival and at Cannes, along with the documentary *Unser Nazi* (*Our Nazi*) by Robert Kramer, which recorded the difficulties in filming *Wundkanal.* The film *Vater und Sohn* (1984) by Thomas Mitscherlich, about his famous father, Alexander Mitscherlich, co-author of *The Inability to Mourn,* is an ambivalent filmic essay on paternal authority that alternates between affection and critical distance. Bernhard Sinkel, born in 1940, the great-grandson of one of the founders of the I. G. Farben petrochemical company, made a conventionally narrated and filmed three-generation family saga, *Väter und Söhne* (*Fathers and Sons*), which dramatizes (and personalizes) the gradual entanglement of the industrial complex in the crimes of the Third Reich. The eight-hour, four-part television mini-series, with an international cast headed by Burt Lancaster and Julie Christie, premiered on West German television in November 1986; it was also shown in English on Showtime cable under the title *Sins of the Fathers* in July 1988. At the end of the film, the son testifies against his father at the Nuremberg trials with the following words: "The truth is that we became guilty. The only thing that can extinguish our guilt is to look at it with open eyes and to see what we have done. Our victims, all these dead, do not ask for revenge. They ask for something quite different. They are waiting for us to mourn."

8. Thomas Brasch, *Vor den Vätern sterben die Söhne* (Berlin: Rotbuch, 1977).

9. Karin Struck, *Die Mutter. Roman* (Frankfurt am Main: Suhrkamp, 1975);

Helga Novak, *Die Eisheiligen* (Darmstadt: Luchterhand, 1979); Elfriede Jelinek, *Die Klavierspielerin* (Reinbek: Rowohlt, 1983); Waltraud Mitgutsch, *Die Züchtigung* (Düsseldorf: Claassen, 1985). On literary representations of mother-daughter relationships, see *The Lost Tradition: Mothers and Daughters in Literature,* ed. Cathy N. Davidson and E. M. Broner (New York: Ungar, 1980); see also Helga W. Kraft and Barbara Kosta, "Mother-Daughter Relationships: Problems of Self-Determination in Novak, Heinrich, and Wohmann," *German Quarterly* 46 (January 1983): 74–88; Benjamin Henrichs, "Mütterdämmerung," *Die Zeit,* 22 July 1983.

10. The numbers in parentheses refer to the published filmscript, which includes pictures from and materials about the film: Helma Sanders-Brahms, *Deutschland, bleiche Mutter: Film-Erzählung* (Reinbek: Rowohlt 1980). Dialogue passages (with page numbers) will be quoted from the book only when they also appear in the film.

11. On the theory of autobiography, see Rolf Tarot, "Die Autobiographie," in *Prosakunst ohne Erzählen: Die Gattungen der nichtfiktionalen Kunstprosa,* ed. Klaus Weissenberger (Tübingen: Niemeyer, 1985), pp. 27–43; Paul de Man, "Autobiography as Defacement," *Modern Language Notes* 94 (December 1979): 919–930; Barbara Saunders, *Contemporary German Autobiography: Literary Approaches to the Problem of Identity* (Atlantic Heights, N.J.: Humanities Press, 1985). On the specific problems of filmic autobiography, see Elizabeth W. Bruss, "Eye for I: Making and Unmaking Autobiography in Film," in *Autobiography: Essays Theoretical and Critical,* ed. James Olney (Princeton, N.J.: Princeton University Press, 1980), pp. 296–320.

12. The allegorical subtext of the film shines through in word associations like "My father. Fatherland" (112). The German fatherland seems to be embodied in the narrator's own father. See E. Ann Kaplan, "The Search for the Mother/ Land in Sanders-Brahms' *Germany, Pale Mother,*" in *German Film and Literature: Adaptations and Transformations,* ed. Eric Rentschler (New York/London: Methuen, 1986), pp. 289–304. A similar equation of father and Germany is found in Peter Krieg's 1987 film, *Vaters Land.*

13. In her later film, *Flügel und Fesseln* (*Wings and Bonds,* 1985), Sanders-Brahms returns to the autobiographical treatment of the mother-daughter relationship, dealing with the difficulty of being an artist *and* a mother.

14. Jean-Louis Cros, "Entretien avec Helma Sanders," *Image et son* 361 (May 1981): 47. See also the interview in Renate Möhrmann, *Die Frau mit der Kamera: Filmemacherinnen der Bundesrepublik Deutschland* (Munich/Vienna: Hanser, 1980), p. 152: "And when I had a child myself . . . I felt an incredibly strong need to tell history not from the perspective of the men, the soldiers, the generals, the important years, but from the perspective of a child. It became enormously important for me because I wanted to leave the film to my daughter as a kind of work of memory, a testament. Everything I can give my daughter in terms of rearing is in this film."

15. Christa Wolf's autobiographical narrator in *Patterns of Childhood* problematizes the representation of memory and history throughout her book. On Wolf see Bernhard Greiner, "'Mit der Erzählung geh ich in den Tod': Kontinuität

und Wandel des Erzählens im Schaffen von Christa Wolf," in *Erinnerte Zukunft: 11 Studien zum Werk Christa Wolfs*, ed. Wolfram Mauser (Würzburg: Königshausen and Neumann, 1985), pp. 107–140; Anna K. Kuhn, *Christa Wolf's Utopian Vision: From Marxism to Feminism* (Cambridge: Cambridge University Press, 1988).

16. Christa Wolf, *The Reader and the Writer: Essays, Sketches, Memories*, trans. John Becker (New York: International Publishers, 1977), pp. 190–191.

17. See "Christa Wolf—Documentation (Interviews)," *German Quarterly* 57 (1984): 114: "Everyone learns—if he has any self-knowledge at all—that he has a blind spot at each stage of his life. Something he does not see. That is related to his perceptual capacity, his history. And a society or a civilization also has a blind spot. Precisely this blind spot brings about its self-destruction. In my opinion the task of literature is not only to describe it but to enter it, to go into the eye of the hurricane. This often happens by means of self-exploration, because I, you, each of us, our education and socialization, are all a part of this civilization. This blind spot has not been addressed by education, because education is concerned only with human reason."

18. See the critical report on the present-day popularity and marketability of autobiographical literature by women in Jutta Kolkenbroch-Netz and Marianne Schuller, "Frau im Spiegel: Zum Verhältnis von autobiographischer Schreibweise und feministischer Praxis," in *Entwürfe von Frauen in der Literatur des 20. Jahrhunderts*, ed. Irmela von der Lühe, *Argument* 92 (1982), p. 156. For an overview of the emergence, motifs, status, and function of women's literature in West Germany during the 1970s, see Sigrid Weigel: "'Woman Begins Relating to Herself:' Contemporary German Women's Literature" (part 1), *New German Critique* 31 (Winter 1984): 53–94; (part 2), *New German Critique* 32 (Spring/Summer 1984): 3–22.

19. Christa Wolf, *The Quest for Christa T.*, trans. Christopher Middleton (New York: Dell, 1972), p. 45.

20. Reprinted in Bertolt Brecht, *Gesammelte Werke in 20 Bänden*, vol. 9, Werkausgabe edition suhrkamp (Frankfurt am Main: Suhrkamp, 1967), pp. 487–488. See also Brecht's other poems on Germany, "Deutschland, Du Blondes, Bleiches" (vol. 8, p. 68), written in 1920, and "Deutschland" (vol. 10, p. 843), written in 1942.

21. Heine's famous poem "Night Thoughts" begins with lines that are also quoted in Syberberg's Hitler film:

Thinking of Germany in the night,
I lie awake and sleep takes flight.

The rest of the poem plays with the associations of "mother" and "father-land":

I would not yearn for Germany so
Were not my mother there, I know.
The fatherland will live forever—
That dear old woman may die, however.

Quoted in *The Complete Poems of Heinrich Heine,* trans. Hal Draper (Boston: Suhrkamp/Insel, 1982), p. 408.

22. Bertolt Brecht, *Poems 1913-1956,* ed. John Willett and Ralph Manheim (London/New York: Methuen, 1987), pp. 218-219.

23. Ibid., p. 220.

24. "Lamentations," in *The New English Bible* (New York: Cambridge University Press, 1972), pp. 836-837: "I have become a laughing stock to all nations / the target of their mocking songs all day / . . . See how, whether they sit or stand, they taunt me bitterly."

25. See Ehrhard Bahr, "Der Mythos vom 'anderen' Deutschland in der Kontroverse zwischen Bertolt Brecht und Thomas Mann," in *Kontroversen, alte und neue,* ed. Albrecht Schöne, vol. 9 (Tübingen: Niemeyer, 1986), pp. 240-245.

26. See, for instance, Irmgard Reichenau, *Deutsche Frauen an Adolf Hitler* (Leipzig: Adolf Klein, 1933). Sanders-Brahms tries to take issue with this interpretation in her introduction to the filmscript (pp. 25-26): "Fest's Hitler film acts as if women submitted themselves to the superphallus Hitler in wild hysteria, as if they were the guilty ones for what happened in Germany at this time. To be sure, women cheered for the strong man who seemed to solve Germany's problems with ease. But in all my interviews I have come across many men who mourn for this time of heroism for everyone as a kind of adventure. Women experienced it differently, more objectively. They did not care about heroism, they would have preferred to have their men at home."

27. The reactions of both male and female film critics after the premiere at the Berlin Film Festival in 1980 were almost universally negative. Few responses, however, were as aggressive as Caroline Neubaur's review, "Wenn Du noch eine Mutter hast," *Freibeuter* 4 (1980): 168-169. Olav Münzberg investigated the premises and intentions of the numerous critical responses to the film in a reception study, "Schaudern vor der 'Bleichen Mutter': Eine sozialpsychologische Analyse der Kritiken zum Film von Helma Sanders-Brahms," *Medium* 10 (July 1980): 34-37. A critique of the ideology of motherhood in the film from a feminist point of view is found in Ellen E. Seiter, "Women's History, Women's Melodrama: *Deutschland, bleiche Mutter,*" *German Quarterly* (Fall 1986): 569-581, as well as in Angelika Bammer, "Through a Daughter's Eyes: Helma Sanders-Brahms' *Germany, Pale Mother,*" *New German Critique* 36 (Fall 1985): 91-110.

28. Interview with Sanders-Brahms in Möhrmann, *Die Frau mit der Kamera,* p. 155; see also the interpretations of the fairy tale by Irene Heidelberger-Leonard, "Brecht, Grimm, Sanders-Brahms: Drei Variationen zum selben Thema: *Deutschland, bleiche Mutter,*" *Études Germaniques* 39 (1984): 51-55; and by Barbara Hyams, "Is the Apolitical Woman at Peace? A Reading of the Fairy Tale in *Germany, Pale Mother,*" *Wide Angle* 10/3 (1988): 40-51.

29. On the distinction between speech/man; speechlessness/woman, see Christina von Braun, *Nicht ich: Logik, Lüge, Libido* (Frankfurt am Main: Verlag Neue Kritik, 1985), pp. 162ff.

30. Julia Kristeva, "Produktivität der Frau," quoted in Brigitte Wartmann, "Verdrängungen der Weiblichkeit aus der Geschichte: Bemerkungen zu einer

'anderen' Produktivität der Frau," in Wartmann, *Weiblich-Männlich: Kultur-geschichtliche Spuren einer verdrängten Weiblichkeit* (Berlin: Ästhetik und Kommunikation, 1980), p. 9.

31. See *Mutterkreuz und Arbeitsbuch: Zur Geschichte der Frauen in der Weimarer Republik und im Nationalsozialismus,* ed. Frauengruppe Faschismus-forschung (Frankfurt am Main: Fischer, 1981); Rita Thalmann, *Frausein im Dritten Reich* (Munich/Vienna: Hanser, 1984); Marianne Lehker, *Frauen im Nationalsozialismus: Wie aus Opfern Handlanger der Täter wurden—eine nötige Trauerarbeit* (Frankfurt am Main: Materialis-Verlag, 1984); *When Biology Became Destiny: Women in Weimar and Nazi Germany,* ed. Renate Bridenthal et al. (New York: Monthly Review Press, 1984); *Unsere verlorenen Jahre: Frauenalltag in Kriegs- und Nachkriegszeit 1939–49 in Berichten, Dokumenten und Bildern,* ed. Klaus-Jörg Ruhl (Darmstadt/Neuwied: Luchterhand, 1985); Gerda Szepansky, *Blitzmädel, Heldenmutter, Kriegerwitwe: Frauenleben im zweiten Weltkrieg* (Frankfurt am Main: Fischer, 1986); Claudia Koonz, *Mothers in the Fatherland: Women, the Family, and Nazi Politics* (New York: St. Martin's Press, 1987).

32. Sybille Meyer and Eva Schulze, *"Wie wir das alles geschafft haben"—Alleinstehende Frauen berichten über ihr Leben nach 1945* (Munich: Beck, 1984); *"Der Krieg ist aus—und nun?" Sommer '45—Berichte, Erfahrungen, Bekenntnisse,* ed. Sybill Gräfin von Schönfeldt (Munich: dtv, 1984). See also Ulla Schickling and Doris Weber, "Jetzt lebe ich—ob ich morgen noch lebe, weiss ich nicht. Die Zeit der Angst: Frauen erinnern sich an den Krieg," *Frankfurter Rundschau,* 4 May 1985: "Up to now we had not thought about our mothers' experiences in the war. They didn't tell us anything and we didn't ask. When war stories were told, they were told by men. War is men's affair, it was said. But war has many faces. One of them reflects the story of women and mothers. We began to research this aspect of war. And we encountered a wall of silence. The women who experienced the terror and the fear of nights of bombings and of flight did not want to talk about it. But a few did talk after all. Stories of survival . . ."

33. The extent of the physical destruction is difficult to imagine today. In Berlin alone more than a million railroad cars were needed to carry away the rubble, which was largely cleared by women. See Luise F. Pusch and Bernd Bredemeyer, "Trümmerfrauen," in *Die Unfähigkeit zu feiern: Der 8. Mai,* ed. Norbert Seitz (Frankfurt am Main: Verlag Neue Kritik, 1985), p. 109: "At the end of the war 400 million cubic meters of rubble covered the area of the former German Reich. 55 million cubic meters, more than one eighth of the total, covered Berlin, the city in which the 'rubble women' became a myth and a symbol of the 'German will to survive.' Forty-one percent of all living space, about 6.5 million dwellings, as well as the most important transportation routes were damaged or fully destroyed. The centers of most major cities were merely fields of ruins."

34. Judith Mayne, "Visibility and Feminist Film Criticism," *Film Reader 5* (1982): 122. See also Margarethe von Trotta, "Female Film Aesthetics," in *West German Filmmakers on Film,* p. 89: "If there is such a thing at all as a female

form of aesthetics in film, it lies for me in the choice of themes, in the attentiveness as well, the respect, the sensitivity, the care, with which we approach the people we're presenting as well as the actors we choose . . . The most essential thing is that we make no distinction between reason and emotion, and between large and small events."

35. See Catharine A. MacKinnon, "Feminism, Marxism, Method, and the State: Toward Feminist Jurisprudence," *Signs* 8 (Summer 1983): 636: "If the sexes are unequal, and perspective participates in situation, there is no ungendered reality or ungendered perspective." See also Georg Simmel, "Female Culture," in *On Women, Sexuality, and Love,* trans. and ed. Guy Oakes (New Haven, Conn.: Yale University Press, 1984), p. 67: "The belief that there is a purely 'human' culture for which the difference between man and woman is irrelevant has its origin in the same premise from which it follows that such a culture does not exist—the naive identification of the 'human' with 'man'" (first published in 1911). On the concept of "collective memory," see Maurice Halbwachs, *The Collective Memory,* trans. F. J. Ditter and V. Y. Ditter (New York: Harper and Row, 1980).

36 Christa Wolf, *Cassandra: A Novel and Four Essays,* trans. Jan van Heurk (New York: Farrar, Straus and Giroux, 1984), p. 259.

37. On the mother-daughter relationship, see the introduction to *Theorien weiblicher Subjektivität,* ed. Barbara Naumann and Elisabeth Böhmer (Frankfurt am Main: Verlag Neue Kritik, 1985), pp. 19–20: "The relation between mothers and daughters is fundamental to female subjectivity, because it is one of the earliest social experiences in which at the very beginning of our lives a woman, our mother, confronts us with and teaches us to handle the satisfaction of needs and renunciation, power and sensuality. It follows that women, consciously or unconsciously, are decisively involved in the individuation process of their daughters and sons, as well as in the formation of gender identity."

38. Christoph Meckel, *Suchbild: Über meinen Vater* (Darmstadt/Neuwied: Luchterhand, 1980), p. 143.

39. Helke Sander, "krankheit als sprache," *frauen und film* 23 (April 1980): 25. The negative characterization of the father is a conscious construct: see Sanders-Brahms's "Kleine Nachrede, hinterher," in *Deutschland, bleiche Mutter,* p. 117: "This film is not fair to my father. I beg his pardon. My father had and has many qualities I respect, even honor. I was not fair to him; this is Lene's film."

40. Margarethe Mitscherlich-Nielsen: "Rede über das eigene Land: Deutschland," in *Reden über das eigene Land: Deutschland* (Munich: Bertelsmann, 1985), pp. 76–77.

41. The history of the student movement and, connected with it, the women's movement, is presented from a feminist viewpoint in Helke Sander's semi-autobiographical film, *Der subjektive Faktor (The Subjective Factor,* 1981). Helke Sander was the founder of the "Action Committee to prepare the Liberation of Women" and spoke at the delegates' conference of the Socialist German Students (SDS) in 1968. In 1972 she founded the influential feminist film peri-

odical *frauen und film*. *The Subjective Factor* is meant to awaken the viewer's own memories through its open, fragmentary form: scraps of memory, Helke Sander's aphoristic commentaries in the voice-over, interposed titles and text, documentary newsreel footage, acted scenes, different time levels; the open, "Klugean" form tries to promote a dialogue about the problems addressed without providing solutions.

42. Quoted in "Feministischer Film," in *rororo Film-Lexikon*, "Filme," ed. Liz-Anne Bawden and Wolfram Tichy (Reinbek: Rowohlt, 1978), p. 200. See also Gudrun Lukasz-Aden and Christel Strobel, *Der Frauenfilm: Filme von und für Frauen* (Munich: Heyne, 1985); for an overview of the gradual emergence of feminist film in West Germany, see Renate Möhrmann, "Frauen erobern sich einen neuen Artikulationsort: den Film," in *Frauen Literatur Geschichte: Schreibende Frauen vom Mittelalter bis zur Gegenwart*, ed. Hiltrud Gnüg and Renate Möhrmann (Stuttgart: Metzler, 1985).

43. Among the flood of literature on this subject, see *Women and Cinema: A Critical Anthology*, ed. Karyn Kay and Gerald Pearly (New York: Dutton, 1977); "Women and Film: A Discussion of Feminist Aesthetics," *New German Critique* 13 (Winter 1978): 83–107; Judith Mayne, "The Woman at the Keyhole: Women's Cinema and Feminist Criticism," *New German Critique* 23 (Spring/Summer 1981): 27–43; Annette Kuhn, *Women's Pictures: Feminism and Cinema* (London: Routledge and Kegan Paul, 1982); E. Ann Kaplan, *Women and Film: Both Sides of the Camera* (New York/London: Methuen, 1983); *Re-Vision: Essays in Feminist Film Criticism*, ed. Mary Ann Doane, Patricia Mellencamp, and Linda Williams (Los Angeles: The American Film Institute, 1984); Gertrud Koch, "Ex-Changing the Gaze: Re-visioning Feminist Film Theory," *New German Critique* 34 (Winter 1985): 139–153; Teresa de Lauretis, "Aesthetic and Feminist Theory: Rethinking Women's Cinema," *New German Critique* 34 (Winter 1985): 154–175; Mary C. Gentile, *Film Feminisms: Theory and Practice* (Westport, Conn.: Greenwood Press, 1985).

44. Claire Johnston, "Women's Cinema as Counter-Cinema," in *Notes on Women's Cinema*, ed. Mary Ann Doane, Patricia Mellencamp, and Linda Williams (London: Society for Education in Film and Television, 1973); Laura Mulvey, "Visual Pleasure and Narrative Cinema," *Screen* 16/3 (1975): 6–18; Mulvey, "Feminism, Film, and the Avantgarde," *Movie* 22 (1976): 3–10. See also E. Ann Kaplan: "Is the Gaze Male?" in *Women and Film*, pp. 23–35.

45. Helke Sander, "feminismus und film: 'i like chaos, but i don't know whether chaos likes me,'" *frauen und film* 15 (February 1978): 10.

46. A related example of this formally radical direction in feminist film is Michelle Citron's film collage, *Daughter Rite* (1978), which analyzes the relations between mother and daughter in an American family, using autobiographical voice-over, home movie footage, and fictional scenes. Other examples are Laura Mulvey and Peter Wollen, *Riddles of the Sphinx* (1974); Helke Sander, *Die allseitig reduzierte Persönlichkeit—Redupers* (*The All-round Reduced Personality*, 1977); Lizzi Borden, *Born in Flames* (1983); and Yvonne Rainer, *The Man Who Envied Women* (1985).

6. Germany as Memory

1. Franz A. Birgel, "You Can Go Home Again: An Interview with Edgar Reitz," *Film Quarterly* 39 (Summer 1986): 5.

2. *Heimat* was produced for television, but shot on 35-millimeter film. It premiered at the Munich Film Festival in July 1984. Its enormous popular success in Germany was largely due to its airing during prime time; it was also extensively advertised in the print media. Although *Heimat* was produced as a miniseries for West German television, Reitz wants it considered as a film or "filmic novel" composed of eleven chapters—not as a television serial. *Heimat* is now available in West Germany for rental on videocassette through educational media services and in libraries; it can also be obtained in the United States through the West German Embassy.

3. Reitz had adhered to this principle from his very first feature film, *Mahlzeiten*, in 1967. See his plea for the *auteur* film in "Wie sie filmen—wie sie filmen möchten: Gespräch zwischen Edgar Reitz und Johannes Schaaf," *Film* (September 1967): 20. See his other essays supporting the *auteur* film, for example, "Das Kino der Autoren lebt," in Edgar Reitz, *Liebe zum Kino: Utopien und Gedanken zum Autorenfilm 1962–1983* (Cologne: Verlag KÖLN 78, 1984), pp. 117–124.

4. Martin Raschke, "Man trägt wieder Erde," quoted in *Weimarer Republik. Texte und Dokumente zur deutschen Literatur 1918–1933,* ed. Anton Kaes (Stuttgart: Metzler, 1983), p. 675. "If you look at the list of publications during this year, one would get the impression that Germany is inhabited by farmers."

5. Ibid., p. 676.

6. Ernst Bloch, *The Principle of Hope,* trans. Neville Plaice et al., vol. 3 (Cambridge, Mass.: MIT Press, 1986), p. 1376.

7. Martin Walser, "Heimatkunde," in *Heimatkunde: Aufsätze und Reden* (Frankfurt am Main: Suhrkamp, 1968), p. 40.

8. See especially Dieter Bellmann et al., "'Provinz' als politisches Problem," *Kursbuch* 39 (April 1975): 81–127. See also *Aufstand der Provinz: Regionalismus in Westeuropa,* ed. Dirk Gerdes (Frankfurt am Main: Campus, 1980); Jochen Kelter, "Provinz—Aufmarschbasis gegen die Metropolen? Zur Renaissance von Heimat und Dialekt in der westdeutschen Linken," in *Literatur im alemannischen Raum: Regionalismus und Dialekt,* ed. Kelter and Peter Salomon (Freiburg: Dreisam Verlag, 1978), pp. 97–102; Norbert Mecklenburg, "Regionalismus und Literatur: Kritische Fragmente," ibid., pp. 113–124; Hermann Lübbe, "Politischer Historismus: Zur Philosophie des Regionalismus," *Merkur* 372 (May 1979): 415–424; *Die Literatur blüht im Tal (Literaturmagazin* 14), ed. Jürgen Manthey et al. (Reinbek: Rowohlt, 1981). Michael E. Geisler reconstructed in detail the leftist encounter with the concept of Heimat in order to locate Reitz's effort in that context. See Michael E. Geisler, "Heimat and the German Left: The Anamnesis of a Trauma," *New German Critique* 36 (Fall 1985): 25–66.

9. See Winfried von Bredow and Hans-Friedrich Foltin, *Zwiespältige Zufluchten: Zur Renaissance des Heimatgefühls* (Berlin/Bonn: J. H. W. Dietz,

1981); Ina-Maria Greverus, *Auf der Suche nach Heimat* (Munich: Kohlhammer, 1980); Peter Rühmkorf, "Heimat—ein Wort mit Tradition oder vom Angriff auf unsere Lebenszusammenhänge," *Frankfurter Allgemeine Zeitung*, 29 November 1980; *Heimat: Sehnsucht nach Identität*, ed. Elisabeth Mossmann (Berlin: Ästhetik und Kommunikation, 1981); Hermann Bausinger et al., *Heimat heute* (Stuttgart: Kohlhammer, 1984); Walter Jens, "Nachdenken über Heimat," *Frankfurter Allgemeine Zeitung*, 9 June 1984; *Worin noch niemand war: Heimat: Eine Auseinandersetzung mit einem strapazierten Begriff: historisch—philosophisch—architektonisch*, ed. Eduard Führ (Wiesbaden/Berlin: Bauverlag, 1985). For Wolfgang Pohrt, Heimat is "a euphemism for resignation, failure, and exile. And that is the reason that 'Heimat'-loving filmmakers and writers find so many adherents among the members of the educated classes." In *konkret* 11 (November 1984): 21.

10. Examples of the critical Heimatfilm include Peter Fleischmann, *Jagdszenen aus Niederbayern* (*Hunting Scenes from Lower Bavaria*, 1968); Reinhard Hauff, *Mathias Kneissl* (1970–71); and Volker Schlöndorff, *Der plötzliche Reichtum der armen Leute von Kombach* (*The Sudden Wealth of the Poor People of Kombach*, 1971). See Wolfram Schütte's criticism of these films, "Linke Flucht in die Vergangenheit," *Frankfurter Rundschau*, 19 May 1971: "But what is the subject matter of these 'Heimatfilms,' these German social westerns, these leftist history films? Only the past? Not also the present, defeat, resignation, the latest rebellion, the last protest, and the current despair? The blind rage, and failed revolution, the sense that nothing changes or has changed, that everything has remained the same? Now that rage is projected backwards and can exhaust itself in the past. No vision for the here and now and what it could become . . ."

11. Edgar Reitz, "Made in Germany," *tip-Magazin* 16 (1984): 23.

12. "Geh über die Dörfer," *Der Spiegel*, 1 October 1984. The cover of this issue shows the face of the actress who plays Maria, Marita Breuer, superimposed over a blue, cloudless sky with the idyllic rolling hills of the Hunsrück landscape: one sees a valley in the distance, a church and several houses, surrounded by green meadows, a forest, and well-tended fields. The caption reads: "Sehnsucht nach Heimat" ("Longing for Heimat"). These images of Heimat—the virgin landscape, the small village, the benevolent motherly face hovering over it all—clearly illustrate the potential for kitsch and cliché.

13. Edgar Reitz in a conversation with Armin Weyand, "Heimat: Eine Entfernung," *Frankfurter Rundschau*, 20 October 1984.

14. This contrast also has a long tradition; see the critical novels about America (which are disguised novels about Germany) such as Ferdinand Kürnberger's *Der Amerikamüde* (1855), in which the protagonist, the famous poet Nikolaus Lenau, can no longer stand being in "soulless" America without the song of nightingales and repentantly returns to Germany. The contrast between the Old World and the New, between Heimat and distant lands, is a motif in Wim Wenders's films as well, for instance in *Alice in den Städten* and, above all, in *Paris, Texas*, where the title alone signals an ironic tension between home and far away. The inner strife between longing for Heimat and the knowledge

that this longing can never be stilled characterizes Reitz's protagonist in *Heimat* and is varied in *Paris, Texas* when Travis chooses to leave and to be lonely and on the road again, at the very moment when he has arrived home.

15. Press kit for *Heimat,* Westdeutscher Rundfunk, 1 August 1984.

16. On the difference between the urban (linear) and rural (cyclical) experience of time, see John Berger, *Pig Earth* (New York: Pantheon Books, 1979), especially his "Historical Afterword," pp. 195–213.

17. Page numbers in parentheses refer to the published filmscript: Edgar Reitz and Peter Steinbach, *Heimat: Eine deutsche Chronik* (Nördlingen: Greno, 1985). The script is meant to be a "reading version" of the film; it deviates from the final version of the film, especially in the order of the episodes. Dialogue passages are quoted from the book only if they are identical with the dialogue in the film. A volume of pictures from the film was also published: *Heimat: Eine Chronik in Bildern* (Munich: Bucher, 1985).

18. Anna Mikula, "Edgar Reitz, ein Deutscher," *Zeit-Magazin,* 26 October 1984, p. 42. Asked whether he thinks of himself as a German again today, Reitz answered: "The images in my memory are German, I produce German memories because you cannot invent memories. 'Heimat' and nation, however, are contradictory terms."

19. Quoted in *Kino-Debatte: Literatur und Film 1909–1929,* ed. Anton Kaes (Munich: dtv, 1978), p. 23.

20. This is strongly evidenced by the emergence of the American film, whose rise is unthinkable without the mass audience of 23 million (mostly illiterate) European immigrants who settled in the large industrial centers on the East Coast between 1890 and 1912. The silent images of the film, understandable without a knowledge of English, acquainted the immigrants with everyday life in America. The populist and anti-authoritarian dimension of these slapstick films (for instance, in early Chaplin films) was repressed only as cinema increasingly catered to a bourgeois audience. Literary adaptations then replaced the minute (and usually critical) observations of everyday life. The various German attitudes toward the new medium are documented in *Kino-Debatte,* ed. Kaes, especially pp. 59–81.

21. Siegfried Kracauer, *Theory of Film: The Redemption of Physical Reality* (London/New York: Oxford University Press, 1965), p. 304.

22. Ibid., p. 309. See also the thesis of the art historian Erwin Panofsky, quoted by Kracauer in support of his position: "The processes of all the earlier representational arts conform, in a higher or lesser degree, to an idealistic conception of the world. These arts operate from top to bottom, so to speak, and not from bottom to top; they start with an idea to be projected into shapeless matter and not with the objects that constitute the physical world . . . It is the movies, and only the movies that do justice to that materialistic interpretation of the universe which, whether we like it or not, pervades contemporary civilization" (p. 309).

23. A. T., "Entretien avec Edgar Reitz," *Jeune Cinéma,* no. 125 (March 1980): 20.

24. Ibid., p. 19.

25. Edgar Reitz, "Unabhängiger Film nach Holocaust?" in *Liebe zum Kino*, p. 102.

26. Concerning the debate on the history of everyday life, see *Lebenserfahrung und kollektives Gedächtnis: Die Praxis der "Oral History,"* ed. Lutz Niethammer (Frankfurt am Main: Syndikat, 1980); Thomas Schmid, "'Oral History' und die Kultur der Unterschichten," *Merkur* 397 (June 1981): 613–620; Jürgen Kocka, "Klassen oder Kultur?" *Merkur* 412 (October 1982): 955—965; Martin Broszat, "Plädoyer für Alltagsgeschichte," *Merkur* 414 (December 1982): 1244–48; Hans-Ulrich Wehler, "Neoromantik und Pseudorealismus in der neuen 'Alltagsgeschichte,'" in *Preussen ist wieder chic . . . Politik und Polemik* (Frankfurt am Main: Suhrkamp, 1983), pp. 99–106; Klaus Tenfelde, "Schwierigkeiten mit dem Alltag," *Geschichte und Gesellschaft* 10 (1984): 376–394; Jürgen Kocka, "Zurück zur Erzählung? Plädoyer für historische Argumentation," ibid., pp. 395–408; Martin Broszat et al., *Alltagsgeschichte der NS-Zeit. Neue Perspektive oder Trivialisierung?* (Munich: Oldenbourg, 1984); Carlo Ginzburg, *Spurensicherung: Über verborgene Geschichte, Kunst und soziales Gedächtnis* (Berlin: Wagenbach, 1983). For an English review of recent developments, see Martin Jay, "Songs of Experience: Reflections on the Debate over *Alltagsgeschichte*," *Salmagundi* 81 (Winter 1989): 29–41.

27. Volker Ulrich, "Den Namenlosen eine Stimme verleihen: Die 'Barfusshistoriker' machen von sich reden," *Das Parlament*, 17–24 May 1986. See the oral history research in the book series on life in the Ruhr district, "Lebensgeschichte und Sozialstruktur im Ruhrgebiet 1930–1960," coedited by Lutz Niethammer: *Die Jahre weiss man nicht, wo man die heute hinsetzen soll* (1983); *Hinterher merkt man, dass es richtig war, dass es schiefgegangen ist* (1983); *Wir kriegen jetzt andere Zeiten* (1985).

28. Theodor W. Adorno, "Amorbach," in *Parva Aesthetica* (Frankfurt am Main: Suhrkamp, 1968), pp. 20–21.

29. See Walter Benjamin, "Der Erzähler," in Benjamin, *Gesammelte Schriften*, vol. 2/2 (Frankfurt am Main: Suhrkamp, 1977), p. 439: "Didn't we notice at the end of the war that people came back from the front mute? Not richer, but poorer in their ability to communicate their experience."

30. An example: Eduard (reading the newspaper): "In Munich the Spartacists robbed the passengers on the streetcar." Pauline: "Thank God we don't have streetcars in Schabbach."

31. "I'm pleased about the irritation," Reitz said in a conversation in the *Frankfurter Rundschau*, 20 October 1984. "Black and white does not mean either present or past, dream or reality. It remains a peculiarity of this film." The French documentary filmmaker Chris Marker, who is admired by Reitz, also uses alienation effects achieved by means of unmotivated changes from black and white film to color, as in his *Le fond de l'air est rouge*. Reitz experimented with the technique as early as 1974, in *Cardillac*.

32. See Pier Paolo Pasolini, "Das Kino der Poesie," in *Pier Paolo Pasolini*, ed. Peter W. Jansen and Wolfram Schütte (Munich/Vienna: Hanser, 1977).

33. Georg Wilhelm Friedrich Hegel, "Vorlesungen über die Philosophie der Geschichte," *Werke in 20 Bänden,* vol. 12 (Frankfurt am Main: Suhrkamp, 1970), p. 42.

34. Edgar Reitz, "Das Unsichtbare und der Film: Reflexionen zum Handwerk, angeregt durch Chris Markers *Sans soleil,"* in *Liebe zum Kino,* p. 127.

35. Susan Sontag, *On Photography* (New York: Farrar, Straus and Giroux, 1977), p. 15. See also John Berger and Jean Mohr, *Another Way of Telling* (New York: Pantheon, 1982), p. 89: "A photograph preserves a moment of time and prevents it being effaced by the supersession of further moments. In this respect photographs might be compared to images stored in the memory. Yet there is a fundamental difference: whereas remembered images are the residue of continuous experience, a photograph isolates the appearances of a disconnected instant."

36. Walter Benjamin, "Theses on the Philosophy of History," in *Illuminations,* trans. Harry Zohn, ed. Hannah Arendt (New York: Schocken, 1969), p. 255.

37. Quoted in Reitz, "Das Unsichtbare," p. 131.

38. Roland Barthes, *Camera Lucida,* trans. Richard Howard (New York: Hill and Wang, 1981), p. 88.

39. On the interdependence of war and cinema, see Paul Virilio, *Guerre et cinéma* (Paris: Editions de l'Ecole, 1984).

40. In contrast, television appears in a completely negative light. When Anton gives his lonely old mother a color set for her birthday, she leaves it unpacked.

41. Reitz, "Das Unsichtbare," p. 130.

42. Ibid., p. 131.

43. Wolfram Schütte, "Neue 'Heimat,'" *Frankfurter Rundschau,* 24 October 1984.

44. Anna Mikula, "Edgar Reitz, ein Deutscher," *Zeit-Magazin,* 26 October 1984, p. 42.

45. See, for instance, the lecture series "Nationalismus und Identität" in the Goethe Institute in Turin (1985) or the conference on "Heimat" sponsored by the board of trustees for "Unteilbares Deutschland" in 1986; see also the highly popular Sunday Speech series in Munich, entitled "Reden über das eigene Land: Deutschland" ("Speeches about Our Own Country: Germany"), since 1983.

46. Gertrud Koch, "How Much Naiveté Can We Afford? The New *Heimat* Feeling," *New German Critique* 36 (Fall 1985): 13–16; see also the transcript of a debate on *Heimat* with Friedrich P. Kahlenberg, Gertrud Koch, Klaus Kreimeier, and Heide Schlüpmann, originally published in *Frauen und Film* 38 (May 1985). An abbreviated translation appeared in *New German Critique* 36 (Fall 1985): 16–20. The same issue of *New German Critique* includes a dossier on *Heimat,* edited and introduced by Miriam Hansen, with contributions by Karsten Witte, Jim Hoberman, and Thomas Elsaesser. See also, for a historian's view of the film, Kenneth D. Barkin, "Modern Germany: A Twisted Vision," *Dissent* (Spring 1987): 252—255.

47. Henri de Bresson, "Un pays se trouve âme et refuge," *Le Monde,* 22 November 1984. The same issue of *Le Monde* also includes an interview with Reitz and Marita Breuer and a long essay by Jacques Siclier, which concludes

by saying: "*Heimat* ... is the great German film of the century. The film of Germany." See also the detailed discussions and interviews in *Libération*, 24–25 November 1984; *Nouvelle Observateur*, 23 November 1984; and *Télerama*, no. 1819 (21 November 1984).

48. Jordan Mejias, "Ärgernisse: 'Heimat' in New York," *Frankfurter Allgemeine Zeitung*, 2 May 1985.

49. James Markham, "West German TV Specials Spark Debate on Reconciliation with Nazi Era," *New York Times*, 24 April 1985.

50. J. Hoberman, "Once in a Reich Time," *Village Voice*, 16 April 1985.

51. Timothy Garton Ash, "The Life of Death," *The New York Review of Books*, 19 December 1985.

52. Edgar Reitz: "Unabhängiger Film nach Holocaust?" in *Liebe zum Kino*, p. 98.

53. Ibid., p. 100.

54. Ibid., p. 102.

55. The title *Made in Germany* was changed to *Heimat* only shortly before completion of the film; the original title can still be seen chiseled into a rock in the opening sequence.

56. Reitz, "Made in Germany," p. 23.

57. Heike Hurst, "Edgar Reitz: Comment être encore un Allemand?" *Nuit Blanche*, no. 21 (1985): 70; translation quoted after Koch, "How Much Naiveté Can We Afford?" p. 13.

58. Ibid.

59. Christian Zimmer, "Our Hitler," *Telos* 42 (Winter 1979/80): 150–151 (translation slightly modified). In *Shoah* a survivor who has returned to the scene of annihilation says: "You cannot recount it. No one can imagine what happened here. It's impossible. No one can understand it."

60. On Claude Lanzmann's film *Shoah*, nine and one-half hours long, presented at the Berlin Film Festival in 1986 and broadcast in March 1986 on German television, see Lothar Baier, "Täter und Opfer," *Frankfurter Rundschau*, 7 September 1985: "*Shoah* is the strongest answer imaginable to Bitburg: the radical, inextinguishable difference between criminals and victims is reestablished. Claude Lanzmann's unique documentary happens to come at the right time for setting the proportions straight in the new German Mickey-Mouse world, where Auschwitz and the expulsion of the East Germans take on the same pastel color." See also Klaus Kreimeier, "Unsagbares sagen," *epd Film* 2 (1986): 24–27; and Heike Hurst, "Gespräch mit Claude Lanzmann, 'Der erste befreiende Film seit 1945,'" *Frankfurter Rundschau*, 1 February 1986.

61. Fechner's *The Trial* was very well received by German film critics; the television audience more or less ignored it. See, among others, Karl-Heinz Janssen, "Über das Böse und das Tugendhafte," *Die Zeit*, 16 November 1984; Volker Hage, "Ich war es. War ich es?" *Frankfurter Allgemeine Zeitung*, 27 November 1984.

62. Sebastian Haffner, *The Meaning of Hitler*, trans. Ewald Osers (Cambridge, Mass.: Harvard University Press, 1983); Hans-Dieter Schäfer, *Das gespaltene Bewusstsein: Deutsche Kultur und Lebenswirklichkeit 1933–1945* (Munich/Vi-

enna: Hanser, 1981). Schäfer speaks about a new "consumer society," an "economic miracle," and "upward mobility" during the National Socialist period. Schäfer's plea for an uncensored coming to terms with the repressed past exactly coincides with Reitz's project: "Only when the Germans begin to tear down the walls they have constructed to keep out their own history and perceive their severed past in context with their present, will they become conscious of themselves" (p. 162).

63. The television film *Regentropfen* (*Rain Drops*), by Michael Hoffmann and Harry Raymon, broadcast in 1982, can be viewed as a necessary supplement to *Heimat.* The film, told from the perspective of the child Benni, provides insights into Jewish life in a small town in the Hunsrück in February 1933. The film deals with the gradual social discrimination against the family and their eventual exclusion, even though they used to be fully integrated into the town's society, spoke the Hunsrück dialect, and so forth. The film ends with the sentence (referring to the news that the family cannot emigrate because of the father's sickness): "Don't worry. We'll make it."

64. The script for *Stunde Null* is by Peter Steinbach, Reitz's co-author in *Heimat.* The film takes place in a suburb of Leipzig (Steinbach's birthplace) during the summer of 1945, just after the American withdrawal from Thuringia and Saxony and just before the arrival of the Russians.

65. Peter Handke, *Über die Dörfer* (Frankfurt am Main: Suhrkamp, 1981), p. 74. Recent Austrian literature abounds in critical descriptions of Heimat and rural life. See Elfriede Jelinek, *Oh Wildnis, oh Schutz vor ihr* (Reinbek: Rowohlt, 1985); Gert Jonke, *Geometrischer Heimatroman* (Salzburg: Residenz, 1969); Gerhard Roth, *Landläufiger Tod* (and *Dorfchronik zum Landläufigen Tod*) (Frankfurt am Main: Fischer, 1984); as well as Thomas Bernhard's confrontation with his "Catholic–National Socialist" upbringing in *Auslöschung* (Frankfurt am Main: Suhrkamp, 1985). Recent West German approaches to Heimat are more nostalgic and ambivalent: Siegfried Lenz, *Heimatmuseum* (Hamburg: Hoffmann and Campe, 1978); Guntram Vesper, *Nördlich der Liebe und südlich des Hasses* (Munich: Hanser, 1979); Peter O. Chotjewitz, *Saumlos* (Reinbek: Rowohlt, 1982); Anna Wimschneider, *Herbstmilch: Lebenserinnerungen einer Bäuerin* (Munich: Piper, 1984).

66. See Martin Broszat, "Plädoyer für eine Historisierung des Nationalsozialismus," *Merkur* 435 (May 1985): 384: "The 'normalization' of our historical consciousness cannot exclude the Nazi era in the long run, cannot succeed by circumventing it. The blanket distancing from the Nazi past is another form of repression and is bound to create new taboos." See also James M. Markham, "West German TV Specials Spark Debate on Reconciliation with Nazi Era," *New York Times,* 24 April 1985.

67. Jenninger's controversial speech, "Von der Verantwortung für das Vergangene" ("On the Responsibility for the Past") is reprinted in full in *Die Zeit,* 25 November 1988. See also excerpts of it in translation in the *New York Times,* 12 November 1988. See further the comments by Richard L. Marcus, "Jenninger Cut Too Close to the Truth," *New York Times,* 22 November 1988.

68. The term is Stephen Greenblatt's in his *Shakespearean Negotiations: The*

Circulation of Social Energy in Renaissance England (Berkeley/Los Angeles: University of California Press, 1988).

7. Epilogue

1. See "Wages of War. ABC Saga Storms the Ratings," *Time,* 28 February 1983. See also the cover story, "The $40 Million Gamble," *Time,* 7 February 1983. The sequel to *The Winds of War, War and Remembrance,* is scheduled to run, with commercial breaks, for a total of thirty hours. The first twelve hours were shown on ABC in November 1988. At a staggering cost of more than $110 million, the mini-series about the events of World War II reportedly took more years to produce than the actual World War II lasted. The ratings for the first parts of *War and Remembrance* were overall lower than those earned by ABC five years earlier with *The Winds of War.*

2. See Theodor Lessing, *Geschichte als Sinngebung des Sinnlosen oder Die Geburt der Geschichte aus dem Mythos* (1927; Munich: Matthes & Seitz, 1982).

3. On the value of film for the historian, see Pierre Sorlin, *The Film in History: Restaging the Past* (Oxford: Blackwell, 1980); John E. O'Connor, *Teaching History with Film and Television* (Washington, D.C.: American Historical Association, 1987); Marc Ferro, *Cinema and History,* trans. Naomi Greene (Detroit: Wayne State University Press, 1988). See also Keith Tribe, "History and the Production of Memories," *Screen* 18 (Winter 1977–78): 9–22; Mimi White et al., "The Conjuncture of History and Cinema: How Historians Do Things with Film," *Iris* 2 (1984): 137–144. The *Journal of Contemporary History* devoted two special issues (July 1983 and January 1984) to the interaction between history and film.

4. Botho Strauss, *Diese Erinnerung an einen, der nur einen Tag zu Gast war* (Munich: Hanser, 1985), p. 49.

5. See Wilhelm Roth, *Der Dokumentarfilm seit 1960* (Munich/Lucerne: Bucher, 1982), p. 194: "Do we have any memories left that are not shaped by film? Isn't everything mediated? How are our own memories and film images connected?"

6. Peter W. Jansen, "Das Kino in seinem zweiten Barock: Aspekte des internationalen Films," *Jahrbuch Film* (1979–80): 23.

7. Max Picard, *Hitler in uns selbst* (Erlenbach-Zurich: Eugen Rentsch Verlag, 1949), pp. 46–47. See also Alexander Kluge, "Die Macht der Bewusstseinsindustrie und das Schicksal unserer Öffentlichkeit: Zum Unterschied von machbar und gewalttätig," in *Industrialisierung des Bewusstseins: Eine kritische Auseinandersetzung mit den "neuen" Medien,* ed. Klaus von Bismarck et al. (Munich/Zurich: Piper, 1985), pp. 51–129; Eric Breitbart, "The Painted Mirror: Historical Re-creation from the Panorama to the Docudrama," in *Presenting the Past: Essays on History and the Public,* ed. Susan Porter Benson, Stephen Brier, and Roy Rosenzweig (Philadelphia: Temple University Press, 1986), pp. 105–117.

8. See Günther Anders, *Die Antiquiertheit des Menschen,* vol. 1, "Über die Seele im Zeitalter der zweiten industriellen Revolution" (1956; Munich: Beck, 1987), especially the chapter, "Die Welt als Phantom und Matrize: Philoso-

phische Betrachtungen über Rundfunk und Fernsehen" (pp. 97–211); Marshall McLuhan, *The Gutenberg Galaxy* (1962; New York: Signet, 1969); Jean Baudrillard, *Simulations,* trans. Paul Foss, Paul Patton, and Philip Beitchman (New York: Semiotext(e), 1983).

9. Chris Marker, as quoted in Edgar Reitz, "Das Unsichtbare und der Film," in Reitz, *Liebe zum Kino,* p. 131. In his novel *The Moviegoer* (1960; New York: The Noonday Press, 1967), Walker Percy refers to the phenomenon of moviegoing as "certification": "Nowadays when a person lives somewhere, in a neighborhood, the place is not certified for him. More than likely he will live there sadly and the emptiness which is inside him will expand until it evacuates the entire neighborhood. But if he sees a movie which shows his very neighborhood, it becomes possible for him to live, for a time at least, as a person who is Somewhere and not Anywhere" (p. 63). Similarly, a Hunsrück farmer is reported to have said about Reitz's *Heimat* television chronicle (quoted in Press Materials on *Heimat*): "I've been living here in the Hunsrück for fifty years, I was born here, it's my home. But I see how beautiful it is only now, after the television show."

INDEX

Hegel, Georg Wilhelm Friedrich, 178
Heimat (Froelich), 181
Heimat (Reitz), 16, 27, 72, 85, 129, 140, 153, 231n9, 231n11, 254n2, 262n9; German reception of, 163–164, 168, 182–183, 254n2; American reception of, 163, 183–184; concepts of Heimat in, 163, 164–168, 170–171, 182, 191, 255n12; as autobiographical film, 164, 169; compared to *Germany, Pale Mother*, 164, 168, 173; cinematic style of, 167, 170, 174–177, 257n31; uses of oral history in, 169–170, 172; image of America, 169, 189–190; as a response to *Holocaust*, 172, 184–187; and depiction of Jews, 178, 188; everyday history, 171–173; photography as memory in, 178–180, 182, 258n35; and exclusion of the Holocaust, 186, 187; depiction of Nazi era, 187–189; destruction of Heimat in, 191. *See also* Heimat; Heimatfilm; Identity, national; Reitz, Edgar
Heimat: leftist interest in, 127–128, 166–167, 254n8; origins of term, 163, 165, 255n9; and Nazism, 165–166; as longing, 165, 168, 255n12, 255–256n14; as contrasted to nation, 171, 183, 256n18; and the Holocaust, 186. *See also* Federal Republic of Germany; *Heimat*
Heimatfilm, 14–16, 167, 181, 255n10. *See also Heimat*
Heimkehr. See Homecoming
Hein, Christoph, 163
Heine, Heinrich, 131, 147
Heller, André, 56, 57, 64
Hermann, Irm, 77
Herrendoerfer, Christian, 6
Herz aus Glas. See Heart of Glass
Herzog, Werner, 8, 59, 76, 227n42
Hess, Rudolf, 13
Heydrich, Reinhard, 29
Hillgruber, Andreas, 222–223n70, 244n65
Himmler, Heinrich, 45, 47, 53, 65
Hiob, Hanne, 147
Historians' Debate, 222–223n70, 244–245n65. *See also* Bitburg; Coming to terms with the past; Federal Republic of Germany; Identity, national; National Socialism; Work of mourning

History: as spectacle, 3–4, 39–40, 43, 45, 49, 119; and storytelling, 29, 83, 86–87, 108, 113, 151, 152, 172–173, 220n53, 239nn4,5; as a construct, 117–119; as a dream, 121–122; and memory, 124, 146, 180, 186, 196–197, 248n14. *See also Alltagsgeschichte*; Coming to terms with the past; Oral history
History Lessons (Straub/Huillet), 20
Hitler, Adolf, 3, 4, 5, 7, 13, 24, 41, 44, 46, 47, 60, 61, 63, 66, 68, 70, 76, 99, 144, 145, 149, 153, 155, 164, 187, 214n8; images of, 6, 40, 43, 45, 49–50, 53–54, 57, 196; as a projection, 51, 53, 57, 69; as a private person, 53–56, 61; and appropriation of German myths, 64–65; prefigured in film, 225n14; as cinéaste, 229n65. *See also* Coming to terms with the past; *Hitler, a Film from Germany*; *Holocaust*
Hitler: A Career (Herrendoerfer/Fest), 6–7, 93, 153, 214n8
Hitler, a Film from Germany (Syberberg), 130, 140; and *post-histoire*, 39, 47–49, 66; German reception of, 40–41, 71, 224n2; foreign reception of, 41, 71, 224n3, 230n30; aesthetics opposed to Hollywood, 41–43, 44, 45, 46–47; and theater, 41, 42, 43–44, 52–53; and use of myth, 42, 58–66; filmic traditions, 42–44; concepts of history, 45–47, 49, 57; "history from below," 53–56, 228n48; irrationalism in, 66–68, 71–72; and work of mourning, 69–70. *See also* Coming to terms with the past; Identity, national; Syberberg, Hans Jürgen
Hoberman, J., 183–184
Hochhuth, Rolf, 109, 139
Hoess, Rudolf, 226–227n33
Hoffmann, Kurt, 217n34
Hoger, Hannelore, 105, 108, 120
Hölderlin, Friedrich, 47, 72
Hollywood, 8, 33, 41–42, 44, 77–78, 97, 107, 114, 129, 159, 185, 197
Holocaust. *See* Anti-Semitism; Auschwitz; Coming to terms with the past; Historians' Debate; *Holocaust*; Jews; National Socialism